Supplying the British Army in the Second World War

Janet Macdonald

Pen & Sword
MILITARY

First published in Great Britain in 2020 by
PEN & SWORD MILITARY
An imprint of Pen & Sword Books Ltd
Yorkshire – Philadelphia

Typeset by Concept, Huddersfield, West Yorkshire, HD4 5JL.
Printed and bound in England by TJ International Ltd, Padstow, Cornwall.

MIX
Paper from
responsible sources
FSC® C013056

Pen & Sword Books Ltd incorporates the Imprints of Aviation, Atlas, Family History, Fiction, Maritime, Military, Discovery, Politics, History, Archaeology, Select, Wharncliffe Local History, Wharncliffe True Crime, Military Classics, Wharncliffe Transport, Leo Cooper, The Praetorian Press, Remember When, White Owl, Seaforth Publishing and Frontline Publishing.

For a complete list of Pen & Sword titles please contact
PEN & SWORD BOOKS LTD
47 Church Street, Barnsley, South Yorkshire, S70 2AS, England
E-mail: enquiries@pen-and-sword.co.uk
Website: www.pen-and-sword.co.uk
or
PEN & SWORD BOOKS
1950 Lawrence Rd, Havertown, PA 19083, USA
E-mail: uspen-and-sword@casematepublishers.com
Website: www.penandswordbooks.com

Dedication

This one is for my dear friend Byrne McLeod –
always encouraging, always enthusiastic.

Contents

List of Plates

New workers training at munitions factory.
Making up Red Cross parcels.
Red Cross ship.
Blood supplies.
Useful data.
Food arriving from Canada.
Unloading biscuits from ship.
Mule train in Italy.
Pigeon loft mounted on lorry.
Parachute hamper delivery.
RAMC burial detail.
Tanks fitted with flails for mine clearing.
Armoured car in South Africa.
Growing vegetables in the moat at the Tower of London.
Interior of an ambulance barge and an ambulance train.
Canadians disembarking on Juno Beach.
Casualties on LCT.
Convoy with barrage balloons.
D-Day DUKW.
Glider offloading jeep and trailer.
Caisson leaving Britain for France; note two tugs.
Supply parcels delivered by parachute.
Lancaster towing glider.
D-Day landing craft.
German PoWs loading onto LCT.
Plan of D-Day harbour.
Sherman tank unloading from LCT.
D-Day transport depot.
Unloading onto floating dock.

Acknowledgements

My thanks for assistance to: Mick Crumplin for medical information and pictures from his collection, Roy Mobsby for parachute information, and the staff at the National Archives, the Prince Consort's Library, the Royal Army Medical Corps Museum, the Royal Logistics Corps Museum, the Imperial War Museum, and the library at the Royal Military Academy at Sandhurst. And, as always, my husband Ken Maxwell-Jones for driving, photography, proofreading and coffee-making duties.

Glossary

Atta – wholemeal wheat flour

Back-loading – sending items back to base stores on transport that would otherwise be returning empty.

Cased vehicles – wheels, axles, and bodies were separated and packed in one case which occupied less space than the assembled vehicle. This was done by packing firms and the cased vehicles were stored in cased vehicle depots to await shipping.

Creosol – one of the constituents of creosote.

Deuce and a half – a truck which could carry 2.5 tons.

Divisional slice – the proportion of teeth (fighting units) to tail (support units).

Drill – type of fabric, a strong cotton fabric with a diagonal bias in the weave.

Duck – type of coarse linen fabric.

Eburite – a type of corrugated paper-based packaging material, used as cases for metal containers of POL.

Fascine – brushwood bundle, used to fill ditches.

Field Parks – mobile distribution and supply centres, to hold stores frequently in demand.

Geodesy – large-scale earth measurements, allowing for the curvature of the earth.

Ghee – clarified butter.

Howitzer – a short squat gun, used for shelling at a steep angle.

Inglis bridge – a bridge made of steel tubes bolted together in triangular sections, bolted together at the top.

Kola nuts – fruit of the tropical rain forest tree *Cola accuminata*. Contains caffeine.

Maintenance – has two meanings, either the regular work done on a vehicle or piece of machinery, or keeping an army in the field supplied with all its wants.

Nullar – a water course or ravine.

Order of battle – basically the various units, formations and equipment of a military force, including hierarchical command structure, strength, disposition of personnel and equipment.

Plane table – a device used in surveying to provide a solid and level surface on which to make field drawings. (Previously 'plain' table).

Prime mover – a truck used to tow artillery pieces.

Puttees – wide strips of woollen cloth, wound round the legs and tied with tapes.

Rhino ferries – barges made of several pontoons and fitted with outboard engines, used to transport heavy equipment or vehicles.

Roof light – an unopenable window designed to allow natural light into a building.

Sommerfeld tracking – a lightweight wire mesh prefabricated originally for airfield surfaces. Strengthened with mild steel rods, this material was un-rolled on the ground when needed.

Spud units – support for earth-moving equipment.

Terneplate – steel plate coated with an alloy of lead and a little tin.

TNT – trinitrotoluene, a common explosive.

Trail – the rear section of an artillery piece, by which it is towed.

Triangulation – the process of determining the location of a point by measuring angles to it from known points at each end of a baseline.

Warlike stores – artillery, small arms and ammunition.

Introduction

Compared to the First World War, in which the majority of troops were operating in trenches or static artillery batteries against an equally static enemy, the Second World War was far more mobile and took place over a much wider theatre of war, from northern Europe to the Far East with the rest of Europe, the Middle East and Africa in between. The bulk of the items transported were carried in or on mechanical land or water vehicles instead of being animal drawn or carried.

Towards the end of the First World War some lorries and a few tanks and other tracked vehicles had appeared, with the bulk of transport power, apart from railways, still being provided by horses, mules, camels and even elephants. During the Second World War there were only a few animals in use in what would otherwise have been inaccessible terrain, and mechanised lorries, tanks, armoured personnel and gun carriers and other mechanical vehicles had proliferated. This meant a vast increase in men to maintain and service these vehicles: the 'tail' of the divisional slice had increased to well over half the manpower.

The supplies to maintain these vehicles had also increased enormously. One might say that petrol had replaced animal feed, but in many theatres the feed could be obtained locally, but the petrol, oil and replacement parts for mechanical vehicles could not.

There had been, and continued to be, many technological developments in all aspects of warfare in the inter-war period. But in the end, it all came down to the basics: get your soldiers, train and equip them, get them to their operating area and keep them fed and cared for while they are there. At the highest point the total number of British troops was close to 3,000,000; after the debacle in France in 1940, few of these were in Europe until the Normandy invasion in 1944. Many were far away from home, in Africa and Asia, which made supplying them even more complex and time-consuming, especially where the enemy had interdicted the quickest routes to the theatres.

Unfortunately, although the lower level workers did their best, their efforts were often hampered by poor planning. From the mounting of the BEF to France, the impression gained is that the high-level planners were taken by surprise and arrangements took a long time to catch up with the reality. Each movement into a new theatre suffered from delays to the supply of equipment and consumable stores, and with the BEF in France they never did catch up before the force had to withdraw.

The exception to this was the 1944 Allied invasion of Europe, where the planning took place in plenty of time and with a couple of minor exceptions the operation went smoothly, despite the appalling weather.

All this was done by what at first glance looks like a simple system: the government and War Office decided what was needed, the Royal Ordnance Corps acquired it and the Royal Army Service Corps moved it to its destination and issued it.

Other smaller organisations did their part in specialised areas such as medical care, catering, signalling and so on, in a complex game of cat's cradle; an endlessly fascinating demonstration of logistics.

Chapter 1

Planning

The Second World War was far larger than the first, and was changed radically halfway through by two events. The first was the entry of Japan into the war by its invasions into British Empire countries in the Far East, and the second was the entry of the United States in two areas: the Far East and Pacific, and the alliance with the UK against the European enemies in North Africa and Europe itself. Both events caused much rethinking of administrative plans at the highest level of government and the military hierarchy. This planning was by the chiefs of staff of each of the military services and it was strategic rather than tactical. It had to start with government decisions on the purpose of the elements of each phase of the war, such as sending an expeditionary force into northern France to repel the Germans who were advancing westwards. From those decisions the planning moved downwards and spread out, covering the number and composition of military forces, their purpose, training and, of course, their supplies.

Strategic planning

The conduct of the war was the responsibility of the War Cabinet. This consisted of the Prime Minister in his secondary role of Minister of Defence, the Secretary of State for Foreign Affairs, the Minister of Production and the three service ministers. They were advised by the chiefs of staff of each military service and the chief staff officer to the Prime Minister. They all met frequently, often daily, and at times more than once a day. Their work was handled by two planning teams, one for strategic planning and one for executive planning. It was the latter section that handled the necessary operations to fulfill the strategic decisions. Later, a third team was added: the future operations planning section, which was to prepare outline plans as the defensive nature of the British strategy changed to the offensive.

Administrative military planning in a wartime situation is the forecasting of the requirements for specific operations or series of operations: the transportation of troops and everything they need to perform their task, from accommodation and rations, through clothing, equipment and weaponry, to medical care when wounded. All this must be in the right place at the right time, which almost always means transporting these essentials from home or a friendly nation close to the theatre of war.

The length of time it takes to prepare all this depends on many factors. The distance from home and the routes to the point of entry, and from there to the areas of operation; the terrain, climate and seasonal weather, the country involved, whether the arrival will be opposed, the transport available for the line of communication and provision for its repair and maintenance. And not least, the size of the force involved and the availability of its necessary weaponry. The larger the force, the more weapons will be needed, and since these cannot just be picked up off shelves in the tens of thousands, the more time is needed to manufacture them. On a really grand scale the availability of the raw materials and the manufacturers to do the work need to be organised well in advance. Usually the activities of very large campaigns will be staggered and thus the preparation for them can be too.

One final aspect which has to be worked into any plan is that of allies. In the British case, although various allies were involved, the largest was the United States. This meant that their senior planners had to be part of British planning. In north-west Africa this was comparatively easy as the US forces, although with some British and French troops, were operating in a specific area, but the 1944 invasion of Europe was very much a joint operation, and the first step was the movement of US forces into the UK.

The planning for the movement of the British Expeditionary Force (BEF) into and through northern France in 1939 was comparatively simple. The movement across the Channel was unopposed and the French ports which were the point of entry were adequately equipped and largely manned by civilian labour, as were the French railways which moved the force onwards. The whole operation took twenty-four days, landing 150,000 men, 25,000 vehicles and guns and 140,000 tons of stores.

It was thought at that time that the total force could be over 2,000,000 men, using some ten French ports including some on the north-west coast and it was obvious that this build-up would take time due to the need to find, equip and train the new men.

This phase was never completed, for the Germans encircled the British and French armies resulting in the collapse of France and the need to evacuate the British army and many allied troops. There was little time to plan this evacuation; five days were all that the situation allowed. The plan, such as it was, relied on two aspects: the organisation at Dunkirk and the adjacent beaches, and the collection of troops on whatever ships and small craft could be found. It was hoped that 40,000–50,000 troops could be saved; in the event it was 225,000 British (including 13,000 casualties) and 112,000 allied troops, most of whom were French. They were unfortunately not able to save all the equipment and weaponry and this meant the planning of the next phase had to include much manufacturing of these essentials.

The process of making a plan starts with a tentative intention of the government and joint chiefs of staff to perform a large-scale operation. They instruct the planners to examine this proposition. The first task is to check the relevant facts, including the latest intelligence. This covers what is known of the enemy's strength, its internal makeup and current location, the need for it to receive reinforcements and where they will come from, the terrain and weather conditions at the desired time of launch, and finally our own resources. The object at this stage is to assess the possible success of the proposed operation, what resources will be needed and how soon these can be assembled to launch an assault. Finally, a check is made of whether there are currently any special conditions which would affect not only the outcome of the operation, but also the general strategy.

If the operation seems feasible, the next step is to prepare an outline plan. This is not intended to be fixed, and it will probably be altered several times. As an example, Field Marshall Alexander's comments on the invasion of Sicily in his despatch are demonstrative:

> It was an essential element of amphibious warfare that sufficient major ports must be captured within a very short time of the initial landings to maintain all the requirements for the attainment of the objective.

It was first held that it would be desirable to concentrate the forces in the south-east corner of Sicily, but that area had ports that would only support six divisions when the overall plan required ten divisions. There were two options available: to utilise Palermo (on the north-west corner of the island) thus splitting the invasion force, or to use beaches to make up the supply requirements.

Alexander decided to recast the whole plan, cancelling the American assault in the west and transfering them to the south-east on the immediate left of the Eighth Army The risks of this were high, but two factors influenced his decision. The first was the probability of good weather to assist beach maintenance. The second was the availability of the new amphibious vehicle, the DUKW.

This emphasises the importance of the early stages of the plan, covering not only the availability of shipping to move the troops and their equipment, but also the need for sufficient landing ports big enough to handle those items. Further, whether the plan would stand the landings being staggered was important. This was not a problem when the BEF first moved into France, but it was when the enormous invasion took place in 1944. For this reason beach landings, with all they involved, were chosen. The issue of maintenance had to be dealt with in outline planning, and in some cases, required no more than some simple arithmetic borne of experience. Apart from the physical items which had to be provided, there were the ancillary and support troops and their vehicles required to aid the front line troops. This is called the 'divisional slice', or the proportion of tail to teeth.

Once the plan had moved on from the somewhat speculative outline to a definite intention, the planning process moved into the executive stage, for which many more people of various departments were needed, and some time-critical issues were brought up. There are several important points to consider:

- In a military situation, what intelligence was there on the capabilities of the enemy? (For instance, would they use tanks? If so anti-tank weapons will be needed.)
- Can the requirements be broken down into specific sections, e.g. types of motor vehicles needed?
- A time-scale for the delivery of such items should be obtained.
- The best delivery locations and potential difficulties which will need to be ironed out should be calculated.
- Shipping requirements and availability should be calculated.
- Regular consultations with the military commander to ensure tactical feasibility and desirability are necessary.
- If the time involved is long, are suggested completion dates acceptable?
- The need for administrative personnel at point of entry and after.
- Times for results to be reported should be set, and a means of 'dating' these devised so the latest version is always the one used.

To avoid failures in supply, long-term planning was necessary. This was often done in twelve-month increments. For manufactured goods agreement as to capacity was reached with a large number of firms, and details of supply were arranged between the firms and the service.

For controlled commodities which the Director of Army Contracts purchased, it was necessary to arrange for the supply of the raw material in advance. This applied to:

- Timber for cases, which was dealt with by Timber Control.
- Steel for banding, tinplate and terneplate which was handled by Iron and Steel Control.
- Tobacco which was handled by Tobacco Control.
- Hexamine for Tommy cookers, which was handled by Molasses and Alcohol Control.

There were several plans, especially in the first half of the war, which, although basically workable, had to be postponed for lack of resources. Some operations based on these plans never took place; others, when the resources were available, were dusted off and updated according to the current or future conditions. Enemy strength and current locations might have changed, seasonal weather might not be the same for the new start date, and new techniques or weaponry might be available.

Since the activation of the planned operation could be imminent, the next step would be to decide the order of battle and which specific 'teeth and tails' would take part. Tail units would include the Royal Engineers, who might be needed immediately for transportation facilities (docks, railways and airfields); the Royal Army Service Corps (RASC) for storage, handling and distribution of petrol, oil and lubricants (POL), stores and equipment and food; the Royal Army Medical Corps (RAMC), the Royal Army Ordnance Corps (RAOC) and the Royal Electrical and Mechanical Engineers (REME); plus others such as the pay corps, and staff for headquarters and the line of communication. Shipping availability would have to be updated and the loading plans might have to be altered according to tactical considerations.

The proportion of tail to teeth during the course of operations could be a source of contention. This happened in the Middle East command in 1940, when General Wavell (the commander-in-chief) was insisting on additional administrative staff to handle the maintenance of the reinforcements of fighting troops arriving, and later for the additional units in Crete, Greece and the Sudan. In December 1940 General Headquarters (GHQ) sent a demand for additional administration units. This drew a personal response from the Chief of the Imperial General Staff (CIGS) stating his concern that the immediate reinforcements included so few fighting troops. He had hoped, he said, that the next convoy would include the best part of a division rather than so many administrative units. Could some of these not be delayed?

Wavell's reply pointed out that these administrative units in the Middle East had been inadequate ever since the outbreak of war. This related to base, line of communication and divisional situations and had been exacerbated by the failure of allied forces from Australia, New Zealand and India to bring enough such units of their own. The need for engineering works was because the Middle East lacked sufficient accommodation, roads, rail and port facilities. The climatic and desert conditions caused abnormal wear and tear on motor vehicles and therefore additional workshops were required. His arguments were accepted at the time, but the matter remained controversial for the next two years.

The RAOC units with the BEF in 1939 suffered three main types of difficulty, most of these arising from faulty pre-war planning: a shortage of actual stores, a lack of direction on procedures, and a lack of experienced personnel. They lacked information on the latest organisational methods; the only freely available manual was out of date and the updated version did not arrive until the force had actually embarked.

The RAOC took with it to France numerous workshops, including two Base Ordnance Workshops (BOW), one Advanced Ordnance Workshop (AOW), one GHQ troops workshop, four port ordnance workshops, four AA brigade workshops, army field workshops on a scale of one per division, and light aid detachments as needed by scale. Other small workshops were formed in towns on the line of communication to handle local requirements.

The port ordnance workshops were originally located at Nantes, Cherbourg, Brest and St Nazaire, the latter two being moved to Rennes and Le Havre. Their principal work was clearing vehicles from the dock areas, mainly by making good damage caused on the voyage. Much of this was actually due to clumsy handling on unloading, a difficulty which the port workshop detachments solved by doing the unloading themselves.

An advanced BOW was also set up at Nantes, but then moved to Arras, where it undertook equipment repairs from forward units; repairs from the local units; experimental stores and as far as possible, all wireless repairs for the forward units.

The field workshops suffered from the lack of adequate planning. Most of their personnel were untrained reserves, and the physical workshops were not suitable for their purpose, being too large and thus taking up too much road space on the march and needing large accommodation space when halted. As a result they were frequently put in inconvenient pitches.

Ammunition stocks were based on some assumptions of how much would be used:

25-pounders	35 rounds per gun per day
60-pounders	30 rounds per gun per day
6″ howitzers	28 rounds per gun per day
3″ 20 cwt	50 rounds per gun per day
2-pounder Anti-Tank	5 rounds per gun per day
3″ mortar	13 rounds per mortar per day
2″ mortar	10 rounds per mortar per day
small arms ammunition	6,000,000 rounds per division per month
anti-tank mines	1,500 per division per month.

The administration policy for Tobruk was drawn up on 7 February 1941. It consisted of twelve main points, which included maintenance of Tobruk by rail and then road convoys; rail-head and siding contruction at Capprozo and Mischeifa; to maintain 30 Corps and others in the frontier area; to dismantle and evacuate the Advance Ordnance Depots (AOD) and BOW depots from Tobruk to Matrah; drastic reduction of all non-essential administrative personnel from the Tobruk area; to maintain a seven-day reserve of commodities at Tobruk; to remove by sea and road all unusable tanks, vehicles and salvage as soon as possible; maintain sufficient anti-aircraft and fighter defence in

Tobruk to protect the port; and to close down the hospital at Tobruk as far as possible. All this essentially changed Tobruk from a base to a forward area. All this needed to be completed in advance of the planned attack on 15 May.

The increasing activity in the Middle East required much local administrative planning, most of which centred on Egypt. At the beginning of the war, the possible locations for a main base were those with good 'entry' points. Two of these, Alexandria and Port Said, were seen as being vulnerable if Italy joined the war and interdicted the passage through the Mediterranean. The third, Suez, although limited in capacity, was capable of much expansion. Not only did it give access through the Red Sea, it had a connection through the Suez Canal with the Great Bitter Lake, where jetties could be built on the shore, but also via Lake Timsah and the Sweet Water Canal to the Nile, and the Egyptian State Railway. Roughly parallel to the Suez Canal there was hard-surfaced desert with plenty of space for depots, transit and training camps and other personnel accommodation. Although rail and road routes needed work, it was the best place at which to base operations.

Plans and an estimate were submitted to the War Office, but the Treasury was reluctant to spend the £921,000 involved; at this time £291,000 was all that was approved, and that was to be spent on accommodation for the troops already in, or soon to arrive in, the theatre.

Repair and overhaul of motor transport on a large scale required centralised plants, as some of the overhauling work was done by mass-production methods. This work was mainly carried out at Tel-el-Kebir, where the motor transport spares depot was situated. The RAMC stores depots were located at El-Mahgar (near el-Kebir) and Cairo. The Base Store Depot (BSD) was to be at Firdan and ammunition depots at Abu Sultan and Royal Engineers stores at the Delta Barrage, Alexandria, Fanara and Suez. There was already some ammunition and other explosives stored in the Tara Caves, south-east of Cairo.

The planning for all this construction was done at GHQ. The estimate for the construction work was in the region of £200,000,000, and the total labour force was some 250,000.

All this work in so many different locations required schedule planning. At each location, the first task was the construction of railway spurs, then roads, fencing, water, sanitation, signal communications and generating stations for electricity. The railway spurs, which were essential to the delivery of all construction materials, were unfortunately delayed by the slowness of the Egyptian State Railway, which had this responsibility. There were other difficulties over obtaining materials, especially timber, and substitutes had to be found. There was a prolonged argument with the War Office over the comparative merits of tents and wooden huts. To the War Office, tents had to be the answer if wood for huts was not available, but those on the spot knew that although tents could be erected speedily, their fabric rotted quickly.

Accommodation was needed for the existing garrison and the reinforcements en route, and also for those going on to Palestine. These came in through Alexandria before moving on, and thus needed transit camps. There was also a need for accommodation for prisoners of war, the RASC base depot, and the store depots, and a new 1,200-bed hospital. Other hospitals were planned, some to be situated in requisitioned hotels and other public buildings. By October 1940, the timber shortage meant that much patient accommodation would be in tents, huts being reserved for nurses, operating theatres, sanitary annexes and a few special wards.

None of this detailed planning work could be done at the War Office, but had to be done on the spot by people who understood the local conditions, both topographical and human.

By May 1941 the War Office had realised that the military commander-in-chief in the Middle East had more than enough to do without needing to deal with administrative matters, such as dock and base administration and railway facilities in his rear, and appointed General Sir Robert Harding as intendant-general to take over these tasks and provision of information for planning. His instructions were that he was to go to the Middle East and examine the military administration of the Middle East command, including the working of the administrative staff at GHQ and other headquarters, the size, location and functions of the rearward services and installations and consider the future development of these. He was to pay particular attention to the repair and maintenance of armoured fighting vehicles, and to the custody and evacuation of prisoners of war.

Harding should then produce reports and recommendations for improvements to the administrative machine, sending these to the War Office via the commander-in-chief Middle East, thus allowing him to add his comments. Any matters of prime importance should be reported straight away by telegram. He was also to bring the commander-in-chief up to date with the general progress of the war; since these reports were only to pass between the commander-in-chief and himself, no formal written reports to the War Office would be needed.

Harding did not go out to the Middle East immediately; during this time his staff collected general information while he met with the Prime Minister, the Secretary of State for War, the CIGS and other prominent people, as a result of which he received new instructions which were rather different from the first set. The most important of these was that he was no longer just to observe and report and recommend, but was given executive administrative power in order to relieve the commander-in-chief.

Chapter 2

Movements and Transportation

At first thought, 'transport' stands alone and consists of the means by which supplies are delivered to the army, but there are two other aspects to this delivery work: transportation and movement. Transport was part of the responsibilities of the Directorate of Supplies and Transport and the actual work was carried out mainly by the RASC. It included the use and repairs of motor transport vehicles and, later, water transport vehicles.

Transportation was different. Its main function was 'to ensure, by planning, construction and operation, that the lines of communication of our field forces and garrisons, through ports and overland by rail and inland waterways, are in all respects capable of handling the requirements of the troops based upon them'. This involved the Royal Engineers on a large scale. It operated under the Directorate of Transportation and provided and maintained the infrastructure of the routes along which delivery was made.

Transportation was a situation of prime importance affecting ongoing operations at home and abroad. After the outbreak of war, its importance grew with every new development, as each of these was dependent on the capacity of transportation facilities, existing or planned.

At the start of the war, transportation was a minor branch of the quartermaster general's department in the War Office. It dealt with technical and engineering matters of railways, inland waterway and ports; agreements with home railways; matters involving transportation policy and intelligence; technical training of railway troops; administration of the transportation branch of the supplementary reserve and railway stores. It also handled the movement of stores at home and abroad; provision of vessel and boat equipment and general control of the War Department fleet.

The work included formation and mobilisation of reserve units; the expansion of technical training, interviewing and selecting candidates for emergency commissions and the provision of facilities in the UK for storage and shipment of army requirements. For this it was divided into three branches: policy, training and stores; railways; and ports and inland waterways. Due to the constant movement between military areas, it was decided that the Director of Transport should have responsibility for ensuring that every unit was technically proficient. An inspector to assist in this work was appointed in July 1940 and soon after that, the Directorate was reorganised into five branches: policy, planning, intelligence, organisation and training; transportation stores; railway, port and inland waterway operation; railway construction and repairs; and port construction and repairs.

The Directorate of Movements and Quartering reported up to the quartermaster general. Its task was control of large-scale movements. It was one thing to send off a couple of lorry loads of supplies, and another entirely to deal with a column of fifty or more lorries, often taking their loads to trains or ports, organising their movements to, and then from, the bulk distribution centres, when other large-scale users wanted to use the same routes and facilities. For this reason, a Priority of Movements Committee was set up soon after the beginning of the war to effect control of movements within the UK.

However, this does not mean that the Movements Control staff had complete control. Their work was dependent on military necessity and decisions made by the government and senior military officers.

There were two elements of the control situation in wartime: one was that of the operators of transport systems (rail, road, shipping and air) who had to ensure the greatest use of their medium; and the other was the military user, who had to integrate the use of various transport systems with the operational requirements of the forces.

All this was comparatively easy in the First World War, when the principal army activity was in the north east of France and Belgium, fairly static and well supplied with rail networks, and the enemy had little bombing capacity. The sea route to this theatre was short and simple. The other large-scale activity was in Mesopotamia, where troops and supplies had the use of river transport. However, the Second World War involved troops in numerous locations overseas and with varied transport systems. In all these, technical knowledge of the transport systems was required; for instance how many freight trucks could be pulled by a single locomotive.

To a large extent, once the British forces had withdrawn from France, the principal concern was for the long-distance overseas commands. For these theatres, troops and all their equipment and basic requirements such as rations had to be taken to the ports, embarked on ships and sent off to their base destination, where the local movement control department moved them on. This was time critical, as living facilities for the troops were limited at ports, and the ships had to be organised to sail together, under naval protection, especially if the route took them through areas where enemy submarines were known to be active. There was one class of troop transport which was allowed to sail unescorted because of their higher speeds: converted passenger liners. The fastest of these, with a 30-knot capability, were *Queen Mary* and *Queen Elizabeth*. Others, with a 20-knot capability, included *Aquitania*, *Mauretania*, and *Empress of Scotland*. These vessels obviously required some refitting to allow for much greater numbers of 'passengers' than they were used to, so needed a long lead time for their first use. The main port of embarkation for these liners was Liverpool, and to move between 40,000 and 50,000 troops to this port required over 100 special trains, and, as far as movement control staff were concerned, a detailed knowledge of the rail network and its operating capabilities.

Movement staff thus had to be constantly aware of what transport capacity was available, and what the military chiefs wanted to despatch: troops and/or equipment and supplies. This staff had necessarily to include military trained staff officers who understood how the fighting services worked and what they needed, as well as officers experienced in transport operations. These functions could not be rigidly divided, so it became necessary to provide training for both sections. This consisted of a four- to five-week course for officers and a four-week course for clerks, with a further four-week course for those who would be working overseas. Before the war the courses, which took days rather than weeks, were carried out at the Royal United Services Institute in London, but once the war was in progress the venue moved to Derby.

Before the war started it was anticipated that the enemy would adopt a major bombing campaign on British ports, and it was decided that no large-scale shipping activity would take place to the east of Southampton. With this in mind, the BEF departed from Southampton, Avonmouth and three other ports served by the Great Western Railway in South Wales: Newport, Barry and Swansea. With the threat of invasion in the summer of 1940, Southampton was closed and ports in the west and north-west were used more; mainly Liverpool and Glasgow. Of the smaller harbours, Leith was used to aid the construction of airfields in the Western Isles.

In early 1941, with increasing imports from America, extra berthing accommodation was needed and the north-east ports of the Tyne, Tees and Humber were extended. There were numerous other smaller ports around the coast which were used when small ships needed accommodation.

At the Head Office in London, the work, and establishments of the movement control department, was divided into movements of personnel (i.e. troops) and freight. By 1942 it had become necessary for representatives of both sides to be involved in advance planning as well as day-to-day planning. By this time, the two sides had been organised into separate directorates: personnel movement and freight movement. Before this, the personnel side had been dealt with in two sub-branches, dealing with long and short sea voyages respectively, and another which dealt with rail journeys to the relevant ports.

After the events of summer 1940 at Dunkirk, when several troop-carrying ships were lost, there were few short voyages. At about this time Italy entered the war and the Mediterranean was effectively closed to British shipping, which meant troops and supplies for the Middle East and then North Africa had to go all the way round South Africa and up the Red Sea. This was an expensive route, not only because of the actual cost of the voyages, but also because the long turn-round of the ships at each end and the lack of return cargoes, which meant the ships returned empty except for a few evacuees.

All this required liaison between movement control staff and various other bodies, including the headquarters of the units of troops who were to go, where they helped with completing documentation and issuing instructions to the troops. The Ministry of War Transport arranged the victualling of ships and the Admiralty dealt with the escort and convoy arrangements. And no sooner had one convoy sailed, than work began on the next. During the eighteen-month period from June 1940 to December 1941, some 470,000 military personnel were transported from the UK to the Middle East and Indian Ocean.

In February 1940 an additional department was added to deal with the administrative side of the work and this eventually divided into four sub-departments.

The first dealt with administrative, policy and financial aspects of travel by land, sea and air; travel entitlement and allowances, coordination with the War Office over military families overseas and civilian travel. The second dealt with administrative and welfare matters arising in connection with the running of transports. The third dealt with movement control personnel and war establishments at home and overseas, while the fourth kept records and statistics of movement of personnel by sea and air, and casualties at sea.

One particular problem they had to deal with was the evacuation of soldiers' families from overseas. These included numbers from Hong Kong, Singapore, Burma, India, the Middle East, Gibraltar and Malta. The quarter-master general issued an edict that women and families were not to travel by sea because of the threat from submarines. This threw a greater burden on the rail system until the quartermaster general's ruling was relaxed.

As well as the main office at the War Office, there were movement control offices relating to the military commands at home: London Area; Eastern (which was split into two after Dunkirk, taking Aldershot with the area south of the Thames to form South-East command); Southern (which ranged west to Exeter); Western (which included rail traffic from the Merseyside and Bristol Channel ports); and Northern, Scottish and Northern Ireland.

Northern France

There were also movement control departments in the overseas theatres, starting with the BEF. The first group of movement control staff arrived at Cherbourg, from where they divided into small groups to handle the arrival and dispersal of the force. During the following ten months, 695,115 army personnel, 961 Royal Navy and 56,445 RAF personnel arrived. Motor transport vehicles totalled 68,130 with 20,988 motorcycles, some of these going on the train ferry. There were also a total of 748,000 tons of stores, including some ammunition and petrol,

In the evacuations of summer 1940, over 522,000 troops (including some French, Poles, Czechs and Belgians) arrived in Britain and had to be moved on from the ports to reception camps, while the threat of invasion meant the movement of large numbers of fresh troops to the vulnerable south-east corner of the country.

Middle East

The situation here was complicated, and often confused, with military and civilian transport to coordinate, along with what one officer referred to as 'the curse of Babel'. Some of the overland routes were very long: over 3,000 miles in the case of a divisional movement which took over a month to complete. The main rail routes included the Nile valley and the Western Desert railway, which required major construction works to fill gaps. In the Levant, the Palestinian railway was never really effective, its personnel having become dispirited after several revolutions. Engineering work was required to increase both capacity and efficiency.

By 1942, it was necessary to enlarge the stores branch due to the increase of military activity in the Far East; increasing production difficulties; stores planning for the arrival of American troops; stores planning for new or emergency lines of communication; and responsibility for checking and assisting with stores of equipment needed by the civil railway and port operations round the world necessary to maintain their efficiency for strategic purposes. This led to a staff of sixty-one military and civilian officers.

The policy, organisation and intelligence branch dealt mainly with issues which could not be easily allocated to specific branches. The organisational aspect covered personnel and technical training as well as basic administration. The intelligence function included planning, operations and general research. On the intelligence side, the main need was to work out the speed with which an enemy force could concentrate in a specific area and the size of that force.

Operational work included planning transportation developments in all overseas theatres, and producing, when required, briefs for service officers. Operations staff also liaised with the Director of Public Relations on publicity questions, supplying material for press, radio and film publicity as needed. Assessments had to be produced on the capacities of roads, railways, waterways and ports, including the time required for improvements and repairs, and an estimate of the stores needed for that work.

Organisational duties included preparing and amending details of war establishments for transportation units and other headquarters. Amendments to existing establishments often led to a need to train tradesmen. The number of these increased from nine to sixty during the course of the war. Each of these units also had its own comprehensive listing of all the equipment and plant, tools, machines and other stores known as the 'Vocabulary of transportation stores', which started as a slim pamphlet and grew into a massive bound book.

On the personnel side, this department made recommendations on the selection of transportation officers, and these often required relocation. Each unit needed a balanced complement of officers with different technical skills, and this made it impractical to use the normal system of promoting by seniority.

Another intelligence branch prepared reports on the structual features of ports and inland waterways in case it became necessary to demolish or reconstruct them. One valuable source of information was aerial photography and a transportation section was added to the Allied Combined Interpretation unit at Medmenham, consisting of six transportation officers and seven or eight RAF officers.

The stores branch of the transportation directorate had responsibility for ensuring all materials and stores required for transportation projects were available at all times. This included estimating probable needs and arranging for procurement, storage and shipment.

The main source of supply for transportation stores was the Directorate of Royal Engineers' Equipment at the Ministry of Supply. There were thirty different types of items, particularly powered craft for use in ports and on inland waterways, some obtained from the Ministry of War Transport and others from the Admiralty.

A sub-section of this branch kept records of all receipts, issues, and stocks of transportation stores, and another kept records of spending for the Treasury. This included items that went direct from contractors to users, plant hire, and stores supplied to US forces under Reciprocal Aid; a category which reached almost £5,000,000.

There were four main transportation stores depots: Longmoor, Kings Newton, Marchwood and Richborough. After the evacuation of the BEF, increased storage space was needed for stores and equipment salvaged from France, as well as those still coming off the production lines but not currently needed.

The Longmoor depot, near St Albans, was enlarged by 2 miles of sidings for open storage and five Nissen huts. It was manned by a transportation stores company just returned from France, and this situation remained fairly static until that company was needed for North Africa in 1942. It had five officers, 116 other ranks, and thirty-eight ATS auxiliaries; this increased to sixteen officers, 567 other ranks and forty-three ATS auxiliaries after it was enlarged by setting up numerous sub-depots along the Longmoor military railway, with 270,000 square feet of covered storage holding over 200,000 tons of stores.

The Kings Newton depot, near Derby, was opened in August 1940. A good geographical and railway centre for the north of England, it was served by the Melbourne Military Railway and was close to plenty of technical and labour resources. The objectives of this depot were similar to those of Longmoor; it was enlarged twice until its personnel establishment was fifteen officers, 456 other ranks and fifty-one ATS auxiliaries. It could hold up to 122,500 tons of stores.

The depot at Richborough was set up in spring 1944 to hold items for special projects, and to take overflow items from the other depots which required covered space.

Earlier, as it had become obvious that war was coming, numerous committees and study groups were set up to deliberate and report on wartime needs. The railways were optimistic about their ability to meet the demand and the government accepted this view. However, the government was slow to realise that rail transport would be short in wartime, especially for coal, and therefore made a faulty assumption that by transferring long-distance traffic to the railways, road transport would manage to function on a fuel allocation reduced to three-quarters of peacetime use.

As the war progressed, the variety and quantity of stores increased enormously, especially when the invasion of north-west Europe drew close. This branch grew from two or three officers in 1939 to fifty-four in 1944. During the course of the war, the transportation service grew from 500 regular and 3,500 reserve Royal Engineer Corps troops to a total of more than 146,000 of all ranks.

By the outbreak of the Second World War, on the assumption that road transport would be used more than rail, many of the world's railways had been neglected. But trains needed coal, and road transport needed oil and petrol; neither were found in the UK and had to be shipped in, as did rubber for tyres. But it was no longer necessary to get close to a fixed front, leaving lorries and buses to cover the final distance.

Railways continued to play a crucial logistics role. What had been tiny stations in the north-west suddenly became major centres of stock-piled supplies in June 1944 in preparation for the Normandy landings. In the early part of the war, the railways branch was mainly concerned with ensuring that adequate railway facilities were available for stores for the BEF; when it withdrew from France in the summer of 1940 and the threat of invasion loomed, its scope increased and it was expanded into two branches, one for railway constuction and one for railway and port operations. As well as serving armoured trains and rail-mounted artillery battalions, they constructed spurlines near the coast to serve both rail-mounted and fixed coastal batteries.

They also helped with emergency repairs to bomb-damaged track and bridges, often using specially designed steel trestling.

When the threat of invasion diminished, the construction of new rail-served army depots and the enlargement of others was started, the work generally being done by railway operating troops under the control of the Directorate of Transportation. These troops consisted of 2,400 all ranks, and were located initially in the UK and later in other theatres.

From July 1942 onwards, much railway construction work was needed on depots for the American forces, and later, as the planned invasion of France approached, on improving facilities at transit depots and embarkation ports. They were aided in this work by mechanical equipment units, using American earth-moving machinery such as bulldozers and scrapers, moving more than 6,000,000 cubic yards of earth. They laid over 680 miles of track, of which 183 were in American depots. The materials and ballast for this work cost £5,810,000.

Building and repairing became more important as the war progressed. With the loss of ports in northern France, Belgium and Holland and the bombing of British south-east and southern ports, the first requirement was for ports for ocean-going ships away from the Channel. It was found that the west coast ports could not carry the extra loads, and it became necessary to build two new deep-water ports on the west coast of Scotland, one at Faslane and the other at Stranraer. With 500ft-long berths with a minimum 30ft of water alongside at low tide, these were designated No. 1 and No. 2 military ports. Each was equipped with roads, railway tracks and cranes. They also had 900ft-long timber lighterage wharves and were connected to main railway lines with some 50 miles of track.

The main theatres where railway expansion was needed were the Middle East, Palestine and Egypt. In Iraq it was mainly a matter of improving the existing lines with a few extensions, but in Egypt there were major building operations. The Egyptian State Railway was good, but restricted to lines between Cairo and Alexandria, and from the Palestinian railway at Kantara to Ismaila and Port Said. It was the lines to the west of those that required concentrated attention, especially during the operations around Tobruk.

Port operations required labour including dedicated stevedore units, and this work, with quay working and maintenance, and the maintenance of other port equipment, including floating cranes, was the responsibility of the Transportation Service. This included work on inland water transport, handling the numerous and varied craft. In August 1943, some 400 Thames sailing barges were brought into use after being fitted with power units and ramps for unloading on beaches. This work was done at the bomb-damaged Surrey Commercial Dock, where 4 acres were cleared and levelled and workshops and other essential buildings, including huts for housing, were erected. This section also dealt with 400 prefabricated 'Minea' barges from Canada, this work being done elsewhere in the London Docks and at Southampton. A hundred ramped cargo lighters arrived from America in sections. These were intended for use in the invasion, but arrived too late and most were sent to India.

After the evacuation of the BEF from France, the German occupation of France, Belgium and Holland made the ports of London unsuitable for large shipments and much material was sent via freight agents for shipments in commercial vessels as space was available. Plans had to be made for maintaining armies at home in the coastal sections. A system of main supply depots for supplies and petrol, and sub-depots for ammunition, was set up, mostly 70 to 100 miles from the vulnerable south and east coasts. Each depot was mainly supplied by rail. Although the invasion on which this system was based never came, it did create a situation where stocks were dispersed in locations which could rapidly supply any port.

Thirty-nine 'Rhino' ferries, made of American pontoons, were originally intended for use by American personnel, but were transferred to the British inland water transport organisation. The crews completed their training just in time to join the invasion.

Before the war, and until April 1942, when the name of the Railway Training Centre at Longmoor was changed to the Transportation Training Centre, it dealt mainly with railway trades. There was no regular docks training unit. The peacetime facilities consisted of the 18-mile-long Longmoor Military Railway. When the war started the numbers arriving for training were so large that many of them had to be sent to Derby, where they were able to use the traffic school of the London, Midland and Scottish Railway. Stevedores and dock-crane drivers were trained, rather unsatisfactorily, in a mocked-up ship's hold until 1943 when they were sent to Penarth Docks while an additional wing was added to the Longmoor establishment. Serving as the depot for all transportation troops, Longmoor trained some 20,000 troops in 1943, and had a ration strength of some 10,000.

The work of the branches overseas was much the same as at home. In some places, notably France, they worked in conjunction with local organisations, operating from headquarters in or near the headquarters of the local military command. The priorities of specific repairs and development projects did vary according to military action. For instance, with the deterioration of the situation in the Mediterranean, deep-water berths and additional railway constructions were needed south of Suez. In other places, such as North Africa, the local rail lines and roads were so limited they had to be augmented with new developments. In fact, the majority of the work abroad was with railways, although there was a fair amount of work on ports, particularly in the Mediterranean where the enemy conducted extensive bombing campaigns.

In 1939, Royal Engineers transportation units were the first to land in France. There they issued the stores and vehicles needed and built and maintained railway lines and communications. When operations in France collapsed, the main centre of activity was the Middle East, where they constructed 170 miles of the Palestine-Syria railway, including a mile-long tunnel, and extended the Mersa Matruh to Tobruk railway in the Western Desert, completing some 2 miles per day. In Egypt they built new ports and developed existing ports and repaired the ports of Libya and Tripolitana. From 1941 the transportation service was kept busy in Persia and Iraq working on the Trans-Persian Railway to increase the supply of deliveries to Russia.

In North Africa, then Sicily and Italy, some 20,000 transportation troops helped support the British armies, and with the Americans developed the port and railway facilities. Using specially developed unit construction for bridges and trestles, they were instrumental in repairing enemy damage.

In Persia and Iraq, the military force, which was known as British Troops Iraq (BTI), had responsibility for the south and east of Persia; the north and west being managed by the Russians. BTI's tasks were to protect the Anglo-Iranian oil fields from ground and air attack, and the development of the Persian Gulf ports and the routes from them.

A big problem in these two countries was a lack of adequate communication systems. In Iraq, the telephone system was both inadequate and liable to frequent interruption, sometimes from floods but more frequently from theft of the copper wires. In Persia it was the same but worse. There was no telephone communication between Teheran, Baghdad and the Gulf ports until 1943. A messenger service between Teheran and Baghdad took some thirty-eight hours by a combination of rail, ferry and car. The whole trip could be done by road, but took two days without stopping. All this was alleviated when the American force took over in Persia, bringing large quantities of the latest construction equipment.

The East Africa command covered an area of almost 2,000,000 square miles between the Great Lakes and the Indian Ocean, from Kenya to Abyssinia. The military movement was north-south, a direction in which railways and good roads were almost non-existent. There was some use of rivers, and steamers on the lakes, and the sea as the main line of communication; the latter took in the islands of Madagascar and Zanzibar.

The first task for the movement control staff was disembarkation and dispersal of the brigades from West Africa, and the South African divisions in 1940, and later that year a vast number of motor transport convoys moved from South to East Africa with supplies for the invasion of Italian Somaliland. This was successful, and added more ports, but meant numerous prisoners of war had to be sent to South Africa, and their families sent home to Italy.

The three principal roads (the Great North, the Great East and the Abyssinian Road) were in poor condition. At best they were beaten earth tracks, degenerated in some places to sand and boulders, and in others, after rain, to quagmires. There were some steep gradients which required more experienced drivers than the local Africans who were used. There were no transit camps, and the convoys were liable to be stopped by vast herds of wild and sometimes unfriendly big game.

Before the war there was little air transport in East Africa, but this soon changed as numerous air services sprang up, based at places such as Pretoria, Elizabethville, Stanleyville, Leopoldville, Nairobi, Juba and Khartoum. The chief routes were the Cairo-Nairobi-Durban service operated by the British Overseas Airways Corporation (BOAC) and the RAF, each of which provided two Dakotas a week in each direction. The Belgian company Sabena operated the Lagos–Cairo service, using Junkers 52s and Lockheed Lodestars. Useful though these services were, they were only small scale. During 1945, BOAC moved 1,875 and the RAF 4,972 military passengers.

The four countries which made up the West Africa command were widely spaced over a distance of some 2,000 miles by sea. Each of these countries was bordered by other countries, some of which were under French control. There were no railway connections between them, and few within them except in Nigeria. In Gambia and Sierra Leone the rivers were used for transport up country. Nigeria was the largest of all these countries, and the best for internal transport systems when the war started. It had a good port at Lagos and a good railway system. BOAC used Lagos as a staging post for their land and flying-boat services.

In West Africa it was difficult to prevent pilferage. The RAOC was not able to maintain a large enough guard to stop it fully, but alert officers and NCOs did much to reduce it. In this theatre there was a large light-fingered local population and it was found important to build adequate perimeter fences, with guards and security checks.

There were several expeditions from the Middle East to the eastern Mediterranean islands and Greece, none of them easy, as enemy activity had trapped shipping in the Suez Canal. The two main ports for Greece were Salonika and Piraeus, serving the northern and southern areas respectively. British involvement in Greece started in November 1940, but the supply situation was chaotic. Secrecy had required that the imminent arrival of store-ships should remain unannounced, so there were no arrangements to unload and store the cargoes. The racecourse at Athens was chosen for the depot for RAF stores, but an early visitor told of what he saw: the grandstand piled to the roof with supplies, detailed issues being handled in the totalisator hall and the racetrack itself a solid stack of supplies for half a mile, all mixed and with a high percentage of broken cases. Petrol and lubricants were on the far side of the course, next to several thousand gallons of what was described as 'Molotov cocktail mixture'. The depot staff had no idea of what stock was there.

Within six months enemy mining and bombing took their toll at Piraeus, where there was a large build-up of shipping and inadequate safety equipment. The ammunition ship SS *Clan Fraser* took fire and, despite several hours of attempts to isolate the blaze, she blew up, destroying several sheds on the quay and seriously damaging other parts of the docks. Pieces of the hull were blown over a wide area and since they were red-hot they set fire to whatever they hit. As well as full-size ships in the harbour, there were lighters full of inflammable items such as tents, which caught fire, then drifted alongside other ships and set light to them too. It was impossible to move the shipping as many basins in the port had been mined; within a week of the German entry into the war in Greece, Piraeus and other coastal areas were unusable, and by the middle of April it was obvious that the British could not remain in Greece and evacuation orders were given.

The islands in the Aegean and Crete required comparatively little work from the movement control staff, but the island of Malta, and its neighbour Gozo, were, given their position in the comparatively narrow channel between Italy and North Africa, strategically important and thus constantly attacked by the enemy. Escorted convoys were the only possible way to get supplies to Malta, and these, too, were attacked by the enemy from the air and on (and under) the sea. Between December 1941 and November 1942, only fifteen cargo ships reached Malta, and three of these were sunk in the Grand Harbour on their arrival. This situation continued, with many of the ships that did reach the island being sunk in the harbour. For those ships which did reach the harbour, special arrangements were used. Four vessels were unloaded simultaneously and the contents were immediately moved from the quays to dumps, where it was later sorted and moved to depots under a civil police escort to avoid pilfering.

Operation Torch was the name given to the Allied (American/British) invasion of North Africa, and its commencement on 8 November 1942 was the result of much planning at Allied Force headquarters, at that time based in Gibraltar. Part of this was the supreme commander's ruling that staff sections should be integrated to cover the allied aspects of the operation. However, many of the British functions did not have parallel functions in the US Army; movements was one of them. It was finally agreed that the operation should be divided into three sections: the assault on Casablanca by the US Western Task Force, mounted in the USA; the assault on Oran by the Centre Task Force mounted in the UK and supported by the Royal Navy; and the assault on Algiers. This was a combined operation, initially commanded by an American general but then transferred to the commander-in-chief of the British First Army.

All assaults were to be made on 8 November 1942. The first assault is not covered here as the British army was not involved. The second assault was assisted by the military landing officers who liaised with the Royal Navy and the British dock operating personnel on landing the motor transport. There were some difficulties with the motor transport landings on the beaches. One beach, known as X, was found to be of very soft sand and 'Sommerfeld' track had to be laid to provide a durable surface. Some heavy swells caused delays in landing, but even so, the task was completed within four days. On a second beach, known as Y, it was found that there was a sand bar about 25 yards short of the low water line; when the amphibious landing craft encountered this, they thought it was safe to drive the motor vehicles off, but found it was not, and several sank. This meant the discharge was slowed as fewer vehicles were taken each time, to lighten the load and allow the landing craft to clear the bar and get right in. On the other beaches, the task took six days to complete, landing 35,508 men, 12,878 tons of stores and 2,629 motor vehicles.

The line of communication between Tangiers and Tunis included a single rail line and a single road, both running roughly parallel to the sea, but much of the way climbed up into the mountains. Neither was capable of moving large amounts of freight, partly because of the distances, but mainly, on the railway, because of a shortage of locomotives, wagons, coal and railway operatives. Although demanded from the UK immediately, these all took weeks to arrive.

The ports along the coast tended to be too shallow for the larger ships. At Algiers there were berths for eighteen freight ships, but limited clearance facilities which could handle no more than 3,500 tons per day. The other three ports had even less capacity: Phillipeville 1,100 tons per day and Bone 2,500 tons per day. The capacity of Bougie had been reduced to just 1,200 tons per day as a result of air raids. Once it was cleared of sunken ships and the quays repaired, this amount rose to between 4,000 and 5,000 tons per day.

British army staff in Washington

At the beginning of the war, the Ministry of Supply was responsible for purchasing, management and despatch of bulk food products such as wheat, vehicles, spare parts and lubricants, in and from the US and Canada. They were able to arrange for lubricants to be standardised across the range of vehicles. After September 1939 the Ministry set up a purchasing organisation for trade with the two countries. America passed the Lend-Lease Act in 1941, under the terms of which they would supply Britain with many of her needs in exchange for the use of bases in British territories and other services. The original arrangement was that the supplies and material should be shipped from North America to the UK, but it was soon decided that stores should be sent direct to theatres of war from North America, thus saving shipping space.

This was one of the responsibilities of the quartermaster general and so a military staff was established in North America to take over the material procured in the US and Canada and to be responsible for shipping it to the required destinations. This was amalgamated with other British military missions to the US into a new headquarters which bore the title of British Army Staff (BAS), Washington.

The supplies and transport branch of BAS took over the functions which had previously been handled by the Ministry of Supply, including the maintenance of reserves in North America and the shipping of these to the UK and other theatres of war when needed. They also had to organise and maintain liaison between the War Office, the British food mission in North America and the US Service departments to ensure the coordinated action of the various ministries and other bodies concerned in provision and shipping, to place War Office demands, and to oversee the RASC maintenance of the Caribbean area and Bermuda.

BAS did not have control of inland movement of goods to ports, which was done by an American organisation, the War Forwarding Corporation. The loading of ships, which were owned and operated by commercial companies, was done by the owners, despite the British Ministry of War Transport (BMWT) having responsibility for it. This meant that the BAS military control staff had to coordinate the work of these organisations, and several others.

On the British side there were the BMWT, the British Merchant Shipping Mission, the British Supply Council, the British and Dominion Supply Mission, the UK Commercial Corporations and the NAAFI. On the American side there were the War Department, the Transportation Corps, the Port Agencies, the Navy department, the War Shipping Administration, the Foreign Economic Administration, the Commercial Corporation, and the State Department. There was also the Middle East Supply Council and United Nations Rehabilitation and Relief Administration, and they were also involved with intelligence services, including the navy, military and air intelligence branches, the Joint Intelligence Committee and the Inter-Service Topographical Department Liaison officer.

At the start, Priority of Movement Meetings were held weekly in New York, but once the BAS had moved to Washington the meetings were held fortnightly. A further meeting was held monthly when US agencies advised the tonnages of cargo for dispatch direct to theatres, and another weekly meeting related to the large amounts of cereals being transported internally and overseas.

In the early months, shipping did not cause any problems as Lend-Lease had only just started and there was sufficient space for military cargoes. One problem was that these cargoes were produced and forwarded by commercial firms, which had no knowledge of military procedures. Embarkation Staff Officers (ESOs) had to be sent to all ports to observe the loading and ensure that 'linked' components were in the same vessel, and that items such as tanks and guns were properly stowed to be quickly usable at their destination. The principal ports where ESOs were posted were Philadephia, Baltimore, New Orleans, San Francisco, Los Angeles and Portland, Oregon. There was a lot of activity at the start, with stores going to India and personnel to Australia, but this gradually reduced until the end of 1943 when the offices at Philadephia and Los Angeles were closed and staff reduced at San Francisco. This was partly due to the opening of the Mediterranean and a decision by the US War Department to use the East Coast ports for military loading. To compensate for this, the office in Baltimore was enlarged and the port at Savannah was taken into military use.

Until 1942 sailing cables were sent by the British Ministry of War Transport and the British Ministry of Supply Mission, but it was found that these did not include enough information to allow the recipients to identify the stores on arrival. The movements staff then sent their own sailing cables, having organised a system by which bills of lading would be passed to the head office in Washington. Over 4,000 such cables were sent in 1943.

In September 1942, despatches of stores by air started, first through the RAF to the UK, and through the British commission to the Middle East and India. Early shipments were as little as 2,000lb per month. These increased until by the end of 1943 the average monthly amounts were over 120,000lb.

The system in Canada was very different from the American system as the Lend-Lease, where it applied at all, was only for small tonnages. The authority for freight movements lay with the transport controller, whose office was in Toronto. Until the autumn of 1941 there were no British movements officers in Canada; the transport controller made all the arrangements for internal and overseas transport. Once movement officers had arrived, BAS headquarters was set up in Ottawa and from there and Montreal the transport controller was informed of BAS requirements, of priorities and component matching. This soon led to more movement offices in Halifax, St John, and Vancouver.

No records are available for shipments from North America in 1942, but in 1943 the total was 3,832,264 tons, and in 1944 it was 4,302,154. In each of these years the bulk of the shipments went to the UK, the Middle East and the central Mediterranean. In 1945 it was just 486,653 to the UK, 1,589,371 to the British Liberation Army, 1,128,777 to India and 640,114 to the central Mediterranean and various others, giving a total of 4,286,196 tons.

The BAS also had a transportation branch in Washington. It started out in July 1941 as the engineers' section at the British Military Mission before it became the BAS, and it dealt with procurement through the Engineer Corps of the US War Department, and within a month acquired a transportation technical supply officer who had handled the procurement of railway and dock equipment, railway locomotives and other rolling stock, track, and cargo-handling equipment. The purchase of portal wharf cranes for the Middle East and Persian Gulf ports was handled by a second officer.

When the US joined the war, what had been equipment built to British specifications was superseded by items of American design, a not unreasonable situation given that the US was going to be using most of this equipment, even though it was meant for common use. The US War Department took the position that the war would be short, and production was based on speed rather than durability. This inevitably led to a need for spares, and a scale for each item of spares was produced for items needed for a year's operation. In November 1942, the US Transportation Corps was formed, with its own procurement division. At about the same time, a Joint Standardisation Committee was set up to deal with items in common use and production priorities for them. It was estimated at this point that some 2,000 locomotives, 40,000 trucks, hundreds of cranes, 2,000 miles of track and numerous other items would be needed, and action was taken immediately to obtain the necessary raw materials for production. Production of tugs, barges and ramped cargo lighters was accelerated to boost supplies of water-borne transport.

By 1943, railway bridges had become a major item. They had not been of particular interest to the US until they had to provide a portion of the joint stockpile for Europe and the central Mediterranean. This involved some 39,000 tons of British steel bridging and trestling supplies, a figure which soon increased to 109,000 tons when the enemy began targeting bridges.

In 1943 the various sections which dealt with the movement of freight came together as a formal Directorate of Freight Movement. Its terms of reference were two part: the movement of all War Department material by land, sea and air, and the coordination of the quartermaster general's services in respect of war maintenance. Its staff included officers experienced in traffic operations by road and rail, and Merchant Navy officers qualified in sea-borne cargo-handling.

War maintenance related to shipments for major operational locations and the routes to them from the beginning of the war. Movement by air was a special task, including the shipment of spare parts for tanks in North Africa, which would not have been able to continue their work without them.

An air despatch section was organised, consisting of freight collecting centres next to the principal airfields that would be used for the flights. A special transport column carried out collection of the cargo and loading the aircraft; particular railheads were designated for special collections. In emergency situations, bomber aircraft were also used to move freight from alternate airfields. The speed with which material was moved was impressive:

demands could be received at the War Office one evening, cargo moved overnight and the cargoes sent off the following morning. Over the course of one year, when this system was in full operation, some 50,000 tons of freight were sent in almost 20,000 flights.

As early as 1939, staff officers were recruited from British railways to handle problems arising with rail freight. Until the evacuation most of the traffic was outward, with such return traffic as there was consisting of salvage, vehicles for repair, and empty packing cases. During the evacuation, export movements were suspended in favour of repatriating as much material as possible to prevent it falling into enemy hands. Between 28 May and 12 July 1940, some 70,000 tons of material was unloaded at the various ports and sent on by rail to War Department depots throughout the country. Over 11,000 wagons were used, most going from Southampton and Newport. Ammunition was the greatest item, with 2,075 wagons going to Cosham and 1,165 to Longmoor. Congestion at terminals was eased by 'stabling' trains at intermediate points along the routes, and diverting traffic between receiving depots. Each War Department depot telegraphed a daily traffic report to the War Office Movement Directorate; this proved so effective as a basis for controlling the day-to-day flow of traffic that it was continued throughout the war.

Merchant Navy officers were seconded; one of their main duties was known as 'pre-stowage'. Service branches in the War Office submitted full details, including weights and dimensions, of what they wanted to be shipped, and this, with priorities, was passed to the stowing officers. They worked out the best way to split the total cargoes (allowing for the possible results of a ship being lost at sea) and submitted a plan, with a separate list of vehicles to be shipped 'on wheels' (as opposed to 'cased'). They also sent detailed plans of all the ships in the convoy, showing dimensions of the cargo space, the size and position of hatches and coamings, derrick capacities and the positions of all potential impediments in the holds such as stanchions and bulkheads. They were aided in this task by a set of scale model vehicles, from jeeps to the largest lorries, which allowed them to ensure that each could be got into (and out of) the position allotted to it in the plan. This allowed the cargoes to be despatched to the ports in the correct sequence for loading. As well as the vehicles, priorities were set for stores: those for discharge at the same time as the vehicles, those for discharge immediately after the vehicles, and those for later discharge.

When the United States entered the war, their equipment and other stores required a substantial proportion of world tonnage, and it was necessary to create a set of priorities. The three main items in this were imports for domestic use in the UK, for military operations, and the military export programmes for maintenance of our British overseas; on a much smaller scale there were other export programmes to locations such as Australia and Africa.

As the size of the forces to be maintained in the Middle East and North Africa increased, the long voyages round the Cape with supplies put an enormous strain on available shipping resources, and it was decided to investigate the possibility of an overland line of communication across central Africa. The only route suitable for moving large amounts of stores was from Matadi at the mouth of the Congo River across the centre of the continent by river, rail and road to Juba on the Upper Nile and then by rail and river to Egypt and the Mediterranean. This route was designated the Congo-Nile Trans-African Line of Communication (AFLOC). It consisted of eight different sections, each with a different transport method.

The first 228 miles, from Matadi to Leopoldville, was by 3ft 6in gauge railway; the next 1,012 miles to Aketi was by river, followed by 410 miles of 60cm railway, 360 miles by road, another 846 miles by river, 860 miles by 3ft 6in gauge railway, 223 miles by river and finally 550 miles by standard gauge (4ft 8½in) railway to Cairo, making a total of 4,489 miles. The Directorate of Transportation had to ensure that all sections were able to handle the target tonnage of 30,000 tons of stores and 800 cased vehicles per month. They had to provide wharf cranes for the ports at Matadi and Leopoldville, locomotives and wagons for the rail sections, arranging for the building of some of those sections, and providing barges and tugs for the Congo River section.

However, it was found that the targets were not achievable: in November 1942 the monthly capacity was only 3,000 tons and 400 cased vehicles. By the spring of 1943 the situation in the Mediterranean had changed and the AFLOC route became less important. The Americans, whose shipping also had to go round the Cape, pulled out of the scheme. The British carried on for a while with much reduced targets, but in March 1944 all work ceased and the route was abandoned.

Chapter 3

Transport and the Royal Army Service Corps

As well as the Directorate of Transportation, there was also a Directorate of Supplies and Transport (DST), which formed another layer between the concept and administration of moving things around and the actual physical movement of those things. The actual detailed work of these movements was done by the RASC.

Although the supply aspect included food, it also covered all the other items which the army needed, including Petrol Oil and Lubricants (POL) and vehicle spares and consumables such as tyres, without which nothing else could have been moved. Once Japan entered the war and overran several countries in the Far East, it cut off much of the supply of important material such as rubber. The main producer of rubber at the time was Malaya, although a little was produced in Ceylon. Since the raw material for rubber came from trees, increasing production was a slow process. Although rubber itself was not much used in armaments, it was essential for the tyres of the transport which delivered small arms, ammunition and other stores.

Before the war, the DST was responsible for mobilisation, planning and peace organisation of road transport, hiring of civilian transport where needed, impressment of vehicles and the administration of these. They also advised on Road Traffic Acts as they would apply to military transport in wartime.

On the outbreak of war, these responsibilities changed somewhat, to include the provision, maintenance and repair of military vehicles, the preparation of those vehicles for service, the impressment of civilian-owned vehicles and, when necessary, the local hiring of vehicles at home and abroad. In September 1940, the activities were divided into three sections: general policy, organisation, planning and operating war establishments; provision, maintenance and repair of vehicles, spare parts and other stores; and the administration of transport at home including staff cars and War Office transport.

In June 1942 heavy repairs were passed to the newly formed Royal Corps of Electrical and Mechanical Engineers (REME), leaving organisation of vehicles, including amphibian and air transport; and administration of home road transport services.

There were just five base supply depots in 1939, each designed to maintain 85,000 troops. Each divisional RASC organisation consisted of a head-quarters and three companies, each dealing with a specific commodity: one for supplies, one for petrol and one for ammunition. The latter was itself divided into three sections, each with twenty-five load-carrying lorries. These carried fixed amounts of all the various types of ammunition and explosives. Delivery was usually made to first-line unit transport at ammunition points, but gun ammunition was often taken direct to batteries, especially when a major bombardment was planned.

In the Middle East, where there was no railway network and where divisions often operated as independent units, the system was to dump stocks of the three commodities in the forward areas until a certain number of department reserves had built up.

For vehicles there was a general principle that specialised vehicles should be avoided as they could not be used for other purposes, but this could not eliminate them completely. The principle was relaxed when the vehicles requested were for tasks which were on a sufficiently large scale that they could be fully employed, and thus release the general types for other work.

The first specialised vehicles were bulk petrol carriers. Some of these were utilised for carrying water, occasionally overseas but mainly at home during the Blitz to provide water for civilians. The next were tipper lorries, used by the Royal Engineers in the construction of roads, airfields and other places where large areas of flat surface were needed. Other specialised vehicles included troop-carrying lorries and motor coaches, amphibians, snow tractors, jeeps, refrigerated lorries, mobile cranes, tank transporters and assorted trailers.

Tank transporters

Tank transporters were introduced late in 1940. They saved wear on the tank tracks on long trips in non-operational situations, not to mention allowing the crews to rest. Taking no longer than fifteen minutes to load or unload a tank, these transporters included ramps and winches. Most were operated by the RASC, but the RAOC had some for recovering non-running tanks. As the number of tanks in an armoured brigade or tank brigade was 1,040, this was the number of transporters thought to be needed: 715 to carry between 18 and 25 tons and 325 to carry up to 40 tons. The smaller type was included because 300 American vehicles of this sort were available for immediate use. One of these, the 18-ton White transporter, was tried but found unsatisfactory, but a related type, the White-Ruxill, was found to be suitable for loads up to 24 tons.

A demand in April 1941 in the Middle East was filled by sending improvised transporters: 10-ton Mack lorries with hinged ramps. Their theoretical topload was 15 tons, but they were often used for Honey, Valentine and Crusader tanks of up to 20 tons. They lacked winches and inoperable tanks had to be towed up by two 10-ton lorries, an operation which could take up to an hour. A couple of months later a further urgent demand was met by fitting 10-ton lorries with drawbars and trailers. For the heavier loads (up to 40 tons), after some experimentation, a tractor design with a wheeled trailer was adopted. Fitted with winches, it could load a 'dead' tank in less than ten minutes. However, these vehicles were less useful in desert or muddy conditions as they had a tendency to bog down.

The original basis of one transporter for each tank in use was soon modified in the interests of economy. The light type of transporter was abolished and converted into 15-ton load-carriers for use on lines of communication and for heavy loads at home. Lighter tanks could be, and were, carried on the heavy transporters.

The tank transporter companies had five main functions: strategic (taking tanks to assembly areas before action); tactical (taking tanks to their initial action positions, complete with a full load of fuel and fresh crews); reinforcement with replacement tanks; salvage of damaged tanks; and mobility (moving damaged tanks which might otherwise have had to be abandoned). The transporter drivers were trained in the main elements of recovery and the handling of damaged tanks. The transporters were also used for other 'heavy lift' tasks.

In the Middle East, replacement tanks went by sea or rail to Tobruk and were loaded there for onward delivery to their operating units. On landing tanks at the docks at Suez, it was found that the tanks did not have brakes and should not be attached to the truck with ropes. Informal instructions for loading were 'stand on the platform, guide the RASC driver up the 30-degree ramps with hand signals and then jump down as the tracks crash down where you had been standing.'

During the battle for the Mareth Line, transporters travelled to Tripoli and Medenin, a total journey of 1,140 miles. This took twenty-two days for the delivery and return, with rest stops at convenient camps, many of which included workshops.

Motorcycles and jeeps

In 1940 the army used Ariel WMG (350cc) motorcycles, but after Dunkirk all those still in use were passed to the RAF and the army got more powerful versions including the BSA WD M20 (500cc) from 1942. They also had Matchless 350cc and James ML motorcycles for airborne service, and a smaller version known as the 'clockwork mouse' (125cc) which could be dropped by parachute or carried in gliders. These were used in Operation Market Garden.

By August 1941 there was an estimated shortfall of 50,000 motorcycles for the following year, and the possibility of setting up a new factory was considered, as well as asking Canadian manufacturers to produce a motorcycle to the War Department pattern, but this involved a nine-month delay for setup.

An alternative to the motorcycle, especially those with an attached sidecar, was the American jeep. With four-wheel drive and capable of carrying 5cwt, it was an effective cross-country vehicle. In trials against motorcycles and sidecars, the jeep came out on top; it was then calculated that a minimum of 15 per cent of motorcycles could be replaced by jeeps (60 per cent in the Middle East), where motorcycles had been found unsuitable for convoy control in the Western Desert. They could be carried in lorries for communication work when units were stationary. This suggested a saving of 15,000 motorcycles by using 12,000 jeeps. An order for 10,000 was placed immediately.

The Willys jeep, first used in 1940, was originally called a 'utility car': it had four-wheel drive, a top weight of 1,300lb and a payload of 600lb. Although over 100 companies were invited to quote, all but two felt they could not meet the specifications in the given time. One of these two, the American Bantam Car Co.'s version, was thought in road tests to lack power and robustness. The other was Willys Overland Co. The upper weight limit was revised to 2,160lb. Ford made many jeeps to Willys' design. Many thousands of these were given to the UK under the Lend-Lease Act. An amphibious version was produced but not popular; known as the 'Seep' (sea-going jeep), it was difficult to handle in the water. Its maximum speed in water was 5.5 miles per hour; on land it was 50 miles per hour.

Jeeps were shipped in two forms: 'partly knocked down' and 'fully knocked down'; both had to be assembled on delivery. It had a 4-cylinder side-valve engine, with a top speed of 60mph, and its range was 300 miles. By the end of the war 640,000 had been built. They carried four men plus the driver and their equipment; some had provision for mounting machine guns.

Jeeps proved extremely popular with the troops, who tended to 'borrow' them for improper use such as trips into the nearest town, and by July 1943 it became necessary to fix a policy for their use. This was restricted to fighting headquarters and units in the field; other administrative headquarters and units were to continue use of the usual two-seater cars rather than jeeps. Jeeps with trailers were found to be extremely useful in Italy, where the Royal Engineers immediately saw their usefulness in carrying road-building material and personnel.

Trailers had already demonstrated their usefulness in civilian commercial situations. They gave economy of petrol, personnel and vehicles as they only required one prime mover. However, they were not always as useful to the military. If they bogged down in soft ground or sand, they were difficult to extract; this made them generally impractical for use in the Western Desert or on beaches. They were deemed only suitable for line of communication transport, but were so useful there that each vehicle was fitted with towbars and and its own trailer.

Tipper lorries were found to be very useful with road repair/construction platoons, carrying stone, and, in the winter in northern climes, sand to spread on icy roads.

Amphibians

There were five types of amphibian craft available: the Landing Craft Tank (LCT), the Z Craft, the Landing Craft Mechanised (LCM), and the Ramped Cargo Lighter (RCL). The LCT was the largest: it was considered highly suitable for its size, range, and ability to operate in rivers and get out to sea. With deck space of 62ft by 26ft, it had plenty of room, a cargo capacity of 150 tons plus a drinking water capacity of 38 tons, and a range of up to 700 miles at 7½ knots when fully loaded (10 knots unloaded). Its ramp was 12ft 6in, and its side walls were 4ft 6in high. The ramps were at the front (bow) and the engines and bridge were at the back (stern) of the craft; they were driven bow-first onto a suitable beach or other landing place.

There was a larger version of this craft called the Landing Ship Tank (LST), at 180ft by 29ft. As well as the lower deck, which was well-ventilated, it also had room on the upper deck.

The Z Craft was larger than LCTs, at 72ft by 28ft, but with lower side walls at only 1ft 6in. The ramp still 12ft 6in wide, and the range was still 700 miles, although with those low sides it was not suitable for high loads at sea. The Z Craft had a sloping hull at the front to allow easy running-up on beaches. They were made in India in pre-fabricated sections, and put together in Egypt.

There were two versions of the LCM: the Mark I at 25ft by 11ft 6in floor space, with a ramp 11ft 6in wide and 10ft long, a carrying capacity of 35 tons and a maximum range of 56 miles at 7½ knots. Its sides were 61in high. The Mark III [there doesn't seem to have been a Mk II in use] was 31ft 6in by 10ft 9in, had a maximum range of 140 miles, a ramp width of 10ft 2in and length of 10ft 2in.

The RCL was intended for inland transport only, such as crossing lakes or rivers, or proceeding along rivers. It had a wooden ramp and floor.

The branch of the DST which handled water transport was formed in August 1940. By August 1944 it had been upgraded to handle all water transport operated by the RASC and the ports from which they operated, as well as the necessary stores. They also dealt with the design, construction and conversion of all vessels, machinery and other equipment. At the beginning of the war, the War Department fleet consisted of sixty-six vessels worldwide. These were owned by the War Department and operated by civilian crews. There were also civilian technical advisers who supervised the maintenance of craft operating at home. These were mainly used to carry baggage, ammunition and barrack stores between military stations on the coast. Some high-speed craft were used to tow targets for sea defence practice.

The first amphibian vehicles in the service were Landing Vehicles, Tracked (LVTs), also known as Alligators. It was originally suggested that they should be manned by the Royal Marines, but in July 1942 it was pointed out that they were to be used for moving stores on inland waterways and on beaches, so they would be better handled by the RASC. Some 300 Alligators were ordered from America and it was decided that they should be operated by three motor-boat companies, with the personnel being drivers and watermen.

During the course of the war, water transport was handled by two separate organisations: the Transport Branch (Inland Water Transport) of the Royal Engineers, and the Water Transport branch of the RASC. These developed from performing routine work with vessels manned by civilian crews, to numerous tasks in active theatres with military crews. The vessels were organised by their type and role.

For non-operational work, whether at home or abroad, they were organised into water transport companies. These were known as the War Department fleet, and moved stores along the British coast and sometimes as far as Gibraltar and Malta. After 1939 the Inland Water Transport service began acquiring special vessels needed for port construction and repair, such as dredgers, and in late 1940 formed two motor boat companies, each with forty launches. The crews might be used to man other craft. In North Africa they used captured and requisitioned craft.

In 1943, several Fire-Boat companies were established, each with six firefighters and a crew of three RASC men: two coxswains and an engineer in the larger vessels (61ft 6in) and five firefighters and two crew in the smaller vessels (45ft).

Ambulance launches were used in the Far East to evacuate casualties in combined operations, and move them from small to larger port hospitals. Each could carry twenty lying or forty sitting cases. The ambulance launch companies had sixteen 112ft launches each with a twelve-man crew. There was also a plan for floating workshops, repair craft and amphibians, but the war ended before they came into use.

DUKW

These amphibious wheeled 2½-ton lorries were first used by the Americans in the North Africa campaign. The British army immediately saw their usefulness and a set of officers and NCOs were trained in their use; they went on to train 700 RASC drivers. Their primary function was conveying cargo from ship to shore without the need for additional handling, but they also proved useful in waterlogged streets after torrential rain, and since they were wheeled, for other load-carrying duties.

The name 'DUKW' was derived from the makers' initial codes:

D – the year of manufacture (1942)
U – body style (Utility, amphibious)
K – all-wheel drive
W – dual rear axles

DUKWs could carry twenty-five soldiers and their equipment, an artillery piece or 5,000lb of general cargo. Their engine capacity was 91 horsepower, with engines made by GMC or Chevrolet. They had a maximum sea speed of 5 knots, a maximum land speed of 50 miles per hour, and an operational range of 400 miles. There was a slightly larger British made version of the DUKW called the Terrapin, which could carry up to 9,000lb of cargo or an equivalent number of men.

In Holland, when the River Maas overflowed its banks after heavy rain (and helped by German demolition crews), DUKWs continued to work in the flooded streets. There were some problems associated with this: hidden pot-holes or other heavy debris hidden below the water led to many damaged wheels and tyres.

A section of DUKWs was used in Burma when all the bridges on the road from Tamu to Kalewa were washed away by floods. The only alternative route was on the River Wu, a journey of about 30 miles, the trip taking four hours downstream and up to nineteen hours upstream, dodging logs and other debris en route. This was not always successful and a water-borne machinery lorry was added to the workshop platoon as it was rarely possible to bring damaged DUKWs on land.

The general policy for amphibians in the Far East was to use two types of amphibians: support vessels including two types of LVTs, and load carriers for use in assault and maintenance. These included DUKWs and Terrapins. Both wheeled and tracked amphibians were used, those for support being manned by Royal Marines and load-carriers by the RASC.

Water transport

The RASC fleet was originally known as the War Department fleet. In 1939, it had seventy vessels; by 1945 this number had risen to more than 1,400. Much of this increase was through requisitioning, mostly of cabin cruisers and launches. The first water transport companies were formed in January 1940, operating in and out of British ports, with one in Singapore. The first big operation for this fleet was the evacuation of the BEF from Dunkirk. During this operation the fleet was badly damaged by enemy fire. With the threat of invasion, the fleet patrolled estuaries and other stretches of water thought likely to be used by the enemy for seaplane landings.

Later tasks carried out by the fleet included cargo-carrying to the Faroe Islands in November 1942, and at about this time the RASC fleet started work in overseas theatres. The first station was on the North African coast, with ten vessels which had been sent in a convoy. There was a strong presence in southern Italy and across the Adriatic, often using chartered vessels with Italian crews. Further afield, there were companies in West and East Africa and the Far East, especially Burma.

Equine transport

In October India provided four animal transport companies, consisting of 1,536 mules and 528 transport carts, each of which was pulled by two mules and carried 800lb. These arrived at the end of December.

In North Africa, pack mules were the only transport able to cope in the mountains in bad weather. Horse transport was much used in the Middle East due to the lengthening of the desert lines of communication and the need to conserve tyres and petrol stocks. The first horse transport company was formed in early 1941 to work in the base ordnance depot, then two more that year, one in 1942 and four in 1943. Each had seven British officers, forty-three British other ranks and 486 local civilians, with up to 200 wagons with a maximum load of two tons. In Egypt the wagons were locally produced and had pneumatic tyre wheels. These units were used for short hauls in base areas and on dock clearance. They were also used on road and airfield constructions, especially at Haifa and Beirut.

When donkeys were needed at Tripoli, they arrived in small groups in lorries with their Bedouin owners, and were put into a hastily constructed 100 square yard corral, male and female and all sizes together, whereupon a battle royal commenced. A second corral was rapidly built to separate the sexes, but no sooner had one jackass been forcibly removed than another mixed load were put in. All this was observed with great amusement by the watching Bedouin.

On home stations, as in the Middle East, rubber and petrol were scarce early in 1942, so horses were used to carry coal and deliver packages. The theory was that one motorised vehicle could be released for each horse-drawn vehicle brought into use. There were plenty of horses but only 560 wagons available.

At the end of the First World War one animal transport company had been retained in the training battalions as a core in case of future needs. The theory at that time was that motorised transport could go anywhere, but this was soon found to be incorrect.

In the Far East, all types of animal were used except camels. Elephants hauled timber for bridge-building, helped make airfields, carried stores, evacuated casualties and were used for shunting in rail-served depots. Most valuable was the mule, but standards of animal management were less than perfect. Shortages of mules meant ponies and donkeys had to be used, but donkeys often proved stubborn under fire and this, as reported by one officer, 'was apt to be awkward for the driver'.

In Malta in 1941 the RASC hired more than 500 mule carts at £5 per week each. On Gibraltar, some parts of the Rock which were essential for defence were too steep for a road, so a small pack company of fifty animals was formed. The UK government objected to sending hay from England, where it was scarce, so Gibraltar had to buy locally or from North Africa.

Pack mules were much used in the Italian mountains, especially the Apennines, where their common and sometimes uncommon sense was appreciated. One such case was the ambulance mule Nina, who took full advantage of her human friends and their chocolate ration, growing quite fat on the proceeds. She disappeared during an attack on Borgo Tossinago and it was thought she was gone forever, but a couple of days later there was a banging on the door and when it was opened, there she stood with an unconscious man in a litter on each side. The patients were too ill to remember what had happened, but it was assumed that the enemy had loaded her and turned her loose. She had found her way home over miles of mountain track in the darkness, an astonishing feat which no doubt assured the continuation of her chocolate ration.

In Assam, in north-east India, the necessity for heavy use of animal transport put great strain on drivers who were then always tired. Some 50 per cent were found to have had no leave for at least 18 months. The commander of 33 Corps agreed that rest for drivers must take priority over operations in the monsoon season, and large numbers were immediately sent on leave. The policy after this was then for 5 per cent of the drivers always to be on leave.

Orders for drivers

Driving military vehicles, especially off road, was not the simplest of tasks, and numerous sets of orders for drivers and training pamphlets were produced. One of these sets of orders, issued for drivers of mechanical transport, said:

- No smoking, neither when driving or within 25 yards of any vehicle carrying petrol or other flammable stores.
- Tarpaulins should be kept well tied down as they are too expensive to lose.
- Know the speed limit for your vehicle, and keep to it.

- Do your best to preserve the tyres and springs of your vehicle by choosing your path when not on a proper road, and drive slowly. Springs and tyres are not only expensive in themselves, they are costly to ship.
- As soon as you finish your detail, fill your vehicle with fuel, oil and water.
- Make sure you know where you are going and how to get there. If uncertain about this, ask an NCO or officer.
- Always report any defects in your vehicle.
- When you halt, get down from the vehicle carrying your rifle, keep off the road but do not go more than 25 yards from the vehicle.
- Never abandon your vehicle without an order from your officer. Treat it as if you had to pay for repairs.
- Your job is to deliver the goods at the right time and place, and keep on doing it. Be prepared to die rather than fail in your duty.

A training pamphlet on driving wheeled vehicles cross-country in the Middle East remarked 'a wilderness of crumbling rock and soft sand may seem uncrossable at the first attempt, but it is surprising how easy it becomes with a little experience and confidence.' It went on:

The cross country driver must remember that he has not only to get to his destination, but to do so without having
- Strained his vehicle or its springs.
- Damaged his cargo by crashing over bumps.
- Damaged his tyres by collision with large rocks.
- Wasted his radiator water by allowing it to leak or boil away.
- Delayed the rest of the column by getting stuck in soft sand when this might have been avoided, or by failing to get on the move again quickly when stuck.
- Before starting, make sure you know your destination and its distance and bearing. Always note the speedometer reading.
- Stay on the alert. Look well ahead and choose the best route to take, don't just follow other trucks.
- Over difficult country, get your passenger to help by standing up and looking ahead; it is easier to spot hazards from a height. The best cross-country vehicles are those whose crews and passengers work together as a team.
- Watch the vehicles ahead for indications of obstacles which you can't see. The depth of tracks they make may indicate soft going.
- Always be ready to brake suddenly, even violently, to avoid unseen bumps and rocks. The safest speed over any surface is one where you can be sure of pulling up in time to avoid a hazard or bump.

- When approaching hazards (bumps, rocks, soft sand or mud) always change down a gear. A higher average speed is achieved by accelerating hard immediately hazards are passed.
- Never stay in high gear at low speeds; the engine is liable to overheat and you cannot be in full control. But don't race the engine in low gear any longer than strictly necessary. This damages the engine and wastes fuel.
- Front-wheel drive should only be used when crossing soft ground or climbing very steep hills, where the rear wheels might otherwise slip.

When driving on soft sand, drivers were warned to avoid getting stuck by avoiding following exactly in previous tracks, no matter how old, where they entered a patch of sand, but to try a different place; when halting on a sand surface, never to brake hard but let the vehicle come gently to rest. When starting, to be gentle with the clutch or the wheels might sink in. To try to avoid halting on soft sand and make a point of approaching a patch of sand as fast as possible and in the most suitable gear, and with four-wheel drive engaged. (There were no speed limits in sandy country.)

If drivers did get stuck, they should:

- Get themselves and everyone else out of the vehicle.
- Unload the sand-trays. Due to the shortage of steel, not every vehicle carries these, so they may have to borrow them from another vehicle. Four is best, one for each wheel.
- Check the extent of the trouble and walk about to find the nearest firm ground.
- Decide whether to get out forwards or backwards.
- Get everyone busy on their knees clearing sand from the wheels with both hands.
- Make sure the front wheels are straight.
- Remove the sand from in front of the driving wheels so the sand trays can rest in grooves, with the lower ends under the wheels and level with their bases and with the other ends level with the general level of the surrounding sand. The driver engages his lowest gear and everyone else pushes.

One experienced driver remarked that with the whole crew practised at the business of inserting sand trays, doing this, even for all four wheels, need take no more than two minutes. An alternative to sand trays was sand mats; these were long flexible mats with ropes at one end for ease of handling. They were for small vehicles (30cwt and under). They were little use for getting a stuck vehicle out backwards. They should be laid in front of the front wheels, rope ends forwards. Two men should manoeuvre them as necessary by pulling sideways on the ropes to keep them under the wheels. After use, they should be rolled up starting at the rope end so that the ropes were securely in the middle of the roll.

One method of crossing large areas of soft sand was to let some of the air out of the tyres, but this was used as a last resort only, and the tyres reinflated as soon as the soft sand was passed. With soft tyres, care should be taken to avoid rocks which might cause tyres to burst.

To prevent the tyres creeping on the wheels, the pressures should not be reduced below:

- For pneumatic tyres fitted to divided type wheels, for 12.00, 13.50 and 15.00 sizes, 20lb, for other sizes, 15lb.
- For pneumatic tyres fitted to flat base wheels, all sizes, 35lb.
- Runflat tyres fitted to divided type wheels, all sizes 5lb.
- These reduced pressures should be identical on all wheels, and should only be done on an officer's orders.

If the leading truck went through the soft sand, the others should follow the same route, but if the leading truck got stuck, the others could either try their luck or halt. The former action might result in the whole column getting badly stuck, especially annoying when an easier route might have been available. The best response to seeing the lead truck getting stuck was for all to halt on firm ground, then one truck go to help. Meanwhile, an officer should go forward on foot to find a better route.

Drivers had to watch for and avoid lateral bumps across the route, as these affected both wheels on one axle at the same time. When unavoidable, the driver should swerve as he approached them so he crossed at an angle. Desert ground is often crossed by numerous steep-sided runnels and 'tacking' in series of diagonals across them was usually the best option. These bumps were prevalent in gravelly ground as well as sandy, and if crossing them in daylight when there was likely to be aerial surveillance, following the crests made the vehicle less obvious.

Muddy and snowy conditions

Wet mud was more dangerous than dry sand. The vehicle might sink deeply, the wheels were more likely to spin and it took more labour to clear them. If they could not be avoided, drivers walked them first with a spade or pick before attempting to drive across. They always crossed slowly, as the mud might hide deep holes or invisible rocks. Crossing was done in low gear and without racing the engine or stopping. If the wheels did start spinning, drivers would try once to get out in reverse, then stop. They would clear away any mud that had built up round the wheels, then use any firm objects such as stones, brushwood or wheel-chains to create a clear track from the wheels towards firmer ground.

Some early trials of machines driven by propellers or screws were carried out in America and Canada, including the Eliason toboggan, which was driven by an endless belt with cleats for grip, but its climbing ability was poor and it was not taken up. Another was the Bombadier snow motor, a half-track vehicle developed in Canada for civilian purposes. It was thought to be insufficiently robust for military use, and although Canada built a few, the British army did not use them.

Several different types of small vehicles for use in muddy and snowy conditions were adopted, including varieties of the Canadian armoured snowmobile: the Mud Cat was a type of snowmobile that could carry up to four men and two Bren guns and could easily be adapted to be amphibious; the Musk-Rat, a smaller vehicle which took only one man (the driver), could carry a 3,000lb payload; and the Weasel could carry two men and a payload of 1,200lb. The Weasel (also known as the M29 Light Cargo carrier) was successfully adapted to be amphibious and was used in jungle swamps and marshes. Weasels could each tow three 10-ton sledges and were themselves sufficiently lightweight to be taken on trailers to where they were needed.

Engines lose water when they boil as the steam expands and pushes more water into the radiator and out through the overflow pipe. To avoid this, most vehicles were fitted with expansion tanks on top of the radiator. Both the connecting tube and steam vent had to be kept clear, as bottled-up steam could burst the radiator. The expansion tank had to be felt at frequent intervals; if it was very hot, the engine was already boiling and the first opportunity to cool it down should be taken. When halted, drivers would turn the vehicle to face into the wind to help the cooling. If the expansion arrangement was working properly, the tank should be empty and the radiator quite full within minutes of halting. Drivers would check frequently that the expansion system was working properly.

Airborne transport

Given that the main purpose of the RASC was to deliver daily requirements to troops in the field, it made sense that they should investigate and adopt useful new types of transport. One of these was the aeroplane. Although at the time the average plane could carry no more than a 3-ton lorry, their speed and range, combined with the use of parachutes where landing was not possible, made them very useful in broken terrain, especially when used in large numbers as aerial 'convoys'.

There were two terms in use for air transport: 'supply by air', meaning the transport of stores from a main base to a forward or advanced base where they were landed at an airfield in the base, and 'maintenance by air', meaning transport of all the items needed by the troops. This might include reinforcements, and evacuation of casualties and prisoners of war. The system evolved gradually, starting with sending food to France in September 1939. The division of responsibilities was not defined until September 1943 when an interdepartmental committee decided that the RASC should handle freight and its packing: this covered organisation of transport from depots; receiving, sorting and packing stores for air transport; moving the cargoes to the loading areas in the airfields; loading the aircraft for landing or dropping; providing crews to handle the cargoes in the air and at the destination; and distributing the stores on arrival.

The pilots and the management of airfields were the responsibility of the RAF, as was the holding, packing and issuing of parachutes. The RASC was responsible for collecting used parachutes for return and reuse. Some of these activities were different from the usual RASC routines and the personnel had to be trained. This included knowledge of how and where storage was appropriate and which were the strong structures in the aircraft for attaching the load. This required a level of skill considered comparable to gun drills.

A specific organisation was evolved to handle all this, based on air despatch companies. These included loading platoons, each comprised of two officers and eighty other ranks, which were expected to be able to load thirty aircraft simultaneously. The personnel also received training to enable them to act as despatchers if needed. Each air despatch company also had up to five dropping platoons, each of one officer and seventy other ranks, to form fifteen four-man crews who loaded the aircraft and ejected the load over the dropping zone. Some air despatch companies also had air transport platoons, which delivered stores via packing areas to loading areas, was well as other duties to relieve general transport companies. Some also had a workshop platoon.

Before December 1944, ammunition and other ordnance stores were the responsibility of the RASC, but the RAOC took over the preparation, packing and issuing of all ordnance stores except ammunition. This was prepared for packing by the RAOC, then packed by the RASC under RAOC supervision.

Air supply in the Far East was different, in that despatch and receipt was handled by a single group of personnel. Air supply was hampered in the monsoon in Assam, although other transport was equally affected; all but the main roads were often unusable with bridges down and landslides causing major blockages. Almost the only transport which worked was pack mules and these were in short supply. As far as air transport was concerned, the continuous cloud cover prevented air drops. This led to serious food shortages and it was then decreed that all units should carry a minimum of three days' supply and that as soon as a scheduled air drop failed, troops should be put on half-rations. On one occasion there was a five-day failure of air drops, but it was possible to buy rice and cattle locally. If all else failed, there was mule meat, although this was a question of whether hunger was more important than transport and long-eared friends.

Each air transport platoon included a twenty-one man defence section to operate three light machine guns, five anti-tank rifles, and three 20mm anti-aircraft and anti-tank guns. Jeeps were provided for platoons; five jeeps for each of seven sections. These were provided with trailers, one 10cwt trailer per jeep. It was then suggested that each should tow two trailers; there were some objections to this idea, on the basis that it would over-strain the towing vehicle and make it difficult to brake on greasy surfaces and hills. After some tests it was found that no serious harm would arise and more trailers were ordered.

Air drops needed crew who were expert in the techniques of dropping. This might be by parachute for delicate loads such as guns, items in containers which might break on landing, troops, and, in Burma, mules (this worked in trials, with the mules in a crate, but was never used in practice). The alternative, for more robust items, was 'free' dropping. Some of these might be double-packed, in two containers, the outer of which was intended to break on landing. Petrol was one such commodity, for which two bags were used. It worked quite well in trials, but was impractical as bags could not be filled in stores or close to the aeroplane. Consequently the idea had to be abandoned. The principal advantage of free dropping was that the load went straight down rather than drifting in the wind when suspended from a parachute, which meant that accuracy was impossible.

These items needed care in packing. Most were secured to a bottom board or pallet which could be slid along the internal runway to the door; all had to be of a size and shape which could pass through that door easily. The target for air drops was to release the whole load in one pass over the designated landing zone. A trained crew could drop the containers in 8 to 12 seconds. In one particular aircraft, the Stirling, considerable practice was needed if the despatcher was not to accompany the container out of the door. This might be caused by getting tangled in the loads, or failing to secure the lifeline, and was derisively known as 'self-despatch'.

Other problems

There were some problems arising from the Ministry of Supply and its attitudes; for instance, in March 1942 it cut the allocation of rubber for tyres for military vehicles, and threatened to cut it further, to 51 per cent, which would have meant a shortage of 320,000 tyres in that year. It got worse: in order to save over 200 tons of crude rubber, the Ministry of Supply proposed a halving of vehicles manufactured in the UK, then remarked that once reduced, production would be difficult if not impossible to increase again as the necessary labour would have moved elsewhere. This time the War Office stepped in and stated that it would not reduce its requirements.

One can see the Ministry of Supply's point, in that the situation in the Far East was threatening rubber supplies. The War Office was, of course, aware of the problem and asked the Rubber Committee for recommendations to save rubber. They had several: vehicles should have two 'rest' days each week, full-scale formation exercises should be reduced by 25 per cent if possible, abolishing the delivery of stores by road and using handcarts in camps and barracks, reducing the number of vehicles in any given unit or establishment, and conserving tyres in all circumstances. The best solution was to recover and reuse worn tyres by remoulding or recapping them. Remoulding was considered to be the best option and it was decided to use remoulded tyres abroad and recapped tyres at home. As a result of all this, instructions were then issued as follows:

- Tyres were to be removed in time to enable them to be remoulded/recapped.
- The vehicle rest day (also known as a maintenance day) was increased to two days a week, neither to be Sunday and not to be consecutive.
- The use of one third of all transport in the UK on the other five days a week was to be banned except where it would interfere with driver training.
- The maximum possible restrictions were to be placed on the delivery and collection of stores.
- The maximum speed for cars and motor cycles to be reduced from 60 miles per hour to 50 miles per hour.
- The practice of keeping vehicles under load continuously was to be reduced.
- Alternative methods of transport e.g. handcarts and animal transport were to be used in barracks and camps.

Other speed limits were revised, and set at:

a)	cars over 10hp	50 miles per hour
b)	cars under 10hp	40
c)	motor-cycles	50
d)	trucks 15cwt	35
e)	load carriers, 3 ton	20
f)	load carriers, under 3 tons	30
g)	coaches and troop carriers	25
h)	tracked vehicles	20
i)	tractors, tracked	15
j)	tractors, wheeled (including tank transporters)	25 miles per hour

As part of reducing petrol consumption, rationing schemes were introduced. Monthly returns of petrol use were sent from each unit and where the ration had been exceeded the commanding officer had to have a good reason, or pay for it himself. A 'blacklist' was kept.

Vehicle maintenance

In January 1941 the system of vehicle maintenance was revised, dividing work between the RASC and the RAOC. The RASC was given responsibility for all its own vehicles, as well as those of the Royal Army Medical Corps (RAMC), Royal Army Pay Corps (RAPC), Royal Army Veterinary Corps (RAVC), Air Defence (AD) Corps and Intelligence Corps, staff colleges, fire services and all ATS units and establishments, War Department Constabulary and military liaison missions. They also provided RASC and Auxiliary Territorial Service (ATS) drivers for those vehicles.

The RAOC had responsibility for all the rest: vehicles of regimental units or establishments, schools and training units except those listed above, headquarters of infantry and armoured brigades, all Royal Engineers establishments including port, transportation and works services, Military Police and pioneer units, prisoner of war camps, and all welfare and Home Guard organisations. Drivers for these were provided by the service concerned, or by the ATS.

The War Office had been considering the matter of vehicle repairs and workshops for some time before it decided that a new corps was needed, and the Corps of Royal Electrical and Mechanical Engineers (REME) was formed. Rather than disrupt the existing system by a complete simultaneous handover, it was intended to do this in phases. The first started in April 1942, with REME taking over the engineering side of the RAOC and all RASC vehicle repairs, with the exception of those done by RASC workshop platoons. REME also took over the provision, storage and issue of vehicles, including spares and consumables, under the Director of Warlike Stores. It was intended that phase two would commence in November 1942, but a review concluded that this should be postponed. It was reconsidered in April 1944 but no more was done before the end of the war.

Women drivers

Women drivers were mostly members of the Auxiliary Territorial Service (ATS) on a volunteer basis. They were not paid, but were trained in driving and vehicle maintenance. Unless driving transport lorries or ambulances they bought their own cars and used their own petrol on a mileage allowance basis, but this created a problem in that it invalidated their insurance, so the War Office issued a statement to the effect that where a policy was invalidated they would cover the risk. ATS drivers also rode motorcycles. The motor transport units of the ATS were called up for service on 25 August 1939.

The lorries considered suitable for women to drive in July 1941 were laden 40cwt four-wheeled lorries, vans and trucks, ambulances, cars and motorcycles, or unladen 3-ton four-wheeled lorries. A year later this was extended to include larger motorcycles up to 350cc, large cars up to six seats, some 3-ton lorries of specific makes (other makes had peculiarities of construction deemed unsuitable for women) and special vehicles for internal depot use, such as electric auto-trucks. Drivers for the heavier lorries had to be at least thirty years old; none were allowed to drive vehicles with trailers.

Regardless of the type of transport used, the RASC was responsible for the delivery of the goods it carried, as well as the maintenance of the delivery vehicles. The RASC had numerous technically fitted vessels, such as mobile workshops, specially fitted pontoon and bridge-carrying lorries, and motor ambulances.

There were constant calls for supplies at that time, but the actual delivery was hampered by a lack of RASC personnel. It was then proposed that the use of special units should be eliminated and all RASC general transport units should be interchangeable, as should loading personnel.

In June 1940 it was decided that motor coaches should be acquired and formed into motor coach companies to convey numbers of troops. This started with the appointment of sixty RASC officers, including some from the Inspectorate of Supplementary Transport, to begin selecting and earmarking the vehicles to be requisitioned. A War Establishment of a motor coach company was created out of redundant BEF units and formed into thirty companies averaging 240 vehicles, each to carry thirty-two passengers. Eleven more companies were added, which, added to the existing 3,000 coaches, gave a total of 5,560 coaches. There was also a reserve of 400 coaches for maintenance and replacement.

These coaches were not new and had generally done a lot of mileage in their civilian roles, so they soon began to give trouble with breakdowns. Much damage was done to them when they made necessary excursions off road, due to their low clearance. They were the subject of continual complaints.

The acquisition of coaches was urgent, because of the perceived threat of invasion, to the extent that the War Office ordered that availability was to take precedence over age. Many needed complete overhauls before they could be put into use. When there was a mass inspection in August 1940, sixty-five were found to require major repairs and were withdrawn and replaced.

In early 1941, the coaches in home defence organisations were removed from RASC handling, but were regarded as first-line transport and driven by unit personnel. At the same time there were major discussions about their proper use; the original idea was that they were only to be used to move troops in the event of invasion, but they were actually used to move troops anywhere at any time. This did not help their condition.

The Home Guard required its own transport. In London, 1,250 taxicabs were requisitioned; these were driven by Home Guard personnel.

Thought was then given to an alternative type of troop carrier, and an experiment was made by fitting new long frames and bodies to a standard 3-ton Bedford lorry. A prototype was ready in April 1941 and was accepted as a good alternative to coaches. It held thirty passengers, who could embus in 24 seconds and debus in 15. A further modification was made to allow loads when they were not being used by men. Once approved, 1,050 of these were produced and an equal number of coaches were released back to civilian life. Further tranches were produced.

Other vehicles were available for use elsewhere when needed. For possible use in an emergency, the privately owned cars and motorcycles of military personnel were assessed for suitability and earmarked. This raised the question of requisitioning tyres from laid-up vehicles by the Ministry of Supply. It was agreed that where evidence could be produced that the vehicle was earmarked, its tyres would not be requisitioned.

There were some common problems with the provision of the fighting, support and ordinary transport vehicles known as Armoured Fighting Vehicles (AFV). At the beginning of the war there were few firms involved in producing these vehicles. The better known of these were Leyland Motors of Leyland, Lancashire, which made engines and transmissions; Ruston & Hornsby and Ruston-Bucyrus of Lincoln and Grantham, which made some components for infantry and cruiser tanks and assembled these; Fodens, of Sandbach Cheshire, which did the final assembly of cruiser tanks; and LMS Railway and North British Locomotives, of Horwich, Lancashire, and Glasgow respectively, which did the final assembly of infantry tanks. Although production was spread between the locations of these and other firms, they were frequently hit by bombs, which actually did little damage.

At the start of the war, although there was plenty of warning that it was coming, the UK lacked the industrial infrastructure necessary to build stocks of standardised military vehicles. When the war started, the policy of requisitioning vehicles from commercial sources produced a heterogeneous stable of different makes, which meant that maintenance/repair personnel had to be trained on the different makes and types, and stocks of spares for them all had to be supplied. The government and the military never did catch up with the desirable standardisation of vehicles.

Research and development

The War Office had always been involved in research and development, an example being the pneumatic tyre, but until 1935 it had tended to let commercial vehicle builders conduct research and testing. There was a difference of opinion on whether military vehicles should be specialised or of the ordinary civilian type, the latter being the feeling of the motor manufacturers. Some of this was due to the taxation of vehicles, which became higher as the size of the vehicle increased. In addition, the army needed high performance cross-country, which was not in the normal repertoire of British manufacturers, but was in America. Until the US came into the war, the War Office relied on British manufacturers.

Ambulances

While some American built ambulances were used, the British built Austin K2Y (nicknamed 'Katy') was preferred. More than 13,000 of these were built during 1939–40. They served in all theatres and could do 50 miles per hour on good roads. They could carry four stretcher cases or ten seated cases. The Katys weighed 3 tons, were 18ft long, 7ft 5in wide and 9ft high. Many ambulance drivers were ATS.

Trucks

Leyland made the Retriever, with a 6-litre four-cylinder petrol engine. Square fronted, it was used for transport and fitted out to serve as light workshops. Montgomery used one as a field caravan mobile base on campaign. Some of these trucks were equipped as searchlight carriers.

Some 66,000 Bedford MW 15cwt trucks were built during the war. They had a 5.5-litre six-cylinder petrol engine, with a top road speed of 45mph, and fuel consumption of 10–12mpg. They did have a solid cab, but no windscreen, open sides, and a canvas top cover. A commercial truck made by Morris was much used in North Africa; like the Bedford this had an open back with a canvas cover.

Other trucks included the AEC armoured command vehicle, at 7.7 tons, with four-wheel drive and a maximum speed of 35mph; the Dodge weapon carrier (WC) series, WC51 and WC52, fitted with .30 calibre machine guns. Also, all the others in this series (WC 54, 56, 57) had a payload of 0.75 tons, and all had a maximum speed of 54mph. As a troop carrier, they could carry six to eight men including the driver and co-driver. An open version of the WE56 with a canvas top was also used as a command car.

These were used as ambulances, this version being just over 16ft long, with a body of sheet metal 6ft 6in wide and 7ft 6in high. They included a heater; most were used by the US army.

There were also M3 half-track troop carriers, with an open load bed and a canvas cover. The front wheels were operated by a standard steering wheel.

Wrecker / recovery trucks

Known to the Americans as wreckers, recovery vehicles were essential for assisting or rescuing damaged or broken-down vehicles and tanks. One version of these, the Diamond T969, was built in America by the Holmes Company, but supplied to the British and Canadian armies. Weighing 9.6 tons and with a maximum speed of 40mph, some of these were fitted with .50 calibre machine guns. Fuel capacity of 50 gallons gave them an operational range of more than 130 miles. Most had four-wheel drive, which made them particularly useful in the desert. A larger version, the M1A1, made by Ward le France or Kenworth, weighed 15.5 tons. All had twin-boom cranes, and many had forward-mounted winches which could haul the damaged vehicle to a positon where it could be lifted onto a trailer or towed. The M1A1 could lift tanks. Some 3,735 of these were produced, some of which could tow a trailer fitted as a workshop, while others were powerful enough to tow tanks.

A later development was the Armoured Recovery Vehicle (ARV) Mk II, based on the Churchill Mk III tanks. This had a winch which could pull 25 tons, and two jibs, one rear-mounted with a 15-ton lift capacity, and another forward-mounted for 7.5 tons.

Prime movers

This was the name given to heavy vehicles used to tow artillery. The American company Mack produced the Mk VII at 14.4 tons, which was fitted with a .50 machine gun. The Mk VII could tow large artillery pieces such as the 'Long Tom'. This gun used shells which weighed 790lb, with a range of up to 14.5 miles. The barrel length was 22.8ft, and it was served by a crew of fourteen, who travelled in the rear of the truck. An experienced crew could fire forty HE shells per hour. The Mack 7 was developed specially as a prime mover for towing large and heavy artillery; it had a five-man crew and a winch at the front with a 40,000lb capacity, to help manoeuvre the gun in and out of its firing position. It had a hoist at the back to lift the gun's trail arms.

Other recovery vehicles were made in Britain: the Leyland AEC Matador and the Leyland Retriever, at 7.5 and 7.7 tons respectively. These could move at 30mph. The AEC Matador could be used as a recovery vehicle, but more often as a prime mover for the 5-ton 5.5in calibre field guns. It had a winch rated at 5 tons with 250ft of steel cable for recovering tanks or other heavy vehicles. It could carry the whole gun crew and their kit. The Matador was built from the early 1930s, and by the beginning of the war vehicles were beginning to show signs of age, although many were still serviceable. They could be fitted up as a mobile workshop, with a crane. Some were used as mobile searchlight carriers.

Morris Motors produced a smaller four-wheel drive truck at 3.3 tons. Known as the Quad, it was designed for use as the prime mover for the 25lb field gun. They were in high demand and other manufacturers built them, including General Motors in Canada. More than 10,000 were built during the war and used by British, Canadian and Australian forces. They were also used to tow 17lb anti-tank guns. They were 14.7ft long, 7.2ft wide, and 7.4ft to the top of the cab roof, could carry two drivers and five other men and had a maximum speed of 50mph.

GMC built what came to be known as 'Jimmy' trucks, aka 'deuce and a half' (for their 2.5-ton payload). As well as carrying or towing loads, they also towed small tanker trailers for water or fuel. Some were fitted with machine guns. Between 1941 and 1945, General Motors produced 562,000 and other manufacturers 250,000. They had a six-cylinder, 91.5hp engine.

Vehicle production in the UK

These figures are for the period September 1939 to September 1945. There were others manufactured before this period, but it is not clear from the sources whether these were intended for war use.

Landing craft	2,379
Tank Transporters	1,317
Lorries – over 10 tons	3,220
Lorries – 6 tons	9,349
Lorries – 1.3 tons	319,825
Lorries – 15cwt	146,956
Ambulances	14,549
Heavy cars	46,689
Light tractors	11,366
Heavy tractors	93,419
Light cars and vans	421,039
Motorcycles	151,070

Chapter 4

The Work of the Royal Army Ordnance Corps

Before the Munich crisis of 1938, the ordnance services at the War Office were part of the department of the Master General of the Ordnance (MGO) and were directed by a Director of Ordnance Services (DOS). He was assisted by a principal ordnance officer (in charge of stores) and a principal ordnance mechanical engineer (in charge of engineering).

Provision of army equipment at that time was spread between several War Office departments. Under the MGO, the Director of Artillery provided guns, small arms, ammunition and optical and chemical defence stores, and the Director of Mechanisation provided all vehicles except those driven by RASC personnel, and all signalling and engineering stores. Vehicles used by the RASC were provided by the Director of Supplies and Transport and the DOS handled the design, provision and inspection of clothing and general stores. These departments were further broken down to provide responsibility for specific items.

As the war approached these various departments were reorganised. The Ministry of Supply was formed in August 1939 and took over all design, production and inspection from the War Office; as a result the MGO and his department disappeared. The DOS (under the quartermaster general) took over responsibility for the provision, storage and distribution of all ordnance stores including mechanical transport and ammunition.

Although all the reorganisations of 1939 had put the RAOC on a better footing, further steps were found to be necessary in early 1940. The control of clothing and general stores were separated from warlike stores and a director put in charge of each of these departments.

Embarkation supply depots had already been set up in the middle of 1939, at Southampton, Avonmouth and Newport (Mons) to handle supplies in the event of an expeditionary force being sent overseas. Depots were also set up at other ports in the early months of the war.

Mobilisation in 1939 caused the removal of the majority of regular RAOC officers and other ranks from their peacetime units; they were posted to field formations and units and replaced with officers from the reserve and untrained militia men, civilians and the ATS. Unsurprisingly, this had a serious effect on efficiency. The main task at this time was the mobilisation of the BEF. A great burden fell on to the RAOC when that force had to be evacuated in June 1940. Not least of this was the shortage of storage space; improvisation created stores in garages, shops, skating rinks, cinemas and even private houses.

As well as dealing with rations, the RAOC received deck cargoes of petrol and put them on board Motor Transport vehicle ships, and arranged the removal and storage of petrol from vehicles before shipment under instructions from Movement Central.

Stores for south-east Asia had to be specially treated to guard against the deleterious effects of the hot and humid climate. Each article had to be coated with a special preservative, have a detailed label attached, be wrapped in greaseproof paper and packed in a carton, which was sealed and dipped in hot wax. The waxed cartons were packed in waterproof bags in cases marked to show not only the contents, but also that they were going somewhere tropical. All this required a complex working area of dipping tanks, packing tables and necessary equipment, all connected by conveyor belts.

The storage for these items was first at Woolwich until a new main depot was built at Donnington (Shropshire). Woolwich provided over 2,250,000 square feet of space, but this was in storehouses with two or three floors served by slow lifts and hoists. They were unsuitable for speedy receipt and issue of stores; the buildings were not contiguous but spread among other stores and some factories, which made efficiency almost impossible. With the exception of officers, the personnel were all civilian.

The depot at Donnington, with its modern layout, commenced operation at the end of 1940 with some 800,000 square feet of covered accommodation. This increased to nearly 2,000,000 square feet by the end of 1941 and half as much again by the end of the war. As Donnington began to operate, Woolwich branches were transferred there.

In 1939 the main Central Ordnance Department (COD) for small arms, machine guns and infantry weapons was at Weedon. By the end of the war this became a sub-depot of a new COD built at Bicester. The old depot at Weedon was like Woolwich, made up of multi-storeyed buildings unsuitable for rapid transactions.

The other categories of warlike stores: workshop machinery, machine tools and test equipment, were handled until 1942 at Didcot and Woolwich. As the war progressed and new equipment was designed, the store-keeping administration became more complex and in order to solve this problem it was moved to Old Dalby in 1942.

After the 1940 evacuation from France, large quantities of repairable equipment were sent to a newly established Central Repair Department at Woolwich. Unfortunately this coincided with heavy bombing, which killed and wounded many of the workers and damaged stock in the depot. As soon as there was space at Donnington, stocks were moved there and to Greenford. Donnington at that time only had two store buildings and the arrival of masses of stores from Woolwich, sometimes as many as 1,000 loaded rail wagons in just a few days, completely disrupted the carefully calculated plans for orderly development. This had to be scrapped and rapid improvisation substituted.

Several sub-depots were established for the main depot at Donnington. The first of these was at Otley (Yorkshire) and this dealt with signals stores for the Northern command, delivering them by binned lorries which called on the units at regular intervals. Ten further sub-depots were opened in Leeds, Bradford and Bingley to handle searchlight equipment. There was also a large Returned Stores Group covered store of approximately 200,000 square feet, where non-serviceable stores returned by units were repaired. This activity was later moved to Woolwich as part of the Central Repair Group.

At the beginning of the war, general stores were handled at the COD Didcot with a sub-depot at Slaithwaite in the Midlands. A further sub-depot was started at Thatcham in May 1940. Didcot was served by rail; its sheds were spread out to minimise the effects of air attacks and this made it difficult to supervise and handle the large volumes of stores going in and out. With the evacuation of the BEF from France, Didcot had the urgent task of supplying those troops with accommodation stores. Staging camps had to be equipped without delay, which depleted stocks at the depots to the point where issues had to be controlled on a priority rationed basis.

When the build-up of American troops began in 1942, the sub-depot at Thatcham was handed over to them for their stores, and a new depot to replace Thatcham was established near Carlisle.

The system for handling and recording the movements of stores was for some time divided into that used at the older stores and that used at the new depot at Chilwell. The latter was based on a new system using NCR systems and Hollerith punched cards; this system gradually took over from the older versions. Under this system, indents arrived at a central point and were given a control number, which was entered on every document involved in the transaction; these could be tracked and delays investigated. Storehouse personnel marked the items issued. For those which were not available in full, new vouchers were created for use when stocks were replenished.

A system known as Visidex, which involved storing cards in cabinets in such a way that the designations and catalogue numbers were easily visible, was in place. The sequence of operations for issuing stores using this system was:

1. Indent registration
2. Indent checking
3. Voucher preparation

4. Selection and despatch of stores
5. Posting of the account
6. Provision action
7. Preparation of vouchers for stores not currently available.

Progressing was effected at each stage.

The storehouse personnel were divided into three groups: selectors, who selected stores for issue and marked up the bin cars; binners, who received stores and placed them to stock; and 'dues out' clerks, who watched the receipt of stores and then released to selectors any vouchers held for stores not previously available.

Small items were kept in bins on steel racking; each of these was given an identification number and a location index allowed speedy location of any given item. Many changes were made in the detailed procedures and by 1941 it became clear that due to the high level of stress involved, and constant changes in storehouse personnel, the actual contents of the bins rarely agreed with the stock listed in the system, and it was finally decided that the use of manpower in keeping these up to date was no longer justified. In future, only one type of record was to be kept, that of the Visidex system. What were then called 'cost control' and are now known as 'time and motion' studies were conducted, and the cost of various functions were listed in terms of manhours used, not actual money cost.

The procedure instructions were constantly reviewed to meet new requirements brought about by new ideas and methods and manpower difficulties. This must have caused severe annoyance to the storesmen; while general instructions on procedures were issued to the departments, the detailed methods of implementing them were left largely to the actual depots, which probably meant the new ideas were ignored and work went on as before.

One area which did benefit from studying the processes was that of packing. A system known as 'flow packing', which standardised the processes and layout of bays, was introduced. Stores and packing materials were brought together on an assembly line. Empty cases and packing materials came from an overhead store and cases went through the processes of packing, fastening, weighing, and marking with stencils, all this done with the stores remaining on the runways. These were mounted on rollers, and packed cases were then moved on their way with forklift trucks of various sizes. However, it was found that for 'hauls' of over 250ft it was better to use industrial tractors and trailers. Various sizes of cranes were also used, large ones operating on railway lines, overhead cranes used for standard routes within the warehouses and smaller mobile cranes for smaller loads.

Between the two wars, successive governments had sought to reduce spending; by 1936 the three fighting services had been reduced to a woeful state. As a result, the peacetime ordnance services were more like a large civilian store-holding organisation administered by a small number of military staff, subjected to continual efforts to reduce staff numbers and depots. Such staff as existed were too busy with their day-to-day duties to devote any time to planning for war. They could not spare the time to join annual manoeuvres and the only place where they could have done so was in Egypt.

Nor was there any provision at the War Office for training RAOC personnel for a wartime situation; such training as was offered was at a School of Instruction organised by the Director of Ordnance Services. Except for a brief period in 1931–1932 there was not even an up-to-date Ordnance Manual. The average commander or staff officer knew virtually nothing about the ordnance services, apart from the occasional lecture given by RAOC candidates at the Senior Officers' School. It was not until 1938 that one place for an RAOC instructor was allocated at the staff college. Given all this, it should come as no surprise that the work of the RAOC field units allotted to the BEF was a matter of improvisation.

But at least there was a new ordnance branch at the War Office, and a new training establishment. Even so, experience in France showed the weaknesses in the field organisation. The ammunition and stores base depots were called on as soon as they arrived in France to provide a full depot service, without even being allowed the usual ninety-day period to organise and house their personnel, stocks and accounting systems. This was not helped by the fact that many of the fighting units were sent out without the proper complement of equipment and promptly called on the BODs to make up the deficiencies.

At the beginning of the war ordnance supplies and store locations were divided roughly into five branches: at Woolwich wireless, signal and engineer stores and artillery stores and ammunition; at Chilwell vehicles and motor transport stores, at Didcot general stores; at Branston clothing and necessaries and at Weedon small arms and machine guns. Inevitably these changed. Ammunition was separated from artillery stores and a depot for it was opened at Bramley. In December 1941, machinery which had been the responsibility of the MGO under the Directorate of Mechanical Maintenance was passed to the RAOC and a further depot was formed at Old Dalby, and this machinery was moved there with plant and machine tools, wireless test gear and optical test equipment.

In mid-1940, high equipment losses in France coincided with disorganised production in the UK, which barely exceeded peacetime levels. Under the threat of invasion it was essential to equip the available forces and the Home Guard to face invasion. It thus became important to find out what was available and which units held it so that it could be relocated to the best advantage. A periodic census system was started. At first, returns covered tanks, artillery, small arms, and a few signal and engineer stores, but were later extended to include various items which were in short supply; items which should be put together with others, such as guns and ammunition; items which were intricate and thus difficult to manufacture; secret items which could not be issued on simple demand, and items considered to be of operational importance and which required complete control of movement.

Controlled stores were subject to War Office allocation. They were classified as Class A stores, which were issued between allies under instructions from the London Munitions Assignment Board; Class B stores, which were of operational significance but in short supply and were allocated to the General Staff branches who knew the operational necessity; and Class C stores, which covered all other items which were still in short supply. The responsibility for coordinating all the items allocated through the Ministry of Supply was held by the Director General of Army requirements and his assistant the Principal Priority Officer. This responsibility covered major items in short supply, items for special operations, items from the US and items with problems of labour or materials.

During the first year of the war, production concentrated on complete equipment and the supply of spares was insufficient. Once the need for spares was recognised, it became standard practice to order them at the same time as the equipment itself. Maintenance supplies of spares were issued on demand, but in May 1942 the force in the Middle East was placed on an automatic maintenance system, and once necessary quantities were ascertained, they were sent out three times a year. Supplies of some types of spares were sent each month on a staggered basis, for instance January, May and September for one type of wireless set, February, June and October for a different type. The object of this scheme, which was entirely successful, was to eliminate the work of submitting demands, economise on issues and enable workshops to plan their work round expected deliveries.

It took a while to coordinate these maintenance schedules with spares for the equipment, as the American system produced fewer spares than turned out to be necessary, but eventually it settled down to a six-monthly schedule. By September 1944 it was possible to make clear estimates of future requirements, in both main items and spares. It became necessary to reduce stocks of most items; future requirements at that time were based on the assumption that the end of the year would see the end of the war with Germany. Reports were called for to assess when production could be stopped and contracts cancelled, taking into account that although the war might have ceased in Europe, it would continue elsewhere. The assumption that the war would be over by the end of 1944 was soon seen to be too optimistic. In April 1945 rationalisation of global stocks was set in place, with surplus items being recalled and reallocated. By the middle of May, India and the south-east Asia command were the only active theatres, and although automatic maintenance supplies were continued for the Allied forces in south-east Asia, they were stopped for India.

South-east Asia command

Once the war began spreading eastwards the strain of providing ordnance supply for the UK and these eastern theatres increased. At a conference in New Delhi it was decided to set up a permanent council of representatives from all the participating countries, in a scheme designed to pool the manufacturing and raw material resources. This council was a civilian body, roughly analogous to the Ministry of Supply in London, and it maintained constant communication with that ministry. There were representatives from the UK, India, South Africa, Australia and New Zealand. At the same time, a Central Military Office was set up to work with the Supply Council. Representatives from the Royal Navy and RAF were divided into sections dealing with the Royal Engineers and Royal Corps of Signals, Transportation, Mechanical Services and Ordnance. Each of the Dominion countries had use of their own production, but in the event their 'estimates' turned out to be no more than guesses, and although a depot was set up near Poona for excess stocks, prolonged teething problems delayed this depot's ability to accept or issue stocks.

As the Japanese forces expanded, first India and then Australia and New Zealand effectively withdrew from the scheme in view of the threat to their territories. All in all, though the whole scheme was laudable in theory, it turned out to be ineffective in practice.

Ammunition

In September 1939 the RAOC had one central ammunition depot (CAD) operational at Bramley and two more nearing completion. There was no separate ammunition branch at the War Office, just sixteen inspecting officers and fifty-one ammunition examiners. At this time, providing ammunition was not within the RAOC's remit. On the declaration of war, with the exception of one inspecting officer and three ammunition examiners at each depot, the depot personnel were generally ignorant about ammunition and its storage, maintenance and handling, beyond what was described in Magazine Regulations. This publication was in two parts; the first did not apply to active service conditions and the other related entirely to the teachings of the previous war, as did the syllabus at the School of Instruction at Bramley. The three Base Ammunition depots moved to France with the BEF, established sites and dumped their ammunition at overly concentrated sites, then waited for standard rail depots to be constructed. After Dunkirk efforts were made to provide ammunition for the threatened invasion, and a series of small ammunition depots were set up to serve the Eastern, South Eastern and Northern command areas, each designed to hold up to 6,000 tons of ammunition. Problems included how and where to store ammunition for the anti-invasion force and the amounts coming off the production lines, how to find and train personnel to man the new field depots, how to administer these new depots and how to frame new safety regulations for storage of ammunition in the English countryside, since the existing Explosives Act and Home Office Regulations were not applicable to current conditions. It was also necessary to consider the implications of ammunition for gas warfare and to produce regulations for its storage, handling and decontamination.

The amount of ammunition stored in the UK in 1940 was 216,000 tons in three CADs, using 2,105 RAOC personnel and 2,400 pioneer corps labourers. By 1945 these figures had grown to five CADs and twenty-one field storage depots (incorrectly called ammunition sub-depots for a while), 13,483 RAOC and 16,000 Pioneer Corps personnel.

The new CADs were required to be rail-served and designed to modern standards. The sites had to be level and flood free, covering up to 1,500 acres, requirements which inevitably pointed to agricultural land and strong objections from the Ministry of Agriculture. Eventually two sites were approved, one at Nesscliff (Shropshire) and one at Kineton (Warwickshire). The depot at Nesscliff was built by the Ministry of Works and Planning and took three years, while that at Kineton was completed in two years by military labour. The field depots were established much more quickly. They often consisted of ammunition stacked on the verges of country roads or in adjacent field margins if the verges were too narrow. Each stack was 400 cubic feet, in a corrugated iron shelter, suitably spaced for safety. Ready-made accommodation for the necessary troops was requisitioned, and the occupants were, as one commentator put it, 'tactfully informed' of the decision.

The RAOC was responsible for the serviceability of ammunition from the time it was delivered to depots from factories to the time when it was either issued to units or handed over to the RASC for transport to units. It was not, however, always under the direct control of the RAOC and it was at these times when it was vulnerable to rough handling and consequent deterioration. At ports in the UK it was supposed to be handled by proper Port Ammunition Detachments, who saw it into ships' holds and supervised stowage. Some items were packed in unwieldy containers and it was these which were most vulnerable to rough handling and often dropped, which meant they had to be set aside for inspection.

Overseas ports where ammunition was off-loaded from ships tended to use more haste than was good for the ammunition, and it was often jumbled up on the quayside, leading to much waste of time trying to sort it out before it could be moved on. Algiers and Bone were notorious for this. Another problem was that the packaging was rarely sufficiently robust to withstand bad roads, free dropping by air, or being tipped into ditches in 10-ton loads. Although there should have been enough tarpaulins or sectional shelters to cover dumps, loading these on ships tended to take a lower priority than the ammunition itself. This was particularly bad in North Africa.

Once the RAOC had handed ammunition to the RASC for movement and distribution by road they were required to deal with it according to the precepts covered by the RASC and did so by distributing training pamphlets. For instance, Training Pamphlet No.6 set out some general principles, the first of which was that ammunition should be passed automatically and systematically from rear to front to replace what had been used. To retain mobility the ammunition should remain on its transport vehicle, except where large-scale operations were expected, in which case dumps might be necessary. If ammunition had been exposed to gas it should be properly decontaminated before it was passed on.

Replenishments of ammunition were forwarded from the ammunition base depot to rail-, road- or river-head by orders from general headquarters. RASC responsibility began when it accepted it from the officer in charge at that head or at a dump, the amounts being those needed to replace expenditure. A proper proportion of personnel should accompany the RASC transport to the rail-head for loading. All vehicles carrying ammunition were issued with a load note to show in detail what they were carrying. Vehicles collected loads from the rail-head then took them to designated ammunition refilling points (ARPs), from which it was collected by other vehicles and passed on to forward areas. These ARPs might have to be moved if found by the enemy and subjected to attacks, in which case motorcyclists would be left at the original site to guide transport to the alternative site.

These sites tended to be along a sufficiently wide road, with 3-ton loads placed on the ground, five of these loads taking up 18 yards, with 50-yard intervals. In view of the weight of ammunition, the distance it had to be carried should be as little as possible, so narrow sites along roads were preferable to deep ones that extended into fields. In rainy weather, wet ground should be avoided, or dunnage used to keep the packages off the ground. The sites should be concealed from air observation, so roads going through woods were preferable.

There was a great deal of concern about the way ammunition was treated in the field, even by the officers who controlled dumps. In North Africa, for instance, many unsuitable dump sites were chosen, including one in a series of nullahs which flooded and submerged several hundred tons of ammunition under five feet of water. In one location in Normandy, knowing of the muddy conditions that followed the autumn rains, a new site was requested but refused. It became necessary to move the ammunition to Belgium, but the lorries promptly bogged down and could only be dragged out by tanks, until the tanks themselves bogged down. It was then decided that the principles of ammunition storage should be taught at staff colleges.

Units were issued with numerous handbooks on weapons, and also copies of 'Notes on the Care and Preservation of Ammunition in the Field'. Training films were made and shown, but few units actually cared for their ammunition properly. As well as opening sealed boxes before their contents were actually needed, the worst faults included transporting ammunition loose or in sandbags after the proper packages had been misappropriated for other purposes.

Before the operation of workshops was taken over by REME in 1942 they were handled by the RAOC. The workshop organisation sent to the BEF consisted of two base ordnance workshops, one advanced ordnance workshop, one GHQ workshop, four port ordnance workshops, army field workshops on a scale of one per division, four AA brigade workshops and some light aid detachments according to scale. Some other small workshops were formed in small towns on the line of communication.

The port workshops performed useful work in repairing the various vehicles that had been damaged on the crossing; much of this damage was caused by careless loading and unloading. Base ordnance workshops were installed at Nantes and another at Le Havre in April. The opening of the former was delayed by accommodation difficulties and was later moved to Arras; the latter was never able to function fully.

Mobilisation plans included the earmarking of personnel for specific units assembling technical equipment and workshop machinery; all these were to be sent to the embarkation ports and despatched co-incident to the main shipping programme. During the Munich crisis a military mission went to France to select suitable buildings for ordnance depots; these were approved by the French military authorities who agreed to their use in the event of war.

When mobilisation came, the RAOC personnel were a mixture of regular, TA reservists and militia, most of whom had no military training. The first few of these went to France on 4 September, the rest following the next week, assembling at Le Mans. The office accommodation allotted was inadequate, and there were long delays before office furniture, machinery and stationery arrived, more than two weeks later, much depleted by pilfering en route.

The headquarters and ordnance services offices were spread out over several villages. Meanwhile, headquarters itself moved from Le Mans to Arras, and by the time I Corps moved on to the Belgian frontier, the line of communication extended over 250 miles. Several of the ordnance depots should have been situated in the Nantes or Brest sub-areas, but it was found that many of the buildings selected by the advance mission were already occupied by French government departments. Others were dilapidated or were lacking structural strength. It was also realised that the storage space required for a BOD for a fully mechanised army had been seriously underestimated. From the start and right through to the end, poor and insufficient storage space was a serious problem.

At the end of September the weather turned to heavy rain, which highlighted the flaws in the roofs and flooring, and led to rapid deterioration in the approach roads.

Finally, in December 1939 a requirement of 1,050,000 square feet of covered storage was worked out for maintaining the stores for twelve divisions, more than half as much again as the pre-war estimates. Part of this was large amounts of bulky stock for anti-gas defences: reserves of uniform clothing, anti-gas clothing and respirators, searchlight, electric light and battery equipment, and motor transport spares.

Many of the storage buildings allocated to the ordnance services in Nantes were in separated scattered buildings. All lacked basic storage equipment and this did not arrive until two weeks after the depot opened: including racking, storehouse trucks, mobile cranes, tools for opening packages, and basic office equipment. Meanwhile, shiploads of stores arrived and had to be housed under cover.

The two BADs were located, according to policy, in forests to conceal them from the air. However laudable this idea was, there were difficulties, not the least of which was the unsuitability of forest roads for continual heavy use. They needed constant repairs and the stacking spaces needed constant levelling. Each depot consisted of three sub-depots, each holding 7,000 tons, a returned empties store and a laboratory. Due to the policy of separating units from their essential equipment on embarkation, personnel of both units were effectively dumped in the forests without blankets, cooking facilities and other accommodation necessaries, and this finally began to arrive six days after their arrival. One major deficiency was the tools to dig latrines, which did not improve the quality of life. Much the same situation applied with the three sites housing Advanced Rail Head (ARH) personnel. At each of these there were two officers and twenty-seven other ranks, and it took a week before they were able to obtain blankets from the RAF. At Germaine they had to be fed from a cafe for three weeks, at first because they had no rations and then because there was no cooking equipment.

The first load of bombs arrived the day after the ARH personnel, and there were immediate problems. The RAF had no lorries or men to load them, and the French stationmaster objected to having a train load of bombs standing in his station. Eventually some French soldiers and lorries unloaded the train and moved the bombs, to the relief of all concerned.

Army ammunition stocks were based on estimated rates of expenditure, ranging from thirty-five rounds per gun per day for 25-pounders to 6,000,000 rounds of small arms ammunition per division per month. At the end of

September an advanced ammunition depot was considered, but the French authorities objected to this, wanting forward reserves to be mobile. This was accepted and quantities were held on trains, each holding a standard pack of all types. By the end of November the two BADs were holding seventy-five days' worth of stock, with no room for more, and had to put a temporary stop on further supplies from home.

The provision of signal stores was equally chaotic due to initial serious shortages and uncoordinated demands by the Royal Signals Corps and the RAOC on the War Office. The initial shortages were a product of supplies needed for the long line of communication, but remained a problem throughout the campaign.

Other items which were in short supply included spares for motor vehicles and technical equipment; the latter mainly because many items arrived in non-serviceable condition due to faulty manufacture and inadequate inspection. This latter situation was reported to the War Office and 100 per cent inspection was instigated at the base.

The main difficulties experienced by the RAOC during active operations were faulty pre-war planning leading to a lack of personnel with the necessary knowledge and experience, lack of directions on RAOC procedures, and shortages of stores. Other arms of the service also suffered shortages of experienced personnel and material. The failure to absorb and impart the current methods of organisation was inexcusable. The only textbook available was out of date, and the revised edition was not issued before the BEF embarked. Since the accounting procedures were based on a new system, the instructions for which were in the revised manual, it is hardly surprising that they got off to a bad start.

The loss of pre-allotted accommodation led to the stores at Nantes occupying some twenty-eight buildings and tents, spread over 20sq mi. An application was made to the French authorities for a further 500,000 square feet of covered space, which threw those authorities into consternation as the original estimate was for only 300,000 square feet.

All the requirements for an advanced ordnance depot arrived, but it was not functional for several weeks, and was lent to No. 1 Base Ordnance Depot pending a decision for its use. It was finally settled at Arras to hold stores required by the forward force. Its covered storage area amounted to 150,000 square feet, but inevitably this proved to be insufficient. All the stores in this depot were eventually lost to the enemy.

When the Germans invaded Holland and Belgium on 10 May 1940, the 1st and 2nd Corps of the BEF advanced to positions on the River Dyle. Considerable amounts of ammunition were held at various locations including mobile reserves on trains. It was decided to use the latter first and then load and send more from the BSDs. Between 10 and 17 May, twenty trains were loaded, but due to interrupted communications definite confirmation of the arrival of only six trains was received.

The Germans continued their advance and by 19 May, when Arras was heavily bombed, the AOD and AOW there had stopped operating and the personnel had been ordered to withdraw towards the main base with all other administration troops not required for defence. The evacuation of the stores at the AOD, which were held in scattered locations, proved impossible and with some of it, especially clothing, destruction was also impossible in the available time. They did manage to dismantle and pack all the machine tools and put them on trains for the main base.

By 21 May it had been decided that further maintenance of the BEF should be through the northern ports of Boulogne, Calais and Dunkirk. By 22 May control of ordnance services had virtually lapsed. An overnight conference on 23/24 May concluded with specific instructions to plan for evacuating certain categories of ordnance stores and ammunition in a defined order of priority.

Despite the need to maintain availability of stores for the units still fighting, orders began to arrive to evacuate certain items to England, including 50,000 rifles, 50,000 respirators and 12,500 tons of ammunition. 'Surplus' personnel were ordered to return to England. On 14 June 1940, the complete withdrawal from France of the BEF was ordered, with the exception of a few of the 52nd Division still under 10th French Army orders. On the same day orders were received to evacuate stores vehicles as well as personnel. In the event, most of the stores had to be abandoned.

Vehicles

The number of vehicles supplied at the beginning of the campaign was insufficient and a census made of them was incomplete and thus of little use. The armoured vehicles were theoretically contained in four light tank regiments (later rising to seven) for divisional reconnaissance, one armoured car regiment, and one battalion of the Royal Tank Regiment. Maintenance spares for these, especially tracks and sprockets, were in extremely short supply. It was some time before stocks of vehicles improved, but that of spare parts never did. During the first three months of 1940, 3,613 different parts were on indent but only 254 of these were ever supplied. By the end of April, No. 1 Base Supply Depot had over 16,000 indents for MT spares, with more arriving at a rate of 1,400 per day, and were unable to supply them all. This problem continued throughout the war.

The situation of inadequate provision of experienced personnel and shortage of vehicle spares was much the same in other theatres. In Egypt and elsewhere in the Middle East this problem was exacerbated by the great distances between Egypt and the sources of supply (Britain and India). This was made worse by the dangers to shipping in the Mediterranean and the alternative six-month journey round the Cape and up the Red Sea. The length of the lines of communication was extreme, there was limited rail and road communication, limited port facilities, a shortage of water and a sand-laden atmosphere.

Palestine

There were two depots, at Sarafand and Haifa. There had been a plan for the development of bases before the war, so that when war did break out, Palestine was able to react quickly when ordered to prepare and extend these to hold reserves for 60,000 troops. Haifa was the only possible port of entry but, due to the topographical nature of the country, was restricted in the choice of locations for the necessary sub-depots. The best choices were in the narrow coastal belt, which was connected by rail as well as sea to Egypt and the Suez Canal. Haifa was the terminal point for the oil pipeline from Iraq.

Egypt and North Africa

In Egypt the command ordnance depot was at Abassia with a camp depot at Alexandria and ordnance dumps at El Daba and Mersa Matruh. Abassia had a main stores depot, four sub-depots and an ammunition depot. The main depot was housed in a small collection of buildings with no room for expansion and presented an easy target for air attacks. The ordnance dumps held stocks of tentage, accommodation stores and ammunition reserves for units going to the Western Desert. The rest of the ammunition was stored partly at Abassia and partly in the new depot in the Tura Caves approximately 5 miles from Cairo.

After the capture of Tobruk in January 1941, an advanced base was established there.

During the advance to Benghazi during the three months from November 1941 to January 1942 the Western Desert force was reorganised into the 8th Army, for which forward reserves were held at railheads.

After much toing and froing across North Africa, the Allies began the invasion of north-west Africa. The intention was to secure Morocco and Algeria, then Tunisia, and safeguard the Mediterranean passages. The RAOC plan was for ordnance units to land on beaches for immediate support to the assault force. For this, new units called Ordnance Beach Detachments (OBDs) were created. Five of these were included in the Order of Battle, as were other RAOC units: two base ordnance depots, two base ammunition depots, eight ordnance field parks which held stores frequently in demand, nine mobile laundries, one base hospital laundry and two shops where officers could replace items of clothing and equipment lost in action.

Stores for the immediate maintenance of the assault force were held by these and known as landing reserves. These were equipment and stores necessary to maintain the force for thirty days. They were landed immediately after the assault troops had gained a foothold and handed over to the ordnance detachment. They were specially packed in lightweight packages with raised markings to facilitate handling and identification.

Beach Maintenance Packs (BMPs) were standard quantities of replacement equipment and spare parts to augment landing reserves and continue maintenance of the force. Again they were designed to last thirty days; they were roughly the same quantity as three landing reserves plus spares for second-line repairs and were landed as soon as facilities for repair were available. Like all issues required to be handled without depot facilities, they were packed in a such a way that issues could be made direct from cases, which were used as store bins.

The first landings were on 7 and 8 November 1942, mostly by American troops, except at Algiers where some British troops landed simultaneously with the Americans. There was little opposition and the harbour at Algiers was reopened to shipping a day later. The five OBDs arrived two days after that. There were considerable losses of ordnance stores caused by enemy action. Other stores were misdirected by the Royal Navy, which sent the ships to ports where they could be unloaded quickly. The result was that landing reserves were often divided between different ports and some ships left before being completely unloaded.

East Africa

Here, the lines of communication were vast and the territory was, to say the least, difficult. Only part of the area had railway transport and that was a single-track small-gauge line with limited rolling stock. Throughout the area few of the roads were metalled and the rest soon degenerated into corrugated and pot-holed dusty tracks which turned into quagmires after rain.

The base depots were at Nairobi and Mituburri (40 miles from Nairobi) and there were few advanced depots elsewhere. Those which were set up were at vast distances, ranging from 324 miles by road or rail from Mombasa, to 2,291 miles by rail, lake-steamer, then road and rail again from Lusaka.

Sicily

It was decided that with the exceptions of ammunition and vehicles, ordnance stores would be handled by what was called the 'short sea voyage' system, whereby AODs were established in the theatre, but were supplied from BODs in Egypt.

Landing reserves and BMPs were packed in advance, but although these were put ashore easily enough, they had been mixed up and were not landed intact on their proper beaches. This meant the ODBs had a major sorting problem. However, this was solved quite quickly and all units were supplied soon after they had gone ashore.

The campaign in Sicily was quite short and the distances small, so full development of the system planned for stores and ammunition was soon seen to be unnecessary. From Sicily, the action moved into Italy and gradually northwards. It was March 1945 before the troops had fought their way up the 'leg' of Italy, when the US 5th Army went into north-west Italy and the British 8th Army into north-east Italy.

Italy

In December 1943, two BADs were operating near Bari and Naples, each with stocks of about 25,000 tons. By the end of the campaign this had risen to 90,000 tons. Both were supplied by road in 10-ton lorries from the docks. The stores were kept in roadside stacks, on improvised bases of empty packing cases or flat stones as no dunnage was available.

Burma

At the beginning of 1941 the only ordnance installation in Burma was Rangoon Arsenal, about 12 miles outside the city, which was served by a special rail branch line from the main line 15 miles away.

After the outbreak of war with Japan on 7 December 1941, stores and ammunition began arriving from the UK; much of this was anti-gas clothing. By 1 February 1942, the Japanese invasion had forced a British withdrawal to the north of Moulmein. During December and January Rangoon and its aerodrome were heavily bombed, refugees on the road made motor transport almost impossible and the number of civilian employees at the arsenal had dropped from 1,300 to 160. Some 200 troops were sent in to assist and some of the civilian workers were persuaded to return, but orders were received to start removing stores as backloads as well as continuing issues. In March, the Japanese entered Rangoon. By September 1942 the ordnance depots had withdrawn into East Bengal, on the banks of the Brahmaputra, on a site which was low lying and subject to flooding in the monsoon season. There had been no floods there since 1937, but in 1943 there were bad floods and 2,500 tons of stores had to be moved to higher ground, into requisitioned sheds. In the Far East generally, the problems centred on the wet and humid conditions. There were few useful roads or railways and much transport was reliant on rivers. Supplies could only be moved in comparatively small quantities.

By November 1944 the offensive against the Japanese was in full swing, many of the supplies being delivered by air and the rest by road convoy. The 15th Corps fought its way down the coast while the 4th and 33rd fought further inland. This eventually resulted in the recapture of Rangoon in May 1945, and the total defeat of the Japanese in Burma. During the period March to August 1945, over 16,000 tons of ammunition and 10,000 tons of other stores were carried by air.

Supplies to Burma from India, including grain for the mules, were mostly air-dropped after careful packing to avoid breakages. They were generally packed in wicker containers covered with canvas, with bags of straw tied to the bottom to act as shock absorbers and the parachutes clipped to the top. For food, each container held a 5-gallon kerosene drum holding ten days' hard ration for one man. Clothing and the grain for the mules were free-dropped in triple canvas bags, packed only two-thirds full to allow the load to shift as it hit the ground instead of bursting the bags.

As well as rations, there were ammunition, mortars, grenades, machine guns and other weapons, gelignite, millions of rounds of small arms ammunition, boots with spare laces and other clothing, safety pins, haversacks and mule saddles. There were 'personal services', which occasionally dropped items addressed to individuals who had requested them. Some of these were items stored at the base before leaving for the field. Among these requests were spectacles, false teeth, tobacco and snuff, a kilt and new books. Every Chindit who had false teeth or wore spectacles had a plate impression or oculist's prescription filed at the base.

They also received post from home, and on one occasion 400lb of chocolate as a special order. Rare in India at that time, the chocolate had to be specially made overnight at the leading restaurant in Calcutta before being despatched to Burma.

Salvage

In July 1939 the Army Council decided that a salvage organisation would be necessary in war, and consulted the Ministry of Supply on the best items to collect. A Directorate of Salvage was set up in the quartermaster general's department in the War Office, consisting of the director and three deputy directors. One of these dealt with salvage at home, one with salvage abroad and the third dealt with statistics. Inspectors of salvage were appointed to each command and one salvage unit per division was organised. This consisted of one officer and forty other ranks. Training and instruction on salvage was carried out in all units so the troops would understand the need for economy in a major war and thus the value of salvaged items.

Many hundreds of different types of salvageable items were collected, but it was decided to classify them under forty-one categories. These ranged from ammunition empties, scrap metal, machine guns and small arms ammunition through clothing, oil drums and sandbags all the way to tinfoil. From March 1940 to June 1945, 1,017,493 tons of material worth £6,713,296 was collected at home and 1,262,400 tons worth £28,695,043 overseas.

At some of the salvage units overseas, workshops repaired salvaged items and in some cases converted them into other things. Damaged barrels were taken apart and made up into new from the usable staves, and scrap timber was made up into packing cases. Glass bottles were cut in half, the top half making hurricane lamp glasses and the bottoms ground smooth at the cut and used as tumblers.

In North Africa in the Western Desert and Cyrenaica in 1942, much of what was recovered was in sufficiently good condition that it could be immediately reissued. This included over 800 guns of various calibres, 1,300,000 rounds of artillery ammunition, 85,000 rifles and over 31,000,000 rounds of small arms ammunition. In the following year, in the advance from El Alamein to Tunisia, the haul included another 660 guns, 510,000 rifles, 4,600 machine guns and over 8,000,000 rounds of small arms ammunition.

When the enemy drove all RAOC units into the Tobruk perimeter there were some 140 repairable tanks and thousands of other damaged vehicles. Of the latter, perhaps 2,000 were worth saving, but there were not enough transporters to clear the tanks and even less for the other vehicles, until GHQ Middle East managed to provide sixty trailers and sixty gun tractors. Drivers to man these were taken first from the workshops and then from any RAOC personnel who had experience of driving a heavy lorry. All the tanks were moved to Sidi Barrani. Most of the other vehicles ended up being towed by any available vehicle going east.

The collapse of the enemy in North Africa was very sudden, and while many units had destroyed their guns and burned their vehicles most had not, so the British army and its allies inherited vast amounts of material. Collecting and sorting this was too large a task for the small salvage organisation, so where they could they delegated the task to the divisions in each area. Precise orders were given on the collection and handling of this material, but there was so much of it that it was not possible for the appropriate service to take over the dumps in time to prevent damage. Such items as gun-sights were broken off and carefully arranged stores strewn about in the search for souvenirs, or, as the perpetrators no doubt thought, prizes of war. This was clearly a discipline issue, as demonstrated by some returns of live ammunition mixed with empty cases and cartridges; this caused some fatal accidents among the personnel working in the dumps.

At the beginning of the final offensive in the Western Desert there were nine salvage units, each consisting of one officer and forty-four other ranks, but it was realised that they could do little more than create the foundation for more detailed salvage work. Their function was defined as:

> establishing and operating dumps on the supply route and at ports, railhead or roadheads; sorting material at these dumps for use forward or for evacuation, as required; collecting special items, and safeguarding captured dumps as far as possible until they could be taken over properly.

The advance to Benghazi was so rapid that the army recovery units had to go forward to continue their operational roles, before the area of the battlefield could be cleared of the large quantities of all types of equipment which were left behind. A few recovery units were able to remain for a while in the rear and collected repairable AFVs, guns and motor transport vehicles (both British and the enemy's) into dumps along the road and railway. The army could not evacuate this repairable equipment, but it was important that it should be removed as quickly as possible to provide useful material to REME base workshops. The problem for GHQ was the need for rapid evacuation to the base of more than 5,000 AFVs, other vehicles and guns, without established units to do the work. The solution was to improvise recovery units with men from base supply depots. Small parties under REME control were put at each dump to sort out and prepare the equipment for removal by rail or road. There was a lack of recovery vehicles, but this was handled by using captured enemy vehicles.

Elsewhere, most theatres had small sections for returned non-serviceable vehicles, but this did not provide any systematic collection and evacuation of broken-down or abandoned vehicles. In the spring of 1944, an effort to solve this problem was made by forming collection points, staffed by joint RAOC/ REME sections. Unfortunately the need for separate collection points for fighting vehicles and others was not foreseen and there was not enough equipment, cranes or towing vehicles. There was an acute shortage of railway flats and it was some months before a methodical system of backloading was organised. However, the situation was eventually brought under control and a complete system organised to deal with this.

Perhaps the most valuable of all scrap material was steel, which was sent back to the UK where it was desperately needed for many purposes.

Chapter 5

Armaments

In order to ensure that the raw materials for the manufacture of the various types of armament would be available, it was necessary to restrict both their export and their use for civilian purposes. Cloth production was increasingly used for military clothing and many other items were necessary to manufacture the explosives for ammunition, but the material most used in military production was metal: steel, bronze, aluminium, copper and tin.

Although export of many products and raw materials was restricted, import was not. Much important raw material came from Canada, including iron and steel, non-ferrous metals and timber. By the end of 1941, some 2,281,200 tons of various materials were imported.

Guns

Guns (which means artillery pieces, not handguns) were made in several calibres. There were field guns and anti-tank and anti-aircraft guns, described either by their bore size or the weight of the shells, from 4.5in and 5.5in bores to a larger one which fired 60lb shells. Some of the guns were howitzers, from 6in to 9.2in. Later developments were 8in guns and 240mm howitzers.

Many of the guns were made at the Royal Ordnance Factory at Woolwich, the rest by Vickers-Armstrong, Beardmore and Nuffield Mechanisation. This does not mean that firms made the guns themselves from start to finish; many made a single part, such as barrels or breech mechanisms, and the whole was assembled by another firm. There were some forty firms involved, twenty-eight of which also made other machinery.

During the course of the war, over 15,000 heavy, medium and field guns were made, plus over 22,600 anti-aircraft guns and 95,000 anti-tank guns. In addition to the anti-aircraft guns, over 30,000 pieces of searchlight equipment were made.

There were also 341 'coastal' guns, twelve of which were to cover the Dover Straits, and almost 800,000 shells were made for them. There were also three 13.5in 'railway' guns on the East Kent Light Railway. These had sufficient range to cross the Channel, and were mounted on railway carriages on short stretches of line to allow for the recoil.

Self-propelled guns came into use in the latter part of the war. With the exception of a 6-pounder mounted on an armoured truck chassis, these guns were mounted on tank chassis. However, they were not a great success and less than 1,000 were made.

Other guns were generally mounted on a two-wheeled carriage with a 'trail' for moving them.

Anti-tank guns were mostly 6-pounders and 17-pounders. The ammunition had been improved, from 'armour-piercing' to 'armour-piercing capped', and then 'armour-piercing capped ballistic capped' which gave a better penetration for targets over 500 yards. A further development was the 'discarding sabot', the sabot being discarded as the missile left the gun, which gave greater velocity and penetration.

Ammunition for guns

Until 1935 the actual manufacturing activity of the three Royal Ordnance Factories (ROFs) was very small. Their real value was in their technical knowledge. It became obvious that more ROFs were needed and by the end of 1939 ten new factories were approved, followed later by another fourteen. The latter consisted of eight engineering factories, three explosives factories and three filling factories. By the end of 1940 the ROFs were employing more than 130,000 people; by March 1942 it was more than 300,000. As well as the guns themselves and their carriages, much of the production of ammunition, especially that of shells and bombs, was dependent on engineering processes. Precise work was required for shell cases and small arms ammunition, but less so for bombs as they did not have to fit into gun barrels.

Besides the ROFs, there were several commercial firms involved in the manufacture of armaments, including BSA and ICI, the latter being mainly responsible for the component chemicals for explosives.

The Royal Filling Factories were the only ones to have a specific title: all the rest, no matter what they produced, were just known as ROFs. Filling shells is a delicate and hazardous process. In addition to handling shells for guns and bombs for the RAF, three of the RFFs also filled and loaded. There were three separate processes: first the actual filling of the missile with explosives (although some projectiles were solid); second the handling of detonators, fuses and other charges; and third assembling all components into a complete round of ammunition. This was usually done in the filling factories. Following some disastrous explosions in the First World War, the requirements for this work were very stringent.

There was a Royal Gunpowder Factory at Waltham Abbey, which was somewhat prone to accidents. On 28 January 1940 there were two massive explosions in the woodland where they manufactured nitro-glycerine; these killed five men, three of whom were never found, having been vaporised. Three months later the same thing happened again and five more men were killed. Production at Waltham Abbey ceased in 1943.

Until 1940, the policy was to obtain TNT from America, but plans to increase the heavy bomber force in 1941 led to the construction of two new TNT factories. These factories required large sites to give the necessary safety distances between buildings. TNT manufacture was the least of these, with a requirement of only 300 acres. Sites should be level, or at worst mildly undulating, and ideally low lying, as high sites would be vulnerable to dangerously low winter temperatures. Effective drainage and a good water supply were also essential.

During the course of the war, the following numbers of filled shells were made:

For field guns	64,494,000
For medium guns	9,829,000
For heavy guns	709,570
For light anti-aircraft guns	43,927,000
For heavy anti-aircraft guns	15,059,000
For tank and anti-tank guns	46,942,000

When the enemy began using mortars on a large scale, rockets were used as an effective counter-measure. They were often fired from multi-barrelled projectors.

Mortars

These medium-calibre weapons consisted of a smooth-bore tube, mounted on a base plate with two supporting legs to make a tripod. They came in two sizes: for 2in 'bombs' and 3in 'bombs'. The bombs had fins to ensure stable flight and a nose landing to detonate them. The tubes could be raised or lowered to alter the trajectory of the bombs. The bombs might contain HE, smoke-producing material or illumination provided by a flare suspended from a parachute. The contents of the bomb were shown by its colour. The 3in mortar fired heavier bombs, weighing 10lb, which might have one of two types of propellant charge for different ranges: 500 or 750 yards. In rapid fire, each tube could fire up to fifteen rounds per minute.

The number of mortars produced is not known, but over 92,000,000 bombs were produced during the war.

PIAT

The Projector Infantry Anti-Tank (PIAT) was produced from the end of 1942, to replace the 5.5in anti-tank rifle. It was effective against tanks up to 115 yards and against houses at 350 yards. It needed two men to operate, and like mortar bombs, PIAT bombs were launched from a large tube with a base 'foot' and a monopod. It had to be cocked before firing the first shot by pulling back a spring. The second man prepared the bomb by screwing the detonating fuse onto the nose. Some 10,405,000 PIAT bombs were produced between the last quarter of 1942 and September 1945.

Tanks

In the First World War production of tanks was exclusively in the hands of heavy engineering firms which made locomotives and other railway rolling stock. In 1937, when orders were placed for light tanks, the contracts went to four firms in the locomotive industry. In the summer of 1939, the increased demand for tanks brought more firms into tank production, two of which, English Electric and Leyland Motors, joined Vickers-Armstrong as the largest manufacturers of tanks during the first part of the war. Other large-scale manufacturers and assemblers of tanks included Harland and Wolff, Nuffield Mechanisation and Vauxhall Motors. By June 1943 there were twenty-eight firms involved.

This does not mean that each firm produced complete tanks from scratch. As with artillery pieces, the work was, in most cases, divided into several types: manufacturing and bench testing of transmission units and engines; various other sub-units; specialised parts such as fuel tanks, radiators and oil coolers; and fabrication of hulls and final assembly.

The first tank that served successfully was the Mk 1 Light tank. It was originally made by the Carden-Loyd Company, which was taken over by Vickers in 1928. Vickers added a fully traversing turret and spring-coil suspension. Vickers then went on to produce several other light tanks based on this design, all with forward-mounted engines. These consisted of the series from Mk 1A to Mk IV, all of which had .303 machine guns. The next in the series, the Mk V, was longer and carried two guns. All these tanks weighed in the region of 7 tons, and had a road speed of about 30mph.

After Dunkirk it was thought that these tanks were not adequate in their armament or offensive power, and tanks generally grew larger (although slower) and carried more powerful weaponry, including bigger guns such as the 2-pounder as well as the .303.

Later developments were the fast Cromwell tank, and the Comet which had heavier armament and a high-velocity 77mm gun. It had good armour-piercing performance, but was best used with HE shells against infantry.

Probably the best known of the British-built tanks was the Churchill. Although slower than the early light tanks, with a maximum road speed of 15mph, its main gun was a 6-pounder. This heavy infantry tank had heavy armour, a long chassis, all-round tracks, and was able to climb steep slopes. It was made by Harland and Wolff, and Vauxhall Motors. It was much used in the North Africa campaign, Italy and Normandy.

There were numerous variants on the basic pattern, including a heavy-duty flame-thrower known as Crocodile. This towed a two-wheeled armoured trailer containing the flame fuel and gas bottles for pressure. It had a maximum range of 100 yards, and could produce approximately 100 one-second bursts before needing refilling. Another variation on the Churchill was the Assault Vehicle Royal Engineers (AVRE), which had its gun replaced by a 4.2in mortar. The projectile for this weighed 40lb and had an accurate range of 80 yards. They could also be fitted with a rotary-flail mine clearer, with a wire-cutter device for barbed wire. Manual mine detectors worked in the Western Desert, detecting a mixture of tank and anti-personnel mines. The detectors came in short and long-armed versions, with a flat plate at the end. When the arm was swept from side to side in an arc and the plate passed over a metal object, its electronics emitted a warble through the operator's earphones. The whole thing could be disassembled and packed into a backpack or a wooden carrying case. The British army also laid mines, both anti-tank and anti-personnel. They produced a total of 62,465,000 mines, but the types are not defined in the available statistics. However, such figures as we do have suggest that they were probably mostly anti-tank mines.

Churchill tanks also served as armoured recovery vehicles, with front or rear mounted jibs, or as an armoured ramp carrier. This consisted of a turretless tank with ramps at each end and trackways across the body, enabling it to be used to form a mobile bridge. They carried short bridge sections, and fascines for craters and ditches, or carpet for muddy or boggy ground. Over 5,600 Churchill tanks were built during the war. As well as the Churchills, almost 20,000 tanks were built in the UK, and a further 33,000 obtained from abroad.

The long-barrelled guns for tanks were made at the Royal Ordnance Factory at Woolwich.

Submersible tanks

There were some attempts to produce a submersible tank, but the War Office could not countenance the cost of fully developing and manufacturing these. It was possible to use them submersed with the addition of flotation devices, but they were not really practical and the idea was abandoned.

Tracked infantry carriers and armoured fighting vehicles

When these vehicles were first introduced, it was unclear whether they were to be a small armoured fighting vehicle (AFV) with fixed guns, or a light armoured front-line vehicle with dismountable infantry machine guns. Its alternative name of 'machine (or Bren) gun carrier' gave a good description of its main role, but it did turn out to be more generally useful as safe transport for personnel who dismounted with their weapons at the desired location, while the machine withdrew to somewhere safe until needed again. This vehicle could also be used to tow 6lb anti-tank guns. Over 74,400 were made by

Vickers-Armstrong in the UK, with a further 52,000 made abroad. Another tracked vehicle was the Loyd, which often carried a 4.2in mortar. A personnel transport version called the 'Kangaroo' was found useful in the later stages of the move into Germany; the 21st Army group had over 400 of these, and over 600 of the larger 'Buffalo' landing vehicle.

Other armoured vehicles (wheeled)

The Rolls-Royce armoured car, originally built and used in the First World War, had some design changes in 1920 and 1924 and then remained in use until 1945. It could carry machine guns, anti-tank rifles and Bren guns. It was not suitable for front-line action, but was used for rear-area security work. Vehicles were protected by riveted steel plates, including one to cover the windscreen, which could be raised or lowered as needed.

There were several types of scout car, including the Dingo, first made by BSA from 1939. After BSA was bought out by Daimler, this vehicle was known as the Daimler Dingo. Over 6,600 were made, along with more than 4,000 Humber Scout cars. Most of these carried .303 calibre Bren guns or other machine guns. The Humber version had a crew of two men, but a third could be carried (usually a forward observation officer). They might have a smoke-grenade launcher, and often carried food, personal kit and weapons.

Rifles

There were two types of rifle: the bolt-action and the self-loading. During the First World War it had been recognised that although more advanced rifles were desirable, the bolt-action rifle worked well enough. At the beginning of the Second World War there was a large stockpile of these ready for use and so production of self-loading rifles was postponed.

Although the bolt action had to be operated each time the rifle was fired, the weapons did have small magazines of five or ten rounds. The self-loading rifles did not need this action of the bolt, automatically loading another round every time one was fired until the magazine was empty.

For the British army, almost all the rifles were the Lee Enfield .303 calibre produced by the Royal Small Arms factory at Enfield, by BSA near Birmingham and by LSA at Old Ford London; various other firms produced components. Some 22,473,221 of these were produced during the war.

Machine guns

Machine guns were designated light, medium or heavy. The Hotchkiss gun was considered light, but was superseded in 1940 by the Lewis gun made by the Birmingham Small Arms Company, and itself replaced by the Bren. All these except the Hotchkiss, which had a slightly larger calibre at .315, were .303 calibre, ammunition being carried in a belt or metal strip of ammunition.

The Bren was air-cooled, used a 30-round magazine, and had a bi-pod to steady the front of the barrel. It was either mounted on a vehicle or used manually by a three-man crew: one to fire, two to refill and pass magazines. They carried ten to twelve of these, short banana-shaped magazines holding twenty-eight rounds. Originally a Czechoslovak weapon, the Bren was modified in the UK and some 226,000 were produced, made at Enfield Lock. In 1940 the entire stock was only 2,300, the rest having been left in France.

Medium machine guns included the Vickers (a development of the Maxim gun) and the Browning (air- or water-cooled). The Vickers was .303 and had a 250-round belt. It was made in Crayford, Kent. Many were refurbished from the First World War stockpiles. Its water-cooled jacket made its barrel look very fat. As it weighed over 88lb and had an equally heavy tripod, it needed a team of at least three men. Its ammunition belt was carried in a wooden box, and this was put by the gun and the belt fed straight in from the box. In rapid-fire mode it used a belt in one minute.

The Browning M2 was a heavy machine gun, of .50 calibre, and with a 110-round belt. It was made in America, the Lend-Lease production of just over 15,000 went mainly to the Free French (7,655) or the 'British Empire' troops (5,233) leaving just over 2,000 for the British army.

Sub-machine guns

There was also a type of gun called a sub-machine gun. The first of these, the Thompson, was purchased from the USA. At the start of the war Britain used the Lanchester 9mm, but it was difficult and expensive to make and was replaced by the Sten gun. At .354 calibre, it had a 32-round box magazine, but this magazine was prone to malfunctions and it was thus necessary to carry several spare magazines. Even so, over 4,000,000 were produced in Britain.

Another variation was the machine carbine. Originally made in the USA only, production was taken up in the UK, making just under 4,000,000.

Grenades

The majority of grenades used during the Second World War were of the Mills bomb type.

Grenades were designed either to explode on impact, or had a timed fuse. The type known as fragmentation grenades had a segmented exterior, rather like a pineapple, which everyone thought was meant to break up on exploding and send lethal fragments flying. In fact this did happen, but some early designers' notes showed that these grooves were mainly intended to give a better grip. An experienced thrower could usually manage 49ft accurately, but the fragments on explosion went further than this.

Several variations of the Mills bomb were produced, including one which could be fitted with a stick to fire it from a rifle. Other variations were the 'sticky' grenade, which had two thin layers of metal over a layer of thin adhesive-covered fabric. This stuck the grenade to the target (usually a tank) for the five seconds required until the fuse detonated. Another variation was a mine-like grenade which was shoved between the tank's tracks and detonated when it was compressed.

Almost 100,000,000 grenades were produced in the UK.

Bayonets

There were various types of bayonet, the blades varying from a straight-sided knife shape to round or four-cornered. They were carried in a webbing sheath which hung on the belt, but were permanently fitted to the rifle when patrolling in the jungle.

Heavy knives

These were issued to troops serving in jungle locations. The American War Aid machete was supplied for British use. It had a distinctive blade with a black plastic handle, and was carried in a standard leather scabbard. The Indian machete had a square-ended blade. The Kukri was issued to British units serving with Indian divisions. Although a fearsome hand weapon, it was more often used to clear vegetation (or its heavy metal pommel for a hammer). Its scabbard included a steel for sharpening and a small utility 'skinning' knife.

Pistols

These were mainly issued to officers, but a few went to specialist troopers who required both hands to operate their special equipment and thus could not deal with a rifle, so needed a pistol for close-range defence. The standard-issue pistol at the beginning of the war was the Webley .45 revolver; later this was superseded by the .38 Lee Enfield.

Enormous numbers of rounds of small arms ammunition were manufactured in the UK:

small arms .22 to .455	8,943,233,000,000
.5 to 15mm	179,962,000,000
2mm	565,449,000

These numbers are almost unbelievable, but it should be remembered that even now vast numbers of bullets are expended for minimal numbers of 'kills', particularly with automatic weapons (never less than 1,000) and that they are often used for 'suppressive fire'.

Chapter 6

Petrol, Oil and Lubricants

During the First World War, the British Army carried with it vast quantities of hay and grain to feed the animals which constituted its transport power. By the time the Second World War started, and during its whole continuation, these animals had been almost entirely superseded by mechanical transport and fighting machines, and the hay and grains had been replaced by what became known as POL (petrol, oil and lubricants). These products were:

- Petrol, often referred to as motor spirit.
- Derv, or fuel for diesel-engined vehicles, often included in 'petrol' or 'motor spirit'. Although referred to under this single category, these two products were not interchangeable in a single vehicle, and if wrongly filled caused major damage to the engines. There is no easy way to say which type of vehicle used which fuel, as all types of vehicle, from staff cars to tanks, might use either.
- Oil meant lubricating oil, the stuff which goes inside engines, gearboxes and back axles to keep them running smoothly.
- Lubricants meant grease, which was applied to external joints to keep them moving smoothly.

The RASC dealt with all these, and also aviation spirit for aeroplanes.

POL needs in the UK were, at the beginning of the war, bought through the civil distribution system. Once enemy invasion was seen as a possibility, each command began to acquire reserves of tinned petrol, and the filling factories were ordered into full production. Arrangements were made to open petrol dumps at each of the eight strategic points where reserves of food were also to be stored. In the event of an invasion, detailed instructions and equipment were issued for the destruction of the stocks in the coastal belts and inland locations which the enemy might target.

Engine fuel and oil came mostly from the Middle East, while most of the lubricants came from America by ship on the Lend-Lease scheme. Other sources were the Caribbean area (Trinidad, Columbia and Venezuela). There was no precedent for purchasing or dealing with the enormous amounts of POL which would be needed. The War Office studied the situation and soon realised that what was needed were experienced personnel from the oil industry, and numbers of these were soon recruited into the RASC.

It was initially decided that 2 and 4-gallon tins were the best method of carrying and storing petrol, but almost immediately there were difficulties in the tin-making and filling factories. Some 5,000 tons of stock had been sent to France before the war started, but it was soon realised that the factories were having difficulties in meeting their targets due to mechanical problems. Shipping waiting to load at Avonmouth and Swansea stood idle, and GHQ BEF began to worry about their stock situation. In the event, the BEF did not use as much as expected. At the same time there were beginning to be adverse reports on the utility of the 4-gallon tins, but these had to suffice until 1941 when they were gradually replaced by the more robust 4½-gallon jerrican.

There was no precedent for planning for the enormous quantities needed, but the War Office had been studying the problem. Supply by road tankers direct to users was soon found to be impractical, so it was decided to use non-returnable tins. The 2-gallon tins were not available in quantity, so 4 gallons was the size used most.

Non-returnable petrol tins, once empty, had many uses, both for cooking and otherwise. They were used to build food stores by filling them with sand and using them as bricks, or flattening them out and nailing them to wooden uprights for walls and roofs.

The jerrican

The jerrican became the most widely used returnable container in the supply of packed fuels and certain lubricants to the army and kindred services, and is still in use today. It was an all-welded container made of heavy-gauge steel, measuring 18.375in × 13in × 6.5in. The sides were embossed to give it greater strength, and its overall shape allowed it to be stacked upright or on its sides. The top of the can incorporated a carry handle, and a man with normally wide hands could carry two cans in one hand.

Thus strongly made, if handled with care, its useful life could be almost indefinite, but in the course of its working life it might need replacement washers, toggles and pins. When these became necessary, rather than try to effect repairs in the working unit, the cans should be sent through normal channels to a petroleum maintenance platoon. Leakage was almost non-existent. The opening/closure was not on the exact top and this made it possible to pour the contents without spillage, and left a space at the top to allow for expansion. For some types of vehicle tank a funnel was needed when filling, but the shape of the opening meant this was not always necessary. The neck of the can is fitted with a special quick-acting closure with a slotted hinge which locks open when the can is tipped to pour the contents. To close the lid it had to be lifted slightly first. Failure to do this and subsequent forcing of the lid was the principal cause of the can having to be withdrawn from service and sent for repair.

It was painted to preserve it from corrosion due to weather, this paint normally being dark green, but it could be other colours to help camouflage it. For instance, this might be buff for use in desert conditions. The interior was painted with a special petrol-resisting paint, but this was poisonous and water should not be carried in petrol cans. For water, different cans were used, painted brown with a large white cross on both sides, and they had a special bituminous lining paint. This was not petrol-resistant, so petrol should not be put in water cans nor vice versa.

Holding 4½ gallons, the jerrican weighed 10lb when empty and about 43lb when filled with petrol, this weight varying with the specific type of petroleum it contained. The only stipulation as to its contents was that they should be of relatively low viscosity to allow them to be poured in all temperatures.

Jerricans were first encountered in North Africa in August 1941 when captured from the German army, but were then manufactured in the UK. Weekly production averaged 18,000 in 1942, 300,000 at the start of 1943 and 500,000 later that year. The total UK production was more than 48,000,000, using 49,000 tons of sheet steel and 5,000,000 gallons of paint.

There were some basic instructions for handling POL containers:

- Sweep out rail trucks and lorries thoroughly before loading petrol containers.
- Examine the interior of the transport vehicle for sharp objects which may damage the cans in transit.
- Pack the containers as closely as possible to avoid movement in transit. If there is space in the lorry, it should be filled with empty containers to prevent movement.
- Where possible, use protective packing or dunnage.
- If upright packing is not possible, stack the containers with the closure uppermost.
- Set leaking containers aside as soon as possible and decant their contents.
- Don't throw the containers about, whether full or empty. Don't leave them about exposed to the weather.
- Don't stack them more than twelve tiers high.
- Don't remove identification tags.
- Walking or sitting on containers should not be allowed.
- Remember the ambition of every container is 'a long life and a quick turnround'.

A further set of instructions on the handling and storage of packed petroleum products was issued in 1942, covering handling and storage of petroleum products in cans.

The storage site should be chosen with care; it should be well-drained, approximately level, within reasonable carrying distance from the road, and in a position which offers concealment from the air or where the stacks could be easily camouflaged. It should be large enough to allow stacks to be sufficiently spread apart from each other.

Petroleum products, although normally stored in the open, can be stored on the ground floor of empty buildings with adequate ventilation, doors and other openings. Derelict buildings are ideal. Lubricants should always be stored indoors unless absolutely impossible. As the fire hazard of lubricants is relatively small, ventilation is less important.

The ground area chosen for stacks should be cleared of vegetation, consolidated and levelled. If possible, a bed of sand or small hardcore should be spread to help drainage and provide a good foundation. The finished level of this layer should be a few inches above ground level. To prevent corrosion a layer of smooth hard material should be laid: wooden slats, rejected sleepers, brick paviors or empty 4-gallon tins filled with sand are all suitable. Ashes tend to be corrosive so should not be used.

Construction of stacks

For petrol and derv, 4-gallon non-returnable tins in cases should be stacked upright and not more than five tiers high. Those not in cases should be stacked horizontally in alternate tiers of headers and stretchers and not more than six tiers high. The tins should be set back half a tin all round at the third and fifth tiers. Four gallon returnable tins should be stacked horizontally in alternate tiers of headers and stretchers, with the opening caps to the top. They should never be stacked more than eight tiers high.

For lubricating oils, 5-gallon drums should be pyramid stacked upright, no more than five drums high and with each tier inset a half drum. Four gallon cans, cased or uncased, returnable or unreturnable, should be treated as for petrol and derv.

For lubricating greases, cases of six × 7lb tins should be stacked upright and not more than eight cases high; 28lb kegs should be stacked upright and not more than five cases high and inset half a keg per tier, or belly stacked not more than eight high.

Petrol stacks should be located not less than 150ft distant from dwelling-houses, public roads, premises occupied by military or civilian personnel, or railway lines where there was a risk of sparks from coal burning locomotives.

To reduce the risk of loss by accident or enemy action, stocks should be divided into at least two separate stacks not less than 100ft apart. The same distance should be maintained between petrol and ammunition stacks. The size of each stack should depend on total stock and local conditions, and on the covering material available.

All stacks were to be covered against weather and for camouflage, but weather protection was more important. Tarpaulins were best but old balloon fabric, corrugated iron sheets, asbestos sheets or similar would serve.* Both top and sides were to be completely covered and great care taken that rain could not seep between the edges of the covering. Barbed wire should be placed round each stack to prevent theft.

When siting stacks, advantage should be taken of natural cover such as trees, high hedges etc. Otherwise nets garnished with rag or bits of vegetation could be used. If in doubt, advice should be sought from a camouflage officer.

Packaged petroleum products should always be handled with care to avoid damage and subsequent leakage. Cases should not be carried by the binding wire. All cans were painted to protect against corrosion, and care should be taken that the painted surface, especially on the bottom of packages, was undamaged.

All leaky packages should be set aside and stacked so as to minimise further loss, then decanted as soon as possible. The contents of leaky petrol and Derv fuel containers should be decanted direct into vehicle tanks or other suitable containers, which were scrupulously clean. The contents of leaky lubricating oil containers should be decanted into scrupulously clean suitable containers. The leaky oil containers might be soldered without emptying, but never petrol containers.

All containers should be wiped clean before decanting, and fine-mesh filters should be used. Four gallon tins should be emptied with the special 'decanter'; if these were not available, a vent hole should be pierced opposite the cap. If packages were suspected of being contaminated, by water or other cause, they should not be issued but set aside for disposal.

The condition of containers should be checked regularly by an officer or responsible NCO. All packages were marked with the month of filling and the oldest should be used first, unless their condition warranted earlier use. A record should be kept of each stack showing daily contents, new receipts and issues. Physical stocktaking should be done at least once a week. A daily record should be kept of the number of leakers, quantities saved and net loss, the monthly net loss being shown as a percentage of the receipts and issues during the same period. When leaky containers were emptied directly into vehicle fuel tanks, only the amount salvaged should be charged.

Loading and unloading should be done under proper supervision. Where possible, dunnage should be packed between drums and flat-sided containers to reduce lateral movement. Rolls of sacking, old eburite cases or sandbags can be used.

* Asbestos was an acceptable material at the time.

Fire precautions were listed as follows:

- A scheme should be drawn up to meet local conditions, personnel should be trained in fire-fighting and fire orders should be posted where all can read them.
- Smoking, carrying matches or cigarette lighters in the vicinity of fuel stacks is absolutely forbidden, and frequent searches of personnel working in these areas is recommended.
- All vegetation or other material liable to start or spread fires should be cleared for at least 50ft from any stack.
- Any spilled fuel should be wiped up or covered with a generous layer of sand or earth.
- Only flameproof types of heating stoves or oil lamps may be installed in guard huts or other buildings within 150ft of stacks or anywhere else where petrol may be present.
- Motor cycles or steam wagons should not be allowed in the vicinity of stacks or decanting points.
- Petrol should not be stored in electrically lighted buildings unless all the wiring, switches, lamps or fittings are of the fully flameproof type.
- Provision should be made for easy access to the top of stacks; emergency steps may be improvised with 4 gallon tins filled with earth.
- A fire alarm should be installed within the vicinity of each stack so warning can be given immediately. A piece of rail or sheet steel can be used for this, with a suitable striker attached.

Firefighting

- Charged foam extinguishers should be kept near each stack with a minimum of four sand buckets. These should also be located at decanting and loading/unloading points.
- At areas liable to heath fires, fire beaters should be provided. These can be improvised by fixing old sacks or bunches of twigs to 4ft long stakes.
- Sand buckets can be improvised from petrol tins with a large opening, and kept two-thirds full.
- Sand should be sifted and dried, and buckets protected by a lid.
- At least one extinguisher should be discharged during fire drills.
- All extinguishers should be re-charged at least once every six months.
- Extinguishers which have been discharged should be washed out before being recharged.
- Extinguishers should be protected in cold weather by placing them in straw or bracken covered pits, or packed in cases with straw.

- The essence of fire-fighting is speed. Anyone who spots a fire, should shout 'FIRE', raise the alarm and indicate the position of the fire, and attack the fire with foam extinguishers and sand. The civilian fire brigade should be warned.
- All vehicles should be removed from the scene of the fire.
- As non-returnable tins of petrol do not explode it is reasonably safe to approach the fire.
- Sand is useful for smothering a spilled petrol fire or to stop petrol from running. It should be applied violently and not just poured out of the bucket.
- Foam extinguishers should be applied round the edge of the fire to prevent further air getting in, not aimed at the middle of the fire, then the jet should be moved to cover the whole burning surface.
- In cold weather the chemicals in foam extinguishers react sluggishly. They should be turned upside down, a thumb placed over the nozzle and the extinguisher shaken violently.
- Water should not be used on petrol fires, but may be used to keep an adjacent stack cool.

POL packaging was:

	Weight filled	Gallon equivalent	Size (″)
Motor spirit			
2 × 4 gall Eburite case	66lb	272	19½ × 10 × 14½
4 gall tin	32lb	280	9½ × 9½ × 13½
Returnable 4 gall tin	40lb	224	9³⁄₁₆ × 14¾ × 9³⁄₁₆
Returnable 2 gall tin	18lb 6oz	242	13 × 6 × 10
Derv fuel			
2 × 4 gall Eburite case	74lb	240	19½ × 10 × 14½
4 gall tin	36lb	248	9½ × 9½ × 13½
Lubricating oils			
2 × 4 gall Eburite case	78lb	232	19½ × 10 × 14½
4 gall tin	38lb	236	9½ × 9½ × 13½
8 gall drum	51lb	220	11 dia. × 17
Grease			
Carton of 6 × 7lb tins	50lb	1,890lbs	20 × 13 × 9
28lb keg	34lb	1,848lbs	10″ dia. × 15½

Home

As part of the anti-invasion measures in 1940, a War Office Mobile Petrol Service depot was formed at Aldershot; RASC vehicles were provided to make it possible to meet all demands at home or at the ports. Reserves of packed petrol were also built up in the ten main supply depots.

In the interests of saving fuel, revised speed limits were put in place:

Cars over 10hp and motor cycles	50 mph
Cars under 10hp	40 mph
Trucks 15cwt	35 mph
Load carriers under 3 ton	30 mph
Coaches and troop carriers	25 mph
Load carriers over 3 ton	20 mph
Tracked vehicles or tracked tractors	15 mph
Wheeled tractors, including tank transporters	15 mph

France

Bulk supply in France consisted of road tanker wagons and a base petrol filling centre to fill and repair returnable tins, but this was too static and its equipment too heavy for use in mobile situations, so mobile petrol filling centres were introduced.

There was a need for speed in getting petrol ashore early in the invasion; this led to the creation of ship-to-shore pipelines called tombolas. Portable 620-gallon petrol tanks installed in 3-ton lorries were tried, but they were difficult to manufacture in quantity and also difficult to secure in the lorries, so were hardly ever used.

By May 1940, the BEF had reserves of 40,000 tons of petrol in containers and 32,000 tons in bulk tanks, plus 3,000 tons of diesel in cans and 4,000 tons of lubricating oil.

Malta

In Malta, petrol supply from outside was difficult; control measures included a total ban on the use of civil transport on Saturday and Sunday. Public vehicles on the road on those days had to carry a special permit. In November 1942 barely eleven days' supply remained and the army's allotment was cut to 6,000 gallons a week. The main civil installation was owned by Shell, at Kalafrana.

Egypt / Western Desert / Levant

A scheme to provide 15,000 tons of tankage in the foothills of Suez and on the borders of the Great Bitter Lake had just been completed at the beginning of the war. Two separate tank farms were connected by pipeline and the intake from ocean tankers could go to either. But this was only sufficient for about fifty days' supply for three divisions. They also supplied returnable containers to the filling plants at Alexandria and Suez, but they could only produce about 15,000 tins per day. In September 1940 it was concluded that a further 155,000 tons of tankage would be needed and authorisation for this was received at the end of the year. However, other operations in East Africa, Iraq, Palestine and Syria and on the Red Sea littoral also had to be considered.

Plenty of refined petrol was available in the Middle East; all was supplied from the output of crude in Iraq, central and southern Persia and a little from Egypt. Refineries at Haifa, Suez and Abadan provided petrol and derv, and aviation fuel was also supplied from Abadan. Early in 1942 the output from Abadan was 300,000 tons; this doubled by the end of the year and was expected to reach 800,000 tons. Most of this was delivered by tanker.

At the end of 1941 the increased demand and some delivery failures from America created a serious shortage of tinplate for petrol tins in the Middle East. Supplies were ordered from various places and the combined output of these was about 3,000,000 tins per month; a year later it was 4,300,000. These cans were referred to as 'flimsies', reflecting the fact that they were not up to rough usage and constant handling. At times losses reached 30 per cent or more. The Middle East command had already recommended the use of jerricans as a standard container, but the War Office delayed and it was not until 1942 that production began. By the end of the campaign in 1943 1,000,000 had been sent to Africa.

There was a gradual transfer of American troops from central and western areas to eastern forces, which also incurred use of petrol. By February 1943 they were using more than 1,000 tons per day.

Ocean-going tankers began to arrive at Algiers. For the final offensive it was planned that half the total fuel required was to be held at the main bases and the rest divided between an advanced base and the forward area, a grand total of 180,000 tons. Much of the storage work was done by American troops, who installed ocean tanker storage at Philippeville, bolting together thirteen 1,000-ton tanks and putting down two 4in pipelines to Souk al Arba. They also installed four 500-ton tanks and completed a 69-mile pipeline from these to Souk el Arba, and imported several 8,000-gallon rail cars from the US and others from Morocco.

The Gebel Dave scheme was a joint army/RAF endeavour, which provided 27,000 tons of buried tankage in the Generfa and Fort Agrud areas, with a pipeline connecting one with a tanker berth in Great Bitter Lake and the other with a tanker berth at the Suez installation, and connecting the two areas.

In December 1940 it was decided that additional storage was needed, on the basis of 45 days' reserve for fifteen divisions covering Egypt, Palestine and Sudan, and Aden for 90 days, some packed, some bulk; and for Greece and Crete 60 days all packed. The scale for diesel fuel was 150 days for compression ignition vehicles. The target for lubricants was 150 days.

By the end of 1941 between 50 and 60 per cent of the maintenance tonnage for the 8th Army was POL. A dump of between 1 and 2 million jerricans was captured in Benghazi, but the hurried retreat prevented removing these.

Four petrol inspectors were appointed in November 1941, one at GHQ and one each to the 8th Army, Egypt and Palestine. Their main duty was to spot and deal with potential losses. As a result of their work, handling cased and uncased petroleum products into and out of ships, trains and vehicles was improved, including ensuring that trucks were tightly loaded and enough dunnage was used, ensuring that proper arrangements were made in depots for inspection of containers and salvaging the contents of leakers.

By 1942 the whole area was supplied with crude oil from Iraq, Persia and Egypt; refineries at Haifa converted this for petrol and diesel north of the canal. Those at Suez and Abadan dealt with the south of the canal. Aviation spirit all came from Abadan.

Fluctuating operating conditions meant that pipelines could not be used as much here as elsewhere, and so they were mainly used in base areas. Several schemes were considered and rejected as impractical, including one between Alexandria and Tobruk.

By April 1943, over 20,000,000 gallons were in returnable containers. But there was much leakage at sea, up to 40 per cent, with another 20 per cent during carriage forward to advance depots. Part of this was due to poor stowage: those loading the ships in the UK and USA did not realise that stacks should not be more than twelve cans high. In some cases they were fifty high with 'disastrous' effects on the lower layers. Some ships arrived with their holds many feet deep in petrol and derv. There were bad fumes, and they had to be pumped out, which presented a high fire risk.

Among the personnel units were the petrol control staff. Among their duties was the supervision of loading and unloading containers and dealing with leakers. The unloading was particularly important as the stevedores, until taught better, tended to throw the containers about in the interest of speedy unloading to turn ships round quickly.

Persia / Iraq

Before the war started, there were three plants for making non-returnable tins, and four more were built during the war. By April 1943 they were producing nearly 3,750,000 tins per month.

West Africa

Before the war, there was no RASC petrol organisation. Civil bulk installations were used at ports in Nigeria, Gold Coast and Sierra Leone.

North Africa

When planning for the campaign, the basis of calculation was 5 gallons of motor spirit per vehicle, per day, derv 50 gallons per tank or AFV per day, lubricants and greases were calculated at 6 per cent of motor spirit and derv.

The first slow convoy carried seven days' maintenance and three days' reserve for vehicles in this column; the second slow convoy carried fourteen days' maintenance for vehicles in first two convoys and fourteen days' reserve for the same, plus fourteen days' advance maintenance for vehicles in first three convoys; and the third slow convoy carried fourteen days' advance maintenance for all forces.

The RAF agreed to accept aviation spirit in containers, not bulk. The RASC was responsible for establishing rail- and road-heads within reach of RAF first-line transport. Once bulk facilities were established, the RAF was reluctant to accept containers and these accumulated at supply depots until there was 3,500,000 gallons in containers. These had to be decanted and issued to local airfields.

Sicily and Italy

The assault plan for Sicily was for all vehicles to land with tanks filled to 90 per cent of capacity, and a reserve in 4-gallon cans plus enough oil for one change. In Sicily there was always adequate petrol. A bulk storage depot at Syracuse was captured intact. Catania was used for aviation spirit as it was only 16 miles from the airfield, to which pipelines were run.

India

Estimated requirements of liquid fuels for the Allied Services in India command and SEAC were coordinated by the petroleum officer of the Defence Department of India, who communicated them to the committee representing the major oil companies. Lubricants were demanded by GHQ India direct from Washington; there was no involvement with the committee in India.

Production of containers in India was disappointing: only about 25 per cent of what was needed. There were many reasons for this, including lack of trained operating staff and the vast areas involved. A new branch in GHQ under the Engineer-in-Chief was set up to organise better arrangements. At the end of 1943 two plants to manufacture jerricans were set up at Madras.

Although not easy to construct through jungles (tigers and wild elephants added to the usual difficulties of working in disputed terrain), long pipelines for petrol were laid in north India. The Americans had already finished a 750-mile 6in pipeline known as 'Infinity' from Calcutta to Tinsukia as part of the 'Aid to China' scheme. The petrol was then flown over 'the hump' (the Himalayas) to China. Work was in progress on a similar pipeline to the same area from Chittagong. The British were also in the process of laying a 4in pipeline from Chittagong to Manipur Road. Much of what it was to carry was aviation fuel for airfields in East Bengal.

Ceylon

Ceylon had been getting 75 per cent of its POL from the Dutch East Indies, but once they were overrun by the Japanese all had to come from the Persian Gulf except lubricants. The Shell Oil Company obtained and stored all service requirements and petrol, kerosene and diesel to an agreed scale of reserves.

North Burma

Jungle warfare did not lend itself to bulk fuel storage, despite the ongoing pipeline-building programmes. One interesting development was the use of urethane-coated fabric petrol tanks holding 800 gallons or 2,500 gallons, with 620-gallon portable steel tanks and 4-gallon single-skin petrol bags for free dropping from aircraft. The 800-gallon tank folded up when empty and in this form occupied little space and was immediately available for use without the need for any construction work. Among other uses, they could be erected in a 3-ton lorry as an emergency bulk road tanker.

After the oil fields in central Burma were recaptured, they were operated on a short-term basis by a civilian oil company on behalf of Allied Forces South East Asia (ALFSEA) until a supply of spirit from Rangoon was resumed.

Solid fuel

The term solid fuel meant coal and coke for use in steam locomotives, and for heating barracks and army offices. There were a few situations where pitch was mixed with coal dust and compressed into briquettes.

In the severe winter of 1939–40 there was some difficulty in getting supplies throughout the UK and France, and reserves were diminished.

In the early stages of the North Africa campaign, coal was shipped from the UK on demands prepared in advance by planning staffs. The Allied Forces headquarters made monthly demands and the coal was obtained through civilian agents. In December 1943, the availability of UK coal was curtailed due to impending requirements in north-west Europe, so until February 1944 most was obtained from South Africa and India. Coal for the locomotives of the Middle East was mainly supplied through India, and from South Africa after May 1942. For Sicily and Italy, an average of 160,000 tons per month was supplied from the UK.

Chapter 7

Works Services and Engineer Stores

Engineering planning

One aspect of planning which needs to be high on the list of priorities for military campaigns, especially those which will take place abroad, is planning for engineering work. During the Second World War this meant that the Chief of Engineering needed to be consulted at an early stage of strategic planning, as his thoughts might influence such things as basic assault plans, for instance, the location for the assault in Operation Overlord. The first idea for this was the Pas de Calais, but it was less suitable than Normandy, where it would be easier to create speedy egress from the beaches and where enemy defences were lighter and there were fewer rivers and canals to cross. It was also a better place to build new airfields. Even in Normandy, some places were less suitable for airfield construction and the country between Bayeaux and Caen was best, partly due to the gentle undulations of the land and partly because of the quick-draining properties of the topsoil.

Once the location for the start of a campaign has been decided, engineers can start gathering intelligence to allow them to make detailed plans for construction projects, with the materials and machinery needed, and the numbers and types of units to work with them. All this may take what the military eye sees as a long time, but engineers know that the more thoroughly the preliminary stages are done, the better (and often quicker) the work will be.

One situation which may take considerable time is where heavy machinery will be required. This may have to be constructed specially and transported to its operating site, with trained operators and service facilities. In some cases, special equipment may have to be designed as well as built, and this may involve disciplines other than engineering. The Mulberry harbours for Operation Overlord were a case in point.

A good engineering plan requires several things·

- A clear understanding of the objective. This will need some detail, for instance with a bridge, what loads is it to carry (weight, width, height etc) and whether there will be one-directional traffic or two. With roads, not only the state of the existing roads, whether they must be widened, and for new roads (as with bridges), what loads they will have to carry and whether there are intermediate destinations that would allow work to be done in stages. And not least, the desired completion date.

- Good details of the physical conditions. For bridges this would have to include details of the water (flow, depth, width, seasonal variations) and the approaches. For roads and railway lines, the levels to be traversed, and whether these will require excavations or infilling.
- What production materials will be needed and where they can be obtained. This might involve hardcore and the machinery to provide and handle it, and top surface materials, drainage materials, timber, and manufactured material such as rails for railway lines. What transport will be needed for this?
- Availability of local labour and its requirements (cash wages, accommodation, hand tools, transport, religious mores etc).
- Accommodation and transport for specialised engineering personnel. Details of available bulk transport in ships, what must be loaded in each and in what order, and which ships must sail together.
- Climate, timing, modern communications, general terrain (desert, hills etc).
- Is this a one-off supply route for an invasion, or a long-term line of communication?

Before the war there was no comprehensive organisation at the War Office to give advice on engineering aspects of plans. The Director of Fortifications and Works could advise the quartermaster general on the quantities of stores for maintenance and work required at the campaign bases and lines of communication. He was also meant to estimate, and organise the supply of, quantities of operational equipment and stores, but this could often be no more than informed guesswork, which had to be based on probable theatres of operations rather than firm plans.

Equally, the Inspector of Royal Engineers could theoretically advise the General Staff on operational engineering matters, but since he had numerous other tasks to perform he was located in London, was rarely consulted on planning and was largely unaware of the strategic plans for the BEF until the day before it sailed. So there was little consideration of engineering aspects, either of the war in general or for the first campaign.

This situation remained static until October 1941 when the main operations in the war had moved to the Middle East and the possibility of trouble in the Far East was looming. Finally, at this time, the office of engineer-in-chief was created at the War Office. His duties included advising the general staff on engineering planning and the provision of resources. The engineer-in-chief's department included an operations branch, known as E(Ops), with responsibility for collecting relevant information, preparing a report following the issue of an outline plan, a listing of units and formations, and lists of stores to be appended to a detailed plan, and finally allocating stores and equipment to engineer units.

Among the defence works along the British coast and in northern France were 'pill-boxes' made of concrete reinforced to withstand shellfire. It was necessary that those in France should be suitable for both British and French weapons, as the two forces might relieve each other. Building with reinforced concrete requires frames into which wet concrete can be poured, with grids of reinforcing rods fixed inside. Known as shuttering, these can be made of wood, but a shortage of suitable timber dictated that standard designs should be created so the shuttering could be reused. Steel shuttering was made for each design in the UK and shipped to France for use there. Work on constructing these buildings was slow to start with, but speeded up as the teams gained experience. With practice, and the necessary jigs for assembling the grids of reinforcing bar, the work could be completed in an average time of less than three days, unless there were problems with the site such as a need for drainage.

Airfields needed joint planning, involving engineers, the army, and the RAF. There were certain constraints that had to be observed, such as wind direction, fuel storage, location of control towers, length of runways for the likely weight of planes, and hangar space for repairs.

In south-east Asia, a timetable was set for the production of amphibious assault plans. In 1945, in Borneo, these were:

- Instructions received by engineers 15 May.
- Outline divisional plan delivered 26 May
- An inter-service conference 27 May.
- Draft operational and administrative plan 6 June.
- Final coordinating conference 7 July.
- Final operational plan delivered 9 July.

The instructions included information on enemy strength, the beaches to be used and possible sites for airfields. The engineers' appreciation of the assault stated the first tasks to be support of the assault brigades, work in the beach maintenance area, and constructing an airstrip for the short takeoff/landing of Auster aircraft.

Early support tasks included the removal of mines and booby traps, other obstacles and enemy defences. Stores for the first day had to be carried by personnel and included tools and demolition charges. These had to be listed, as did the reserves for the next few days, which were loaded in the vehicles that landed on the first day and held at field parks where they could be called for by field companies.

Although most engineering work was construction or repair (sometimes preceded by demolition for clearance), there were some situations where demolition was performed on its own. There was much of this during the invasion of Europe and advance towards and into Germany in order to protect the army's left flank.

In the Far East, sometimes the jungle was so impenetrable that there was neither a point of ingress, nor clearings where equipment could be dropped. The start of projects such as roads or airstrips in such country meant that everything had to be manually carried, and the first task in such circumstances was to work out what tools were essential and how to pack them to ease handling and carrying. Even when a start had been made and further supplies and equipment could be air dropped, they also had to be carefully chosen.

Before the war British construction engineers were not very mechanically minded, except in large public works, where bulldozers, mechanical diggers and pile drivers were used. However, this was on a very small scale and very few items of heavy plant were manufactured in the UK; most came from the USA. Consequently the British Army owned few of these machines and few of its engineering officers knew how to use them and what they could and couldn't do. Certainly other fighting officers had little idea of what bulldozers could do, and some very odd requests were received, such as providing absolutely level surfaces by skimming the tops off rows of felled tree stumps.

When the BEF arrived in France, its engineers found themselves in need of heavy plant for excavating anti-tank ditches, levelling ground for airfield construction and laying concrete on a grand scale. They also had to create accommodation for British troops, and although they realised the need for machinery to help them, airfield construction at home was already using most of what was available. A little was eventually found in the UK and sent to France, and more was ordered from overseas. Even such small amounts as could be produced raised two immediate problems: competent operators had to be trained, and an organisation had to be created to maintain and repair the machines and deliver them to where they were needed.

There were some smaller machines, such as pumps and concrete mixers; these were considered to be engineer stores and loaned to units as needed. It was considered that no special training was required for operation of these machines.

There were quite a few tipper lorries, which had been acquired on the outbreak of war with other commercial vehicles. These were mainly used as basic carriers until their value on construction projects was realised.

Although military engineers were often regarded as miracle workers, they did need equipment and stores to do their work. In peacetime, this work was rarely as urgent as in wartime and essential construction stores could be obtained when each project was agreed. However, they did need to maintain a 'stable' of machinery and other essential equipment and this required its own storage and maintenance facilities. Engineering work, often referred to as 'works services' in wartime, both home and abroad, consisted of the following:

- Communications (construction of airfields, construction and repair of roads and bridges, development of ports, rehabilitation of captured ports and construction of quays and wharves).
- Piped water supply and water storage.
- Oil and petroleum, construction of tankage and pipe-laying.
- Accommodation (hutting on lines of communication and in bases, including welfare accommodation, hospitals and convalescent depots, construction of various types of depots).
- Electrical and maintenance services and supplies, cold storage, repair and maintenance in large towns in operational theatres.
- Provision and distribution of engineer stores and plant, building engineer workshops.
- Other activities, including development of local resources and establishment of local industries, forestry and quarrying.

First priorities were given to provision of depots at home, airfields in northern France in 1939–40, water supply in the Western Desert, roads and airfields in North Africa, bridges in Africa, airfields and oil pipe lines in SEAC, and roads and bridges in Western Europe in 1944–45.

When the war started there was no Ministry of Works and Planning, only a much smaller Office of Works. It was thought that military spending at home would be some £45,000,000 per annum, this being about a quarter of what the civil construction industry thought could be their annual capacity. In the event, it was some £312,000,000 over the duration of the war. This figure does not include the cost of military labour. It does include some £50,000 spent on Operation Bolero for housing and caring for American troops in the UK from December 1941. The £312,000,000 included £14,800,000 for personnel accommodation, £14,300,000 to provide hospitals for 94,000 beds, £12,700,000 for depots and workshops, and £8,200,000 for other services.

The depots provided 18,000,000 square feet of covered accommodation and 45,000,000 square feet for open storage, with 310 miles of roads in the depots.

The number of engineering personnel employed during the war rose from 4,000 to just under 16,000, with engineering troops used as needed.

In July 1943 the two sections, works services and engineering stores, were separated, the engineer-in-chief was appointed and his staff at the War Office were reorganised. Central accounting was introduced. In the field, works sections were formed which provided a mobile trained team wherever needed.

Usually two or three of these were attached to each Corps of Royal Engineers (CRE) unit (also known as sappers). Large-scale use of heavy plant was introduced, especially for roads and runways. The use of local resources was encouraged, especially in the Middle East and Italy. The status of engineering stores was raised with a directorate.

Organisation

Before the war the engineering works situation was rather a 'poor relation' at the War Office as part of the quartermaster general's department, with most work done by outside contractors. The entire directorate in 1936 was 216 men, consisting of thirty-four officers, four civil engineers, four architects and 178 military and civilian clerks and draughtsmen. The whole directorate was organised into five branches:

- QMG7 dealt with all works services at home except fortifications.
- QMG8 dealt with all works services abroad and fortifications at home and abroad.
- QMG9a dealt with military and civil personnel.
- QMG9b dealt with the provision of plant and stores, and electrical and mechanical services and Royal Engineers power installations.
- QMG10 dealt with design, standardised plans and running contracts for the directorate.

Works services were controlled by a system which divided into classes:

- Class 1 was new works estimated at over £2,500. These were listed in the army estimates approved by Parliament each year and could not be transferred to other services without Treasury permission.
- Class 2 was new works under £2,500. These were not shown in the army estimates in detail.
- Class 3 was maintenance services. These were not shown in the army estimates in detail.

In the army estimates for 1938–39, new services totalled £7,797,500 and maintenance £1,638.000.

At the outbreak of war the duties of QMG7 were listed as:

- Finding out what resources and capacity contractors had which would make them ready to undertake various works services.
- Arranging a system of war contracts with the Director of Army Contracts (DAC).
- Consulting with QMG9 on the organisation of additional districts.
- Making preliminary arrangements on finance.
- Consulting with General Staff over AA defences.

- On general mobilisation to arrange for additional camps, hospitals and depots.

All this related to home; for the BEF, QMG8 had to liaise with the Director of Fortifications and Works (DFW)

QMG9 had to:

- Organise personnel for works in theatres of war, and the other personnel who checked shipments.
- Maintain designs for electrical and maintenance installations, and provide ongoing advice on their maintenance.
- Provide, through the DAC, engineering plant and materials except ordnance stores, according to estimates from the field force commander-in-chief.
- Arranging transport of stores from factory to depot and on to overseas bases, while holding some items in reserve.
- Provide a list of all stores needed for the BEF on embarkation.

The pressure of work at this time was very great, and the necessary recruitment of additional personnel never kept up with the demand. With this, and the expansion of actual work and acquisition of stores, accounting staff found it almost impossible to keep up.

Expansion abroad started with the need to bring all port defences up to date, the urgency depending on the location; those in the Far East were not considered vulnerable to attack at the outset. The countries at the eastern end of the Mediterranean did need consideration. In Egypt, the existing 10,000 British troops in the Canal Zone, serving under the terms of the Anglo-Egyptian treaty of 1936, were to be increased to nearly 300,000. The first move was to send twenty-one more works officers, an engineering base stores depot, an engineering base workshop, two engineering and maintenance companies and two army troop companies.

After Dunkirk the concentration was on invasion defences; the total cost of emergency work was £28,000,000. There was some criticism of the War Office on the slow work on the militia camps, so an advisory committee on engineering building made up of civilian engineers (the Jameson Committee) was appointed to advise the DFW, especially on works contracts. A number of civil engineers were appointed to supervise the building of large camps, and a Royal Engineers inspection team was deputed to visit works in progress and report on efficiency. Then, in May 1941, a controller-general of Military Works Services was appointed and ordered to review the position and report. This report pointed out that there was no existing organisation to collect, collate and disseminate engineer intelligence, and he had found no engineer studies having been prepared for projected operations. In at least one case this led to gross underestimates of requirements, which made it clear that they had never been studied. There was no one person at the War Office for field force engineers to deal with. The report suggested that an engineer-in-chief should be appointed with full control over works and stores. This took place in early August 1941, and led to a major reorganisation of the whole, which included a new branch for finance and statistics.

Once appointed, the new engineer-in-chief introduced centralised accounting and stores control in works services. This took place in phases over nearly eighteen months. At the same time there was an acknowledgement of the work to be done and a massive addition to the engineer-in-chief's staff, from 4,000 to 15,800.

The Lend-Lease Act (relating to supplies and American bases on British soil) was finalised on 11 March 1941. Before this purchases of American equipment were limited, as they had to be paid for in cash and British dollar resources had to be carefully used. When America entered the war the scope of Lend-Lease increased enormously and was also altered by an agreement that America should concentrate on warlike stores to a greater extent than the UK.

The Military Mission in Washington was then augmented by four officers with knowledge of both technical and military problems. Before this the British Purchasing Commission had handled requests, but only by passing on demands from London. Specifications had been drawn up by the American procurement agencies and manufacturers, but neither understood military requirements outside the USA.

The British engineering branch in Washington was organised into five branches, one each concentrating on engineering and mechanical stores, construction stores, general stores, transportation, and shipping. In March 1942 the US War Department took over responsibility for supply from the British Treasury, and programmes for the sixteen months to 30 April 1943 were drawn up, estimating the requirements for that period at almost $200,000.

One slight difficulty was what was called the 'forty-five day rule', which said that equipment not shipped within forty-five days after becoming available would be repossessed. Given the shipping difficulties of the time, it was almost impossible to meet this deadline, a situation which could only be dealt with by delaying documentation. In October 1943 the rule was changed to seventy-five days.

Shortly before the war, work commenced for the Air Defence of Great Britain (ADGB), mainly on building new AA batteries. A typical battery consisted of two gun emplacements, spread 90ft to 150ft apart, two magazines, a gun store, caretakers' quarters and living huts for the gun crews. The first of these was at Shoeburyness (south-east Essex). They were built in three phases, starting with finding sites for guns and searchlights, mobile stores, supply depots and ordnance workshops, ammunition magazines and depots. The second phase involved the manning of the site, and thus was not CRE responsibility. The third phase might involve expansion. The accommodation for personnel was provided at first by tents, which were replaced as quickly as possible by huts or brick and concrete buildings. The magnitude of this task can be judged by the personnel strength of the emplacements: 269,000 by January 1941. They were situated all over the country on more than 4,000 sites, including 300 static gun sites, 200 mobile units and numerous light AA units.

Militia camps

It was decided to raise the militia (i.e. start conscription) in April 1939. This meant building accommodation and training facilities on a large scale. The decision was taken in such a hasty fashion that it was some time before numbers of conscripts and thus camps for them could be estimated.

Further decisions were that no conscripts should be housed in tents after the beginning of October and that the accommodation should be provided partly by adding huts to existing barracks and partly by building completely new hutted camps. As the usual procedure for these works was rather long-winded (drawing up general plans, inviting contractors to inspect sites and tender for the work, select firms etc) and the need was urgent, a different procedure was used. Leading contractors were called to a meeting and the situation explained, then contracts were awarded on a cost plus fee basis. The contractors were given specifications and standard plans and made responsible for fitting the plans to the sites. Leading firms of quantity surveyors were appointed to supervise the works, the costs of which were subject to investigation by a government accountant. All this had to be approved by the Treasury Inter-Services Committee.

There were some difficulties (mainly complaints by the public of waste and inefficiency), but also some problems with labour as the sites tended to be in remote locations. Where the work was for training units, these needed to be located well away from population centres. Typical of this was Barnard Castle, where much of the labour came from Darlington, 15 miles away. Until the work was advanced and hutting was available, it was difficult to persuade workers to accept jobs where they had to live in primitive conditions, but in general these camps were found to be very satisfactory. They did cost a little more than the peacetime procedure, but they were comfortable and quickly completed.

Other works followed; because of demand from other government departments, it was not always easy to find contractors for army work, and the DAC, with the assistance of the National Federation of Building Trades Employers, started investigating the available capacity of the larger firms. An advisory committee of contractors was formed, chaired by Sir Malcom McAlpine to plan for use of labour and materials.

A quartering plan gave priority to building training camps. The first phase of this was for 110,000 men; the second, for about twice that number, was due to start when the militia camps were finished. The third was for mobilisation and expansion of storage needs as new equipment came forward, and operational defence movements for aerial attacks or to protect new naval bases.

The shortage of timber and the need to use bricks for these camps did create one problem: with timber construction, when the camps were no longer needed the huts could be dismantled and the land, which had been requisitioned, returned to its former condition. This could not be easily done with brick construction, so the government purchased the land instead.

In the very severe winter of 1939–40, building work had to be suspended and the labour diverted to clearing roads and other civil maintenance.

At the same time as the camp-building programme, there was an equally large programme of depot extension and renovation, and extending and updating port defence in locations away from the south-east coast.

After the evacuation from Dunkirk anti-invasion defences took precedence over other building.

In the autumn of 1940 work began on the big RE stores depot at Long Marston (6 miles south of Stratford on Avon and next to a railway line). Some 350 acres were requisitioned at the start and a further 300 were earmarked for later work. While this was building, in order to relieve congestion at the Donnington depot, temporary storage at Swindon and Garston (on Mersey) was acquired from the GWR and LMS railways.

When the expected invasion failed to materialise in the summer and autumn of 1940, labour was returned to camp and depot building. By the end of January 1941, there were nearly 2,000,000 troops and ATS in the country. 'Austerity' hutting, which basically meant double bunks, was introduced. Ordnance depots were also high priority, starting with the vehicle depot at Chilwell and several satellite depots. Two large ammunition depots at Kineton and Nesscliffe followed, then an enormous ordnance depot at Bicester.

The expansion of ordnance services made it necessary to construct another large depot once Donnington was complete; Bicester was chosen. The site was on the slopes of two facing hills and the valley between (although the latter was prone to flooding and major drainage work had to be done). Close to a point where the GWR and LMS railways crossed, it was organised into six sub-depots; one for each of the specialised uses such as signals.

A lieutenant-colonel was appointed to supervise the work, which was done by a mixture of military labour, civil labour and about 1,000 Italian prisoners of war, who were housed in huts in a detached camp. A firm of consulting engineers and a special surveyor were appointed.

Expenditure on works services in the year 1940–41 totalled £62,347,087, and in the following year approximately £61,750,000.

Other CRE works at that time included reinforcing the neck of land at Kilnsea, which prevented the sea breaking through and turning Spurn Head into an island; and creating road blocks and tank blocks. These consisted of reinforced concrete blocks of varying sizes and configurations, augmented by heavy steel rails. Deep anti-tank ditches were dug in several places, mines were laid and flame-throwers were stored.

The accommodation for the construction workers was in huts and the storage buildings had steel frames and concrete cladding; the roofs of these were corrugated iron covered in bitumen. The original cost was estimated at £5,000,000, but with various additional work the final cost was £6,175,000.

The end 'product' was 6,739,500 square feet of covered storage space and 5,177,025 square feet of open storage space and accommodation for about 14,000 people.

Bolero

When planning for the Allied invasion of north-west Europe, which would leave from the UK, it was decided that the provision of accommodation for troops, support staff and stores would be a British responsibility; that the Australians would assist with manpower and materials for the building, and that the British Treasury would provide all the necessary funds during the project, with a final settlement between the various countries after the war. The numbers of men involved consisted of an air component of 240,000, 2,900 at headquarters; 235,050 fighting troops; 294,050 supporting troops and 277,000 supply service personnel, making a total of 1,049,000. It was estimated that all this would cost £50,000,000. This estimate was prepared on very short notice (less than an hour) but proved to be remarkably accurate, as the final cost was £49,900,000.

Not surprisingly difficulties arose, not least due to the British policy, meant to confuse invading Germans, of removing road signposts. Although it was suggested that these should be replaced, they were not, and much time and petrol was wasted by lost travellers.

There was also much confusion over language (is it a rubber or an eraser?) especially with country dialects. This required the compilation and issue of local glossaries. Glossaries of British storage nomenclature were also prepared.

Other difficulties involved:

- The quality of accommodations. American troops were accustomed to higher standards and more space than British troops.
- Types and standards of construction. The British were used to working with a variety of materials such as brick, plasterboard and

corrugated iron, whereas the Americans were used to using wood alone. Some training courses had to be rapidly organised.

- The Americans were not used to working with clay soil or in the changeable British weather with its intermittent rain.

France / BEF

The original war plan was for a mobile division and two other divisions entering through the ports of Brest and Nantes on the north-west coast of France and Cherbourg on the north coast. All had arrived and disembarked by 7 October 1939.

The main reason for choosing those locations was to site the bases out of the reach of enemy short-range aircraft, but also because at the time of the landing, the role for the BEF had not yet been decided other than to 'support' France against the Germans. It was then decided that British troops should hold the Valenciennes–Armentières section of the Maginot line. This delayed the provision of engineering plans, but it soon became clear that the two main priorities were airfields and troop accommodation. The RAF estimated that it needed twenty-five airfields. Five of these were almost complete by June 1940 and a further twelve were operable in good weather. This also meant a very long line of communication, at 220 miles from Rennes to Abancourt, and another 50 miles to Arras. The most pressing task for the CRE was to get all the line of communication troops under cover before the winter. This meant delays in commencing work on other tasks including depots for supply, ammunition and transport.

It was hoped that the RAF would be able to take over some French airfields and that such other work as was needed could be carried out by local contractors. None of this came to pass, and it soon became obvious that the RAF had underestimated their requirements. They needed twenty-five airfields and twenty-five satellite fields. Concrete runways would be needed, especially due to the mud in Flanders in the autumn and winter; a few fields in the drier Champagne region could be temporarily operated on grass. Work was progressing quite well until 10 May when the German advance began and the tasks, together with the heavy equipment and most of the stores, had to be abandoned.

A reconnaissance party had been sent before the landing but this did not include a RE officer, because it was thought that the General Staff and Transport representatives could get what was wanted, and because the French had promised to provide accommodation for bases at Nantes and Rennes, and to supply the force with all the stores needed.

Neither of these promises was kept, and the two sites given were found to be either hopeless or nearly so. Nantes had been an American hospital in the First World War but had only a few concrete roads and some dilapidated huts. The railway sidings were three-quarters of a mile away, and no other rail facilities could be provided; the site at Rennes was on agricultural land with no roads or buildings and only one shabby siding. It did at least lend itself to development, and railway spurs and sidings were provided, but the heavy demands on railway construction meant that all the lines were single, not double. This meant that unloading and loading the same train simultaneously was impossible, and cranes mounted on trains alongside could not be used.

There were no reserves of hutting at home and it took some time before supplies began to arrive in France, the first order for 500 Nissen huts not arriving until December. Statistics on this are not available, but somewhere in the region of 90,000 tons were sent, which made about 27,000,000 square feet of covered accommodation for troops, hospitals and stores.

Problems with engineering stores included distribution of bulk petroleum products: piping, tanking and pumping plant for the Normandy campaign. Plans were produced for 1,000 miles of 6in and 400 miles of 4in pipe.

Norway

This short-lived expedition in April and May 1940 was not a success for various reasons. The CRE had to do its best without most of their stores and transport which had failed to arrive; they did manage to repair timber wharves, make road repairs and construct hard standing. They prepared the layout of engineering stores and did preparatory work on a transit camp of Nissen huts.

Middle East – Egypt / Western Desert

One of the biggest tasks was the construction of the Middle East base in Egypt. This involved 24,500,000 square feet of covered accommodation, 37,550 hospital beds, 8,820 convalescent beds, 400 miles of roads in hospitals and depots, 2,300 feet of landing wharves and 5,000ft of deep-water berths. There had been little time to make a full plan for this; despite the fluid military situation, the main features of the plan with only a few adjustments were met.

All the operations in the Western Desert were dependent on good water supplies, both for drinking and locomotive supply. Several schemes were proposed, but the best was a pipeline from Alexandria to Mischiefa. The engineers also built factories for local products, which reduced the transport time taken by shipping round the Cape after the Mediterranean was closed to British shipping.

A directorate of works was set up very soon after the outbreak of war. Factories producing cement, oxygen and acetylene and oil refineries were supervised by the War Department. Other items were manufactured by the

Works Services department: anti-tank mines, jerricans and large quantities of joinery and even some Z-craft.

The rapid expansion of activities in the Middle East required almost continuous expansion of the stores section. They covered provision of stores including local purchases, workshops and experiments; and matters which covered the administration of depots, control of stores, inspections and statistics. The principal task of the works services in the Middle East was the construction of more than 26,000,000 square feet of covered accommodation. At the outbreak of war, there were 10,000 British troops in the Canal Zone at Moascar and Fenci.

As for RE stores in the Middle East, at Abbassia, Cairo, Moascar, Haifa and Sarafand the covered space available was just over 100,000 square feet. Early October 1939 planning was for a total of 296,694 troops, of which three divisions were in the Western Desert, two in Palestine and ten in transit, all to be housed in Alexandria or the Canal Zone. The original plans for Alexandria were abandoned when Italy joined the war; instead a new depot for 60,000 tons was built on a 20-acre site.

In early 1940 work started on two new depots to facilitate the work necessary to house and supply the extended troop commitments. These depots included giant cranes, wharves for canal-delivered stores, and road and railway enhancements.

A general purpose depot for engineering stores, occupying 275 acres for stores and 57 acres for workshops, was built at Fantara on the Great Bitter Lake; there was covered accommodation at those sites of 69,000 square feet and 107,800 square feet respectively. There was some docking space, for which 9 miles of standard and light gauge railways served the depots.

The Western Desert force was served by a depot for 600,000 tons at Burg-el-Arab, mostly timber and defence stores.

Water supply and pipelines were provided by repairing ancient Roman rainwater reservoirs called birs; sinking tube wells (the water thus provided tended to be very saline and needed distillation before drinking); and so-called 'aqueducts' near the sea which collected the fresh water which had seeped towards the sea and floated on the heavier salt water in a layer up to 2in deep. A pipeline was built which carried filtered Nile water.

The Tura caves were in the 400ft escarpment running north/south about 15 miles south of Cairo. Originally dug out of the limestone by Pharaonic engineers, these caves were well made, but later inhabitants had extended their width by reducing the inner walls, and there were frequent rock falls. Once cleared and reinforced by concrete, they were used for storage of ammunition and other items. There was plenty of sand and aggregate and bitumen from the oil refineries at Suez and Haifa.

Middle East

The chief use of heavy equipment was for clearing stones and sand from roads and airfields, and levelling uneven surfaces. Bulldozers, scrapers and graders were used for this, and small mechanical diggers were used to create gun-pits, various defensive positions and also to build banks for tarpaulin reservoirs. As well as straight-bladed bulldozers, angle dozers were found to be particularly useful, including shoving abandoned vehicles off roads.

The principal difficulty with such machines was that they had to be transported to their working sites and then away afterwards; this was not always easy to achieve and many had to be abandoned.

Later in the war there was some experimentation with fitting bulldozer blades to tanks. A troop of Sherman tanks with these blades was used successfully in Italy in 1944, but in general the tanks were not fitted with the gears to continually advance and reverse, and thus broke down frequently.

Palestine

A tentative plan for construction of a base had been prepared pre-war; this was for up to eight divisions with auxiliaries, and thirty-one officers in all. A new depot was built at Nabula consisting of 320 acres of 60,000 square feet of covered accommodation. Another at Quryat Motzkin near Haifa was designed for 100,000 tons but often handled 150,000. There was also 120,000 square feet of covered accommodation.

Sudan

No base depots were built here, stores being handled at dumps at Port Sudan, Massawa and Khartoum.

Turkey

The CE here was based at Istanbul and there were two CREs at Izmir (Smyrna) and Kilya. For a while in late 1940, it looked as though CRE work might be withdrawn and in July 1941 the teams based in Izmir were drastically reduced. Meanwhile, in March 1941 a new CE arrived and set up his headquarters at Ankara. By 1942, most of the work was roads and airfields.

Persia / Iraq

Here there were four phases in British operations:

- Occupation, necessary to suppress a revolt which broke out in May 1941 and lasted five months. A force was considered necessary to defend the oilfields and Persian Gulf ports; this required bases.
- By the second phase, what had been an independent force known as 'British troops in Iraq' (BTI) had become the 10th Army, with the

usual CE and staff. Work was started to implement plans for 'Aid to Russia' scheme, with works in northern Iraq. Several bases in north Iraq were started.

- Defence started in July 1944, the need caused by the threat of German breakthrough from the Caucasus into northern Persia. The 10th Army was relieved of responsibility for the base and line of communication, which was then taken over by GHQ Paiforce.
- When the threat of invasion died away, aid to Russia began and lasted two years.

East Africa

There was no organisation whatever when war broke out, so the situation was chaotic.

For the first year, only defensive measures could be taken. When Italy entered the war, a CE with staff was sent from the UK and South Africa provided three CREs and staff. An engineering stores base depot (ESBD) was formed at Thika. During the advance in spring 1941, Works Services followed closely and rehabilitated the ports of Kismaya and Mogadishu and maintained the route from the latter to Addis Ababa. By autumn 1941, when Italian resistance had collapsed, fewer troops were necessary, and some South African troops were transferred to the Middle East. But when Japan entered the war, East Africa became an area of major activity and by the middle of 1943 the CE had three CREs in the central area (Mombasa, Nairobi and the west and north frontier districts) and an independent one as well as three covering works in Somaliland, northern Rhodesia and Nyasaland, and the islands of Madagascar, Mauritius and the Seychelles. There was also a reserve depot about 60 miles north-west of Mombasa at Samburu, which was stocked from South Africa. Until the middle of 1943 the vast stocks captured from the Italians provided almost all the supplies needed.

West Africa

At the outbreak of war there was only one engineering unit, at Freetown, Sierra Leone. This was followed in autumn 1940 by GHQ at Achimota, Gold Coast, and stores at Lagos, Takolari and Freetown.

North Africa

For Operation Torch a shortage of shipping space had some unfortunate effects on CRE. The ESBD arrived late and was badly situated too far from the port of entry; the works directorate of thirty officers arrived in several different convoys. The last had only just arrived when Armed Forces HQ assumed control. There was a dump at Bougie which extended along 4 miles of road, one at St Charles (10 miles from Philippeville), several by road and rail run by a workshop and park company and another similar depot near Bone. This last supplied stores for the final battle.

The main requirements here were for airfields and roads. The natural surfaces deteriorated badly in wet weather, which made airfield location and maintenance extremely difficult until a good source of sand was found.

The line of communication from Algiers was some 450 miles, mostly in mountainous terrain, and heavy use tended to break up the surface. It was difficult to keep roads open for traffic; a shortage of bitumen did not help.

Two types of hospital were built here, one for temporary use with all accommodation tented except the reception block, cleansing block, cook-house and food stores. The choices of site were restricted by water supply; 12½ gallons per bed was the minimum acceptable, while 20 was the ideal. Known as Type A, ten of these hospitals were built, with a total of 9,400 beds.

Type B hospitals were permanent and housed in existing buildings or 24ft Nissen huts. Extension continued with schemes for electrical and water supply, the work being completed in 1942 for 40 per cent of wards and their sanitary annexes, 33 per cent of storage space and dining and recreation rooms, which were tented. Nine of this type, for 10,000 beds, were built, along with four convalescent hospitals with a total of 8,000 beds.

Sicily

In summertime bulldozers were used to create fords, by laying down 44 gallon drums with both ends removed as culverts in river beds, then using a bull-dozer to push soil, gravel and stones over them.

Italy

Many Italian roads were badly damaged and dozers were invaluable for repairs.

Hospitals in Italy were of the same two types as those in North Africa, for a total of 45,000 beds. It was not possible to establish a works services organi-sation until Naples was captured.

Because of the Apennine mountain chain, which runs down the centre of Italy, it was necessary to have a separate supply line on each side, with main bases at Bari and Brindisi on the east, and Naples on the west. Much of the supply and construction work in Italy was carried out by American engineers. Due to a lack of coal, electricity was very important and the Allies worked closely with the main supply organisation, the Societa Meridionale Elettrica. An electric power committee was set up in December 1943 and a few months later a Central Electric Board took over the direction of all power systems. In August 1944 this was superseded by the Electrical Reconstruction Com-mittee. By January 1945 sufficient results had been achieved to allow the system to be operated as a grid.

The role of works services in Sicily was comparatively minor, with no installations. There was some rehabilitation of ports and airfields.

When Vesuvius erupted in March 1944, some eighty USAF aircraft were destroyed by hot ash at the Pompeii airfield near Terzigno, and some engineers' heavy plant was used in attempts to divert lava flows.

The principal engineering work in Italy was bridging, more being used here than in any other theatre. As well as bridge-building by the field engineering units, replacements were the responsibility of the works department. They also removed them and sent them elsewhere for reuse. Bailey bridges were particularly useful, some 2,500 being built. These bridges were made of pre-fabricated trusses, which were light enough to be carried on a truck and placed by hand without the need for a crane. Nevertheless, they were still strong enough to carry a tank, with a maximum load capacity of 70 tons. Between 1942 and 1945 some 695,583 Bailey panels approximately 10ft by 5ft and weighing about 570lb were produced; these were made by over fifty firms. Peak production in mid-1943 was 6,000 panels per week. Other bridging material included 196 complete Inglis bridges, and 65,293 pontoons, all but 5,691 being produced between 1943 and 1945. There was also a light bridge called the Folding Bridge Equipment which could carry loads of up to 9 tons.

The whole programme used 400,000 tons of steel, about half of which was high tensile steel. The first batch of folding bridges were found on delivery to be made of inferior steel or inadequately welded and a testing programme was started.

There was a local version of the Bailey bridge, called the Flambo. Local resources were also found useful in other fields, providing timber, cement, bricks and lightweight steel items. Use of local types of hutting saved about 35,000 tons of material to be shipped from home.

Gibraltar

Most of the work done at Gibraltar was tunnelling in the Rock, but a new landing strip was also built. Because space was so limited on Gibraltar, stores, workshops and offices were quickly built in any space that occurred; there was no possibility of centralisation.

India

There was little British-controlled engineering activity in India until quite late in the war when Japan had overrun Singapore and Burma. The build-up of activity took most of 1943 and concentrated on communications: rail, road and river, then airfields, oil pipelines and troop accommodation. During late 1943 the newly formed South East Asia Command (SEAC) assumed operational control of the campaign in that theatre.

Ceylon

There was minimal threat to Ceylon (Sri Lanka) at the beginning of the war and little work was needed. This situation continued until Japan joined the war in December 1941, when defensive work was accelerated. By the end of the war the operative numbers had risen to ninety-one officers and 3,372 other ranks.

South-East Asia

Dozers and tractors were invaluable for clearing jungle to build roads and airfields. All but very big trees were easily removed by pushing or pulling, and these methods also removed the roots intact, as opposed to the alternative of cutting the trees down and then having to remove the stumps.

Ground communications were sparse here, due to mountains between Burma and India, combined with thick jungle. Air supply was the mainstay, with some 400 airfields built, ninety-five of which could be used in all weathers. It was not always possible to supply fuel for the aircraft by tanker; as a result a pipeline from Chittagong to Tamir was built. This covered 612 miles and another line, from Chittagong to Tinsukia covering 420 miles, was added. Feeder pipelines ran off to the airfields. In all 1,400 miles of 6in pipe and the same of 4in pipe were laid.

Burma

Communications consisted of one single railway line and a single road, and some river transport on the Brahmaputra. Airfield building took precedence, but other communications were also improved, with a build-up of advanced depots. Airfield building by October 1942 was 100 fully developed bomber and eight fighter airfields, sixty-three lay-back airfields, four advanced landing grounds, four reinforcement landing grounds, twenty-six bomber fields for USAF and one armament training unit. A little later, twenty-eight fair-weather landing strips and sixteen emergency strips were added.

Numerous long roads were built, many of which had to be raised on berms where their route was through paddy fields or other low-lying ground.

North Africa

The chief engineer reported that without angle dozers it would have been impossible to complete on time various tasks such as creating diversions and wadi crossings. They were able to work at night.

Other theatres

Small groups of CREs worked briefly on the Faroe Islands, Azores, Falklands, Addis Ababa, and the Cocos Islands, their work consisting mainly of construction.

Chapter 8

Signals and Other Communications

A principle that had existed long before the war was that communications were so important that personnel engaged in transmitting them should be assisted in keeping up with mobile forward troops by giving them free passage. Their status was shown by blue and white armbands. They were also entitled to have the use of whatever fast transport was available; if they did not have their own, they were entitled to demand what they needed. Their own transport in the early days of the war was good-quality horses and mules; light vehicles, including two-seater cars, jeeps, and motorcycles soon superseded equines. In some cases, senior officers rode pillion behind despatch riders.

Wheeled vehicles were needed for equipment transport and cable-laying as well as carrying personnel. Cable-laying vehicles were fitted with special bodies, and the horsedrawn versions were replaced by mechanised vehicles as soon as these were available. One big problem with the horsedrawn versions was that the amount of cable that could be laid was restricted by the stamina of the animals. Another form of wheeled vehicle was the armoured command wireless vehicle. Early versions of these were made by some units, but difficulties with replacements made it desirable to produce a standard type. A second difficulty with the armoured version was its weight: about 18 tons unloaded.

Before the war, experiments had been made to provide mobile signal offices by mounting them on trailers. Commonly known as 'the coffee stall', the operators sat round it under a canvas awning. This was not entirely satisfactory and a better version, known as a 'house' type, was developed. All the equipment and the operators fitted inside this, requiring only for it to be connected to the lines when needed.

These trailers were not popular with the operators who had to use them; they were found to be cumbersome, especially on narrow roads. This restriction did not apply in the Middle East or the Far East, and several different types of trailers were used. A special American jeep trailer, with a pressed steel body, was found to make a useful small boat for crossing water obstacles.

Almost every theatre except the Far East needed larger local carriers for the weighty line construction stores. Ten-ton lorries and tank transporters were used when speed was required during a rapid advance. Sometimes complete RASC companies were loaned to Signals to assist in this.

Other armoured vehicles were needed to provide signals equipment for fighting commanders. The first of these were diesel-powered, but petrol types followed. Reconnaissance parties were equipped with vehicles stripped of all but two wireless sets, the theory being that if there was only room for two operators there would be no temptation for the commander to take too much of his main headquarters with him. In some cases, command tanks fitted up like armoured cars were used, especially in the Royal Artillery, where the unit operators had to be specially trained.

In mountainous or jungle country where there were few roads, pack animals had to be used, although it might be difficult to find a junior officer who rode well enough to command the unit. The animals were provided by the RASC, but had to be loaded by Signals personnel who needed training in how to avoid sore backs when loading. Various animals were used in different places, from camels to large dogs, but not, although it was suggested, goats.

As the war progressed, especially in the Far East, light aircraft were used for reconnaissance, and after a while special light-weight radio units were developed, to be carried by air. The design of the actual wireless sets changed, mainly after Dunkirk where complaints were made that they were too heavy. What was needed was a set which could easily be carried in and out of cellars and dugouts, but not with a case made of aluminium, which was in short supply. A new case, made of pressed steel, was produced and then became the standard.

As is always the case with new technology, wireless set designs kept changing, and the Director of Signals set out some performance specifications. These included the level of command personnel who expected to use the sets, the limitations of size, weight and frequency cover to be applied, climatic conditions which might be encountered, and the methods of transport to be used and the types of power supply. When units set off for operations, they had to ensure that they had sufficient spare batteries. Field charging sets wore out quickly under sandy conditions; their working life was rarely more than 200 hours, after which they had to go in for repair.

Where the location of the sets did not include a fixed power supply, or when on the move, the power supply usually involved batteries. There were two types, dry and wet. The dry ones tended to deteriorate quickly in high temperatures. They needed to be stored carefully and used in rotation. The wet batteries, especially those in use in armoured units and even more in the Western Desert, where they were mainly used in pairs, had to be changed and topped up with acid and distilled water. The 8th Army had high wastage rates averaging four per day for wireless sets and 200 per week for accumulator batteries. Of every eight of these, no more than three were recovered and usually two of those were damaged beyond repair.

In the Far East, where there were some permanent power lines, there were still problems caused by the climatic conditions. These included damage to the lines caused by lightning, loosening of poles by tropical storms and loose earth, oxidisation of open wire joints, rusting of contacts and other metal joints, insects eating the insulation, and even spider webs between open wires, which collected moisture and spoiled the quality of transmissions. Some of these problems were avoidable if components were varnished, but only when this was done in dry conditions, ideally at the point of manufacture.

In the moist jungles of Burma the effective range of wireless equipment was often greatly reduced and in some places non-existent. This was due partly to the height of trees, and partly to the amount of moisture in those trees. The effect could be alleviated to a certain extent by keeping the set in a clearing and keeping it dry.

At the beginning of the war, almost all signals were transmitted by wired telephone, with wireless or radio telephone (RT) in a secondary role, but use of RT was increased after it was found to be useful in the Western Desert. It gradually came to be the only method of mechanical communication for mobile units, mainly because it did not involve lengthy and man-greedy procedures to set it up.

Once the Director of Signals had laid down the General Staff Specifications, approval of new designs of sets went through a fairly prolonged process of production and testing before they could be issued for use. The Director of Signals passed the details to the Ministry of Supply, which either passed them to the Signals Research and Development Establishment (SRDE) to finish the design details; instructed the SDRE to work with one or more manufacturers before selecting those who would build the new design; or passed the whole thing to a chosen manufacturer to produce some new sets for trial within a certain time. The first set to be produced was then tested by the SDRE to ensure that it would work as specified and that the manufacturer had not introduced any modifications to make manufacturing easier. The next stage of tests were made to ensure that the set would work properly when the operator was, perhaps, none too well-trained or liable to panic under battle conditions; in other words, under true service conditions rather than the perfect conditions of a design laboratory.

Once everyone was satisfied, the chosen manufacturers could go through the lengthy process of 'tooling up', or separating the manufacturing process into individual processes and making the jigs and tools that would allow mass production. In peacetime this would take up to a year; in the urgent conditions of war it still took at least six months. The whole process, from having to request a new type of set from the Director of Signals, to having stocks of sets and spare parts ready for issue, took some two years. This would include all the additional items, beyond the set itself, which were needed to make the signal station effective. Known as accessories, these included batteries, head-phones, microphones, wave-nets and aerial gear.

One problem which surfaced in the early stages of each new type was that of spare parts. The manufacturers were unable to produce any spares during the first three months of production; it was therefore decided to send all sets produced during this period to training establishments rather than to field stations. This did allow the instructors to familiarise themselves with the new equipment before it went into general use. After that, a system called 'Auto-matic Maintenance' went into operation, sending a four-month supply of parts with each new station, followed by more at three-monthly intervals.

It was also necessary to produce and send instruction books. Theoretically these should have been supplied by the manufacturers of the equipment, but they did not always understand exactly what was needed, and eventually the whole task was passed to the publication section of the School of Signals.

In theory, provision of bulk supplies of signal equipment, as all other equipment, was the responsibility of the RAOC, which took it to an agreed forward location such as a railhead. However, it was found more convenient for Signals, which originally just handled items in short supply, to take on distribution of the whole of the equipment. The RAOC had had some difficulty in identifying the individual parts which made up a full set. It should have been easy to do this by using part numbers, but it was found necessary to have some trained signals personnel available to avoid errors and delays. There were some items which were ordered by a single number, with the orderers unaware that a crucial part had a separate number.

Equipment which was subjected to long sea voyages had to be tested before issue, ideally on arrival in the theatre. Eventually REME units were involved and the equipment was tested at the end of the line of communication instead of further back.

As well as the actual sets, adequate supplies of cable and line construction stores were essential. In addition to normal wear and tear, it was assumed that field cable used by divisions going into action would be destroyed and a new stock of field cable (some 19 tons) would be made available each evening. When possible, cable was recovered from battlefields. Special cable recovery units operated in the Middle East, but they often found it had been appro-priated for non-military purposes, such as providing trouser belts for the local population.

For beach landings it was necessary to provide some additional items. Handcarts were needed to move the sets up the beaches and waterproof bags were essential to avoid damage to the sets and batteries from salt water. These bags were provided for spare parts, telephones and switchboards, coming in five sizes, one of which was constructed so the set could be operated while still in the bag. All equipment not needed for the assault was sealed in the bags.

Project stores parks were set up, one for each division and sometimes for a brigade group. These were to be landed early in the operations, and not only held the main reserve, but their personnel were also available to search enemy dumps for useful items.

When the Americans joined the war they provided a great deal of signal equipment under the Lend-Lease scheme, to the value of some £30,000,000. Two types were produced: those similar in design to those used by the US Signal Corps, and those produced to British designs. The British Military Mission in Washington kept a watchful eye on this production, ensuring that it was shipped without delay as it came off the production line. Some sets were obtained from Australia, where there was a flourishing wireless industry. Most of these went to India and the Far East.

The Military Mission also had to intervene in a dispute about operational methods and training, which was, of course, different from the British versions. The Americans felt that their methods should be used because of the higher number of American operators. There were also differences in the intonation and pronunciation of letters (for instance, the British say 'zed' while Americans say 'Zee'), partly from regional accents but mainly due to differences in the phonetic alphabet. The British version had just been standardised when the Combined Communications Board in Washington produced an American version and it took some negotiation to arrive at a mutually satisfactory version.

This was incorporated into the syllabus at operator training establishments, where as well as basic repairs and part replacement, operators were taught message protocols for both telephone and radio line communications, Morse code and the use of ciphers and codes. While radio telephone was best for short distance routine reports, when there was a security element to the message, ciphered communication was better where tactical information was given and/or there was a possibility the enemy might be listening. The main School of Signals was based at Catterick Camp, but smaller training establishments were set up elsewhere as needed.

Although the personnel who ciphered and deciphered messages were basically in separate units from the signals personnel, it was necessary for each to have a basic understanding of the other's job. There were two classes of message traffic: that which might give information to the enemy if sent unciphered, and which was passed from the signal office to the cipher office and back; and the ultra-secret, which should not even be seen by the signal operators, which went straight from the originator to the cipher office under sealed cover.

Ciphered messages were created in 'groups' of five letters or numbers, and the messages were designated a priority: OU for Emergency State, O for Emergency operations, OP for Immediate, P for Priority and R for Routine.

These priorities did not refer to the urgency of the message delivery, but to the amount of time before the recipient must act on them. However, a high volume of messages on some stations meant that anything up to 50 per cent of messages were sent by despatch rider. Despite the priority system, messages were often delayed for reasons ranging from high volumes of messages, constant changes of locations or just line breakdowns. It was usually possible to send messages by an alternative route and operators were taught to do this automatically if the message was urgent.

The main method of ciphering was with the Slidex device. This consisted of a card with twelve columns and seventeen rows which gave 204 rectangles, and two coordinating strips, one vertical and one horizontal. These were placed in a metal frame. The coordinating strips also had rectangles, with a random letter, so that each word could be represented by a bigram. Each rectangle on the main card had a word or phrase, and a letter or number; these being those most likely to be used in military matters, such as 'attack at once', or 'artillery'. Other words had to be spelled out by their letters. The cards were only valid for a specified time, and the coordinating strips changed every day. More than 350,000 Slidex units were issued in the latter part of the war.

Unfortunately, German signals operators found it easy to duplicate the Slidex system and did so extensively from late 1943. This gave the enemy useful operating information on tactical operations and requests for RAF support.

Although women were not part of the Signals Corps, some of the ATS were trained at first at Trowbridge and then the Isle of Man. Once trained, they were posted to special intercept establishments at home. In 1943, some were posted to Cairo, thus freeing male operators to serve in the deserts. Later some women were posted to India and Burma.

As well as the military messages, facilities were provided for the Press. This service grew throughout the war until by September 1944 an average of 45,000 words per day were being sent, usually between 4pm and 10pm. There were eight Press centres in south-west of England, all connected to the Press Room in London, from where messages were passed on to newspapers throughout the world. More than half of these were to America and Canada. As an example of the volumes involved, on one day alone in June 1944, a total of 445,000 words of press traffic were sent.

Press facilities were available for representatives of newspapers, the Ministry of Information, the British Broadcasting Corporation, the Psychological Warfare Board, missions to Allied governments and Foreign Office and consular services.

For a reason which has never been satisfactorily defined, radio operators were known as 'Scaleybacks'. One theory says this may have been due to the scars on the backs of operators who had to carry leaking batteries on their backs. At the high point of the war, there were over 150,000 members of the Signals Corp: 8,512 officers and 142,742 other ranks.

Despatch riders, who originally belonged to separate regiments and units, were also part of the Signals Corps, but still stationed with those fighting units. They carried a set of spares for their motorcycles, including a valve and a spark plug, tyre repair outfit and a spare inner tube, and a complete set of tools. The messages they carried would be encoded.

Postal service

Because the Post Office service was deemed to be of the same type as signals, the running of this service was put under the Royal Engineers, who had responsibility for signals.

The home depot for the mobilisation section of this service was based at Mount Pleasant in London before the war, but the space available there was already known to be too small, and on 15 September 1939, after sending the first batch of mail to the BEF, it moved out to the basement and garage of the Post Office at Reading, and subsequently to Bournemouth from where it was easy to get it to Southampton.

Units were organised to accompany the BEF, but after the first units departed, men for subsequent units were bizarrely chosen for the size of their feet. There was a shortage of boots in sizes below 8 and above 9, so unless the men could wear those sizes, they were not sent overseas. Before the war recruits were meant to be a minimum of 5ft 2in tall, but this requirement was soon relaxed. Meanwhile, at Reading, sixty ATS women had been recruited to serve as cooks, clerks and typists. At its peak, there were more than 2,000.

Letters and packets were sorted in the garage at Reading and parcels in the basement. From there, items for the BEF went to the BEF Base Office at Cherbourg on troop ships from Southampton, where it was subject to some confusion as the army Post Office was not provided with up-to-date troop unit locations. There was more confusion after the postal units were evacuated with the troops from Dunkirk, but it was all sorted out eventually.

After Italy joined the war in June 1940 some postal units were sent to the Middle and Far East. Mail for these locations was mainly sent to Liverpool and Glasgow and the main home depot was moved to Northampton. In the years that followed, the work at Northampton became increasingly complex, dealing with airmail post as well as surface mail for twenty overseas locations. The volume of work continued to increase until in 1944 a staff of 3,000 men and women handled 340,000,000 letters, 95,000,000 packets and 13,000,000 parcels. This involved some 2,500,000 mail bags, which once filled had to be stacked so that they were dispatched in the right order.

Routes taken by the mail could be convoluted. After Italy entered the war, the Mediterranean was closed to commercial shipping and the direct air service between the UK and Egypt was cut. Surface mail went via the Cape of Good Hope and air mail was sent by sea from the UK to West Africa and then flown to Egypt via Khartoum. Although thought to be fast and efficient because it was expensive, air mail took between three and six weeks to deliver and surface mail up to three months. Air mail was speeded up by producing lightweight forms (later the Air Letter) which meant more could be carried on each flight. They weighed only one tenth of an ounce, but initially were rationed to one per man per month. Another innovation, introduced with the help of Kodak, was the Airgraph. Letters had to be written on special forms which were then microfilmed at the point of posting and printed at the point of delivery.

The Mediterranean was reopened to commercial shipping in the middle of 1943, and Alexandria and Port Said were then available once again for surface mail. Typically, at El Alamein, mail was delivered by rail from the base Post Office at Cairo to Alexandria, and then onward by road.

Organisation of the mail system in North Africa was slow, the main problem being a lack of vehicles, but there were also some difficulties in delivering mail to casualties, although it was accepted that this should be delivered as fast as possible. The arrangements for casualties of the 1st and 8th armies became confused, with men of the 1st Army being evacuated to 8th Army hospitals and vice versa. The records for the 1st Army were in Algiers and those for the 8th Army in Cairo, and it took some time to redirect mail to men at the 'wrong' hospital. The resulting 2,250,000 letters, 35,000 registered letters and 7,000 bags of parcels to be redirected made the Postal Directorate suggest that this mail should be returned to the sender, but this idea found no favour and army Post Office staff had to persevere.

When the move into Sicily was planned, the army Postal Service was involved from the start. Before embarkation, units were divided into separate parties depending on the time and place they were to go into action. As well as convoys sailing on different days, there were landings from assault craft. The principle adopted was that mail should be delivered to each unit until it departed. Troops completed a 'change of address' form and the Home Postal Centre diverted mail appropriately. Two weeks after the landings an air service was organised, flying mail from Algeria and Tunis to Syracuse, then direct from home to Palermo. It usually took only six days for mail to reach its destination in Sicily.

The invasion of Italy began on 3 September 1943, after the overthrow of Mussolini. The first mail reached Italy two days later, but there were then delays until mid-October when delivery to Naples began and mail went on from there by road, usually taking no more than two days.

For the Normandy landings an additional 600 postal workers had to be recruited; these eventually went to France to work on the lines of communication, and on up into Belgium and Holland.

In the Far East, before the war started, mail for the British army in India was handled by the Indian civilian Post Office, but this was overwhelmed by the increased volume once the war started. The transit time across India was often slower than from the UK; this service was good, usually less than six days. On the lines of communication, the mail was often dropped by parachute, with specialist teams ensuring it was packed well enough to survive the drop.

Printing and Stationery Service

The Army Printing and Stationery Service (APSS) provided everything from printed manuals and forms to simple blank typing paper. This paper, plus office machinery, was first held at Nantes until an advanced storage depot opened at Arras. Requirements were underestimated: consumption of duplicating paper soon reached some 3,000,000 sheets per month. At the beginning of the war the APSS consisted of seven officers and sixty-four other ranks; by the end it was 176 officers, 2,955 other ranks and 2,971 civilians.

The departments were:

- Stationery depots which held and issued paper, army forms and various office supplies.
- Publication depots which received and distributed such items as training manuals, books of regulations and reference and some secret documents.
- Mobile printing sections which did not actually print but duplicated using Gestetner machines (their name was changed to mobile duplicating sections).
- Special printing press units which did actually print items.
- Receipt and issue sections which received and checked work done by local firms.
- Typewriter repair depots and workshops.

The units which went to France with the BEF suffered several weaknesses, including shortages due to what should have been automatic monthly top-ups of stock failing to arrive. When the force had to evacuate, they did manage to destroy all confidential and secret matter before departing.

In the Middle East the service grew from small beginnings to a large organisation which was able to supply the RAF and Royal Navy as well as the army. It had a printing press at General Headquarters in Cairo, stationery depots at Suez, Cairo and Athens and an advanced stationery depot at Jerusalem, publications depots at Cairo and Athens and an Indian base stationery depot at Khartoum.

In static situations, a signalmaster took charge of all communications; his duties included close supervision of all priority messages passing through the office, keeping control of all message traffic and dealing with breakdowns or blockages, and ensuring that staff did not misuse priorities nor create irregularities in message writing. In the largest of such offices a staff message controller was appointed to assist the signalmaster; he dealt mainly with misuse and irregularities.

Precise statistics of use are not available, but as an example, an average of 25,000 long-distance calls per day were made in North Africa, and an average of 100,000 long-distance calls per day by Allied forces in Italy in 1945. The number of telephone sets used in main headquarters offices ranged from 185 for the Second British Army to over 600 in 21st Army Group.

Among other problems was that of mutual radio interference as more and more sets came into use. Inadequately trained operators were also common; they were prone to blame their sets for failures to communicate. During air-raids, the lower frequency transmitters were shut down to avoid giving navigational information to the enemy.

A small and easily carried signalling device was the hand-held Heliograph, which could be used to send Morse messages on bright days when the sun was in the right direction for sender and receiver. It consisted of a mirror with a hole in it, and a wand also with a hole, these being looked through by the sender. The wand was attached to the mirror with a short cord and in use was held at the full extension of the cord to make the correct space between the two holes.

Portable radio sets were made to be carried by one man. They were supplied in two parts: a large one carried in a webbing shoulder sling, and a small one for the headset and throat microphones. Both were supplied in canvas haversacks.

The following statistics are given for production of signals equipment. Some of these figures seem rather high, but the list does not specify army supplies, merely 'munitions' and much of the equipment may have been for RAF installations and shore-based navy installations. The amounts given are for the period September 1939 to September 1945.

Wireless sets	552,810
Reception sets	87,016
Mine detectors	166,422
Charging sets	42,296
Telephones	599,339
Teleprinters	11,623
Switchboards	86,375

Chapter 9

Maps and Surveying

Essential for many purposes, both military and civilian, maps were the responsibility of the Geographical Section, General Staff (GSGS) of the Director of Military Survey in the War Office, otherwise known as MI4. GSGS operated under the Director of Operations and Intelligence and was headed by a Royal Engineers (RE) colonel. Its officer staff were mostly RE officers with surveying qualifications and some Royal Artillery and infantry officers. Other personnel included a few RE other ranks, technical civilian assistants and a few clerks. Just before the war, the total personnel was about seventy. These worked in two branches, one for the UK and one to cover overseas theatres. When America joined the war, they brought some of their own maps and surveyors.

The main function of MI4 before the war started included:

- Preparing and supplying maps for defence, local administration and military training to British forces at home and abroad.
- Preparing and supplying copies of all standard and special maps to War Office staff as needed for their work.
- Building up a map library of copies of all maps produced by foreign countries, and collecting data on foreign survey and triangulation systems.
- To advise the Colonial and Foreign Offices on boundary surveys and any special work needed in the colonies, and providing assistance and equipment for surveying work in the colonies.
- To maintain material so that an operational series of maps could be produced in the event of war.
- To advise the General Staff on training and general instruction on survey methods and practice, and survey policy in the event of war. This included plans for the formation of survey units, and the provision of equipment and stores.
- Generally prepare for the requirements of an expeditionary force on mobilisation.

Even before the war, the existing staff was known to be insufficient and had become somewhat disorganised. As well as survey staff, MI4 had topographical draughtsmen, and a map reproduction section with cameras and printing machines. An organisational sub-section which dealt with all matters of the make-up and mobilisation of survey units and their equipment and stores units was also under-staffed. The mapping sections were divided into geographical areas, which made special studies of their areas, but when this led to unequal division of work, ad hoc arrangements were made, moving staff across the regional boundaries.

It had been obvious since the early 1930s that the increasingly aggressive attitude of Nazi Germany meant a war was inevitable and that Britain and France would be dragged into it. A mapping programme to handle this became urgent and it began with preparation of several map series on the standard scales. The first task was to investigate the existing material and set up staff liaison between GSGS and the French Service Géographique de l'Armée in Paris.

British mapping policy had been set in 1931. This required that maps should be on the standard scales: small scale, (1/250,000) for strategical and general use; medium scale (1/50,000) for use as a tactical map and for general administrative purposes; and large scale (1/25,000) for battle planning, and especially for use by the Royal Artillery, and that these should be gridded and map references given in the current (modified) British system, and that since European allies would be using maps on a metric system, so the British maps were given a metric grid as well.

In 1936, GSGS initiated some new map series known as the 'rearmament' series, contracting the work to the Ordnance Survey. The maps were in three series: small, medium and large. The small-scale version was in two series and covered the whole of Belgium and Luxembourg and the part of France to the north-east of a line from Le Havre to Paris. The medium-scale version, also in two series, covered mainly the frontier areas, but was thought to be too generalised and missing important tactical detail. The large-scale version covered all of Belgium and most of north-east France, but was missing a portion of the Pas de Calais.

There were other maps for ground and air staff use, on a 1/1,000,000 scale. They were for air use, strategic planning and as wall maps.

By the spring of 1936 it was clear that Germany was preparing to start a major new war, and the mapping programme was hastened. This was initially intended to cover north-east France and Belgium on a scale of 1/50,000. Funds were allocated for this and other projects after the Munich meeting in 1938. Two additional officers were added to the establishment, but these were nowhere near as many as were needed.

During the pre-war years the only survey unit was one small training depot. It was realised that much more would be required to meet the needs of an expeditionary force on the Continent, so several survey directorates and field survey units were prepared in August 1939, the personnel being drawn mainly from the Ordnance Survey (OS), the main available source of military surveyors. There were also some civil survey officers employed in the colonies; their practical experience made them a great asset.

The OS had its own extensive map-printing facilities, and there were numerous civilian printing firms, all of which could have produced War Office maps, but it was decided that it was essential for the War Office to retain control of map printing. Even during peacetime there were numerous demands for rapid production of special maps and diagrams, many of which had heavy security requirements which precluded their being produced by outside printers. At the same time, the OS had no spare printing capacity and certainly could not produce maps at short notice; many on this timescale were needed for such operations as commando raids.

Like those of GSGS, many of the personnel of the OS were RE trained. The technical personnel included trigonometry surveyors for work on a new triangulation scheme, levellers for the levelling network, field revisers for revision work on all scales but mainly the 1/25,000, with draughtsmen, photographers and printers.

Before the war it had been accepted that the OS would assist in producing maps for military purposes, and also provide a pool of trained technicians for work at mobilisation and after. Luckily, the OS had, for some time, been recruiting and training young male technicians, and then women, who remained when the men were transferred to the military GSGS. On the outbreak of war, the OS effectively became a War Office map production unit, although it stayed under the administrative control of the Ministry of Agriculture and Fisheries, who took it over from the Board of Ordnance.

Shortly after the outbreak of war, when many of the personnel of the OS had been called up, it set up a recruitment scheme whereby young men aged 16–17 were employed and given a basic training in OS technical work until they were old enough to enlist in survey units, where they received more technical training as well as basic military training.

The OS, which had its main printing works in Southampton, suffered when the main building was bombed in late 1940. At first the OS's activities were housed in requisitioned buildings round the city, but many of these were unsuitable and eventually much of the production was moved to hutted accommodation at Chessington, Esher and Waddon.

It was decided in 1939, against objections that this would isolate MI4 staff from daily contact with the General Staff and from the main map depots at Alperton (north-west London), that the entire organisation should move to Cheltenham; the stated reason for this being to free up space for other War Office branches to expand.

At about the same time, MI4 was reorganised into three sections: one for general organisation and technical stores, one for grids and other records and one for map design and production. The latter included supervision of the map library.

At the beginning of the war, the Air Ministry had its own map section. When MI4 moved to Cheltenham the Air Ministry map section moved to Harrow. This separation between the two organisations made it difficult to centralise operations, a necessity for supplying overseas demands.

It was just a few months before it was realised that the move had been a mistake. Despite the disruption which was likely to occur, it was decided to move the whole organisation back to London, and premises were found at Eastcote (near Ruislip), and MI4, now designated GSGS, moved and, at the same time, absorbed the Air Ministry map section from Harrow. Although larger than at Cheltenham, the new premises at Eastcote were still not large enough to include the drawing and printing section, which ended up at Hanwell a few miles away. This did at least double its space and it was fitted with the latest equipment.

When the BEF was mobilised, several field survey units went with it, most coming from the RE survey battalion. A large training unit was created by the amalgamation of two smaller units and settled near Fareham. The training syllabus included military training as well as technical survey training. The military training included use of rifles, automatic weapons, grenades, anti-tank bombs and weapons, tank traps, booby traps and demolitions. Much of this military training was carried out with the local Home Guard.

There were three main categories of survey training:

- Field survey, including triangulation, topographic surveys and compu-tations. The preliminary stage of this taught the basic principles, including the use of all the necessary instruments. Advanced courses were modelled on field exercises and confined mainly to methods for quick surveys of the type that would be needed under active service conditions. Normal triangulation methods were taught, including section and intersection, levelling and transverse methods. There was also astronomy including star and sun azimuths. They did teach the use of the plane table, but experience in the field suggested there should have been more of this fundamental part of the topographical training.
- Air survey dealt with the production of contoured maps from aerial photographs, emphasising the necessary accuracy of large-scale maps for artillery use.
- Preparation of maps for lithographic printing. Many of the trainees already had some experience in this, but they had to learn to use the

equipment used in field surveys, and the methods which had been laid down as standard operating procedures in military survey.

There were also courses for technical officers, including triangulation, astronomy, topography, compilation of maps from various kinds of materials, and air survey methods. They all received instruction in administration methods, and printing officers had a whole course in map reproduction. Clerks were trained in military clerical work, including regulations, pay, messing and quartermaster procedures.

Overseas theatres

The survey organisation which was mobilised with the BEF consisted of a director of survey (a colonel), two deputy assistant directors (majors), one captain or lieutenant and a few other ranks. There was an operational movement in the eight months before the evacuation from Dunkirk, but the unit was occupied fulltime with sorting out the geodetic systems in Western Europe, the acquisition of air photographs from the RAF and using these to revise existing maps, preparing new and special maps for GHQ purposes and supplying maps to military formations.

The authorised establishment of the No.1 Field Survey Depot at GHQ allowed for one officer and eighteen other ranks and was set up with no responsibility for distributing maps, so had no transport for this purpose or for moving itself. It was not long before distribution of maps was added to its duties, and as the line of communication stretched from Brest through Normandy and Brittany to the Belgian border, it was found necessary to split the depot in two. The main base depot was at Rennes and the other at Doullens, just west of Arras. The main base depot received bulk stocks of maps from the UK and issued them to units on the line of communication.

When active operations started in France, an advance section of the field survey depot went forward to form a semi-mobile map store near Brussels. Unfortunately the bulk map stores at Rennes and Doullens were cut off by the advancing enemy in the early summer of 1940. On the evacuation, all the surveying instruments, except for a few theodolites, had to be left behind.

These existing map series were available:

France
- 1/20,000: a good coloured map covering the whole of France.
- A new version of the above.
- A different version of the above known as *Plans Directeurs de Guerre*. They were not all reliable and some were badly inaccurate.
- 1/80,000: an old staff map dating from Napoleon's day. It had been regularly revised, was reasonably detailed and fairly accurate.

- 1/50,000: a direct enlargement of a new 1/80,000 series. Begun by the French after the First World War, it gave priority to France's eastern borders and the series was not completed until 1940.

The survey directorate went to France on the day after the declaration of war, and concentrated initially on clear road maps for convoys going from their disembarkation port to the concentration area. This was done by making a tracing from the relevant Michelin sheets and having these printed in Rennes, then giving stocks of them to the base commandant at the principal ports so every driver could have a copy.

The concentration areas for 1 and 2 Corps were Rennes, Laval and Le Mans, which was too far west to be covered by the British 1/50,000 series. For billeting and administration, and training exercises while waiting to move forward, a 1/50,000 map was essential. Some copies of the French maps were obtained and distributed.

After the BEF moved to its position on the French/Belgian border, accommodation was sought for the drawing, photographic and printing works. This was eventually found at Frevent, near Arras, where the GHQ survey directorate was located. There were two printing machines there, and four in Paris, all of which had to be left behind on the evacuation. Until then, printing was done on almost continuous shifts to produce bulk stocks of the small and medium-scale maps to meet emergency needs. These were mostly shipped over from the UK, but when urgent supplies were needed they could be printed in situ from duplicate plates supplied by the War Office. The small and medium-scale maps were revised from air photographs. Most of these revisions were sent back to the UK, but road and canal corrections were made to the printing plates to bring them up to date.

As soon as a decision had been made to move forward to the east of Brussels in the event of a German offensive, special map preparation was done to meet GHQ requirements. These included route diagrams, town plans and administrative traffic maps. Some attention was paid to the German defences along the Siegfried line.

Belgium

The principal series were published by the Institut Cartographique Militaire in Brussels. Until the Belgian government decided to cooperate in 1940, the only copies were in the War Office map library. Some were not fully updated:

- 1/20,000, in black or colour. This covered the whole country and was accurate.
- 1/40,000, as above, the latest edition was prepared in 1933.
- 1/100,000 was prepared from the above, in colour, this was highly detailed but clear.

Holland

- 1/25,000 (two versions, old and new). The old version dated from 1904 to 1934; these were detailed, clear, and where modern, accurate. The new series was started in 1934 but only a few were available by 1939.
- 1/50,000, as above.
- 1/200,000, this was the main Dutch series, dated from 1927 to 1938.

The pre-war expansion of the RAF and Bomber Command created a demand for special air navigation maps, with emphasis on features such as woods, water, railways and main roads.

Middle East, Egypt and the Western Desert

Pre-war mapping arrangements for the Middle East started in 1937 when the War Office considered the need for maps for British troops in Egypt in anticipation of war. There were no survey units available to send out to Egypt, but there was an Egyptian government survey department in Cairo, and an officer from GSGS was sent out to check the situation, with special reference to the Western Desert. As a result of this, extra stocks of maps for the Western Desert were printed and stored in Egypt, aerial photography was started by the RAF, and impressions of the available maps were sent to the survey departments in Egypt and India in case of need.

As well as stocks of maps of the Western Desert, the Egyptian government had medium-scale maps of the areas between the Nile and the Suez Canal and Red Sea, and the Sinai peninsula. Larger-scale maps were also available for the cultivated areas of the Delta and Nile valley.

Another field survey unit arrived in the Middle East in the winter of 1940–41 and was immediately sent south to Khartoum to assist with plans to oust the Italians from Eritrea. Quick reconnaissance surveys were carried out and photographs were obtained from the RAF and used to modify the existing inaccurate maps to help pilots use these. Triangulation work started. This unit did have mobile printing equipment, but the advance, when it began, was so rapid that the unit found it difficult to keep up.

On 20 February 1941 the British opened the offensive against the Italians in Somaliland and Abyssinia, entering Abyssinia on 7 March and occupying Addis Ababa on 5 April. Meanwhile a counter-offensive by the enemy forced the British troops to abandon Benghazi and retreat to Egypt. German forces then invaded Yugoslavia and, with the Italians, moved into Greece. An expeditionary force was rapidly assembled in Egypt and sent over to Greece, accompanied by a small survey directorate. Unfortunately the stores and printing equipment were sent on a separate convoy and lost. Some of the survey personnel were taken prisoner and there was difficulty in ensuring that maps sent to Greece were delivered safely. It became necessary to send each batch with a conducting officer who saw them to their proper destination.

Early in 1940 a director of survey was appointed and took a small directorate staff to work with the military headquarters in Cairo. They were soon followed by two survey units, one to perform field survey work, including photography, map-drawing, reproduction and printing, the other to hold and issue bulk map stocks. This consisted of one officer and eighteen other ranks. The director of survey soon realised these were not enough and by October the number had increased to fourteen officers and 350 other ranks.

There was considerable difficulty during that autumn in obtaining aerial photographs due to a shortage of suitable aircraft; these photographs were valuable as they showed enemy gun positions and defences which could be overprinted on maps for the Royal Artillery.

Much of the early work was special tasks for the engineer-in-chief, including surveys for the layout of the bases and suitable locations for anti-aircraft and coast defence gun positions in Alexandria, Port Said and up into Palestine. They also reproduced some of the available small-scale maps of Turkey.

When Italy entered the war in June 1940 it was thought certain that hostilities in Africa would soon follow, in Libya, Abyssinia and the Italian East African colonies. Mapping programmes over this area were intensified. The available War Office maps were out of date and it became necessary to obtain copies of the most up to date maps of those areas and overprint them with a military grid. Local triangulation systems had to be investigated, and the RAF were asked to produce air photographs of certain areas, to enable existing maps to be revised and new ones prepared. All this extended northwards to the Balkans and eastwards to Palestine, Syria, Iraq and Persia.

By September 1940 the Italians had arrived in Egypt and dug in at Sidi Barrani. The first British offensive in the Western Desert was in December and the Italians were quickly driven back. Thousands of Italian prisoners were captured and many useful Italian maps obtained. These were rapidly copied and reproduced in Cairo and stocks sent back to British forces. One found to be particularly useful was a large-scale map of Tobruk, which was promptly copied, and later, when the Germans got hold of one of these copies, recopied by them.

One survey unit went with the Desert Force during the first campaign, and they ran a chain of triangulation points to connect up with the Italian system. The map revisions arising from this had to be printed in Cairo, there being no mobile printing equipment available.

The campaign against the Italians in East Africa covered an area of about 1,000,000 square miles, from the border with Kenya in the south to the northern boundary of Eritrea in the north, and from the border of Sudan in the west to the Indian Ocean and the Red Sea in the east. Little of this area had ever been properly surveyed and there was little cartographic information. The theatre of operations was described as 'primitive and uncivilised' which, with its variety of terrain, great distances and differing climates, made the Survey Service's work extremely difficult. The Survey Service for this task was made up of units from East Africa, South Africa, southern Rhodesia, Nigeria, the Gold Coast and the UK.

The campaign in this theatre consisted of two coordinated offensives, one each from the north (based in Sudan operating against the Italians in Eritrea) and the south (based in Kenya and dealing with Italian Somaliland and Abyssinia).

The British survey contingent had arrived in the Middle East command in the winter of 1940–41 and was immediately sent south to Khartoum, where it was greeted with demands for local surveys and miscellaneous maps, including reconnaissance surveys for the chief engineer. The plan was for an advance on Keren (in the middle of Eritrea) and the unit immediately began work on triangulation. They had lorry-mounted printing machinery and were able to provide sufficient maps to issue to the troops in the field as well as for headquarters planning staff.

Aerial photography was done by the South African Air Force and later by the RAF from Tanganyika. The aircraft involved in this were not the best; three were supplied, one of which was immediately condemned as not airworthy and another crashed killing all occupants. Then weather conditions turned bad and flying had to be suspended. Three more aircraft were provided, but one was soon shot down. The remaining aircraft were then transferred to map delivery duties.

A standard survey directorate served the force in the Western Desert. One unit was at Matruh doing large-scale surveys, drawing and printing sections were at Alexandria, and two topographical sections were surveying the area round El Alamein. Three other field survey companies were delayed in their journey from the UK by a shortage of convoy space, and a fourth, which was originally intended for the Middle East, remained in the UK until Operation Overlord, when it went to France with the 2nd Army.

At the time of the campaign in Greece there was a shortage of survey units and some civil establishments were formed using local personnel with locally purchased equipment. These units were at Cairo, with a drawing office in Alexandria. Stocks of all maps covering the theatre were held at the main base map depot at Abassia (Cairo). The main depot distributed bulk supplies of maps to GHQ for issue to staff, Moascar on the canal and Alexandria, which held reserve stocks of the Western Desert and delta areas. All these were under GHQ control; there were also sub-depots at Jerusalem, Gaza and Tel Aviv, and a forward depot at Nazareth which later moved to Syria. In the summer of 1941 there were numerous mapping projects which covered Egypt, the Western Desert, Cyrenaica, Palestine, Syria, Turkey, Iraq, Persia, Cyprus, Trans-Jordan and East Africa. These included air surveys in the Western Desert, Palestine, Sinai, Syria, El Alamein and the Nile delta.

By September, fifty Indian draughtsmen had joined and were working in the Tura caves near Cairo, preparing for the installation of printing machines and depot stores. Most of the latter had been installed there by the end of the month.

In June 1942 the 8th Army was pushed back from Cyrenaica by Rommel's advancing Afrika Korps, which was reaching for Alexandria. It was necessary to move supplies of maps and destroy some. Some of the stores and equipment were moved from the Tura caves to the eastern side of the canal, and stocks of paper were sent to Palestine and Iraq, and later to Sudan. There was particular concern about theodolites, which were difficult to obtain at that time.

North-west Africa

Anticipating operations in what was at the time French north Africa, the War Office had begun preparation of a map series covering that area. By the time the Americans moved in late 1942, in what was known as Operation Torch, mapping was well under way and a main map depot had been established in Algiers.

There is a security aspect to mapping operations, since if stocks of maps or surveying notes are captured they immediately tell the enemy where advance operations are planned. With Operation Torch, it was decided that a continuous exchange between American and British surveyors would not draw attention to any particular area.

There were other security dangers: on one occasion a consigment of maps was being taken from a War Office map depot to an American headquarters at Cheltenham. Although they mostly covered a wide area, there were some sheets which were more detailed, and these were among some which were inadequately secured in the lorry and fell out unnoticed, ending up strewn along the road. Fortunately the police were notified and managed to recover them all. After this incident, all issues to troop ships were made by road with an officer escort and armed tailguards to ensure nothing fell out of the lorry.

The move from north-west Africa up through Sicily to Italy, then from Sardinia and Corsica to southern France, required some major revisions of the existing maps. The large- and medium-scale maps for Sicily and Sardinia had production dates ranging from 1863 to 1937, although in Sardinia most were dated 1931. In Sicily the medium-scale maps were mostly pre-1900 in the north and 1923 to 1937 in the south. The whole of Italy and Sicily were covered in a series produced for the Touring Club Italiano and dated between 1929 and 1937.

India

Maps of India, Burma, Afghanistan and Persia were produced pre-war by the Survey of India, most of the reproduction work being done in Calcutta. The areas covered extended to Thailand and Indo-China, some of China and Malaya. Ceylon had its own survey department. After August 1942, work on aerial surveys was increased and by the end of July 1943 over 22,000 square miles of country had been photographed. By March 1944 maps for all the countries listed above were available, and also some for Sumatra and the Andaman, Nicobar and Cocos Islands.

After the cessation of hostilities in Italy a conference was held at AFHQ to discuss the needs of map users. On the matter of scale, it was felt that the 1/25,000 large-scale maps (with accurate contours) were the most useful on the ground, but the medium-scale was useful for both infantry and artillery. As far as colours were concerned, if monotone maps were all that could be produced (and they were not liked), black was better than brown. Where additional colours were used, the preference for coloured detail was roads, water, contours and woods. The tactical air force considered that woods were of paramount importance, but the shape of woods was important for identification from above, and if possible these should even show the type of trees.

With water features, when bridging was contemplated, it was desirable that the size of the gap was accurate and that the centre line of the bridge should be marked, together with the direction of water flow. There should be profiles of each bank on the centre line and, if possible, of the river bed; where Bailey bridges were to be erected, fixing the levels on the roller sites for launching the Bailey sections and also the approach roads. Soundings should be taken 250 feet upstream for the anchor line.

The times involved and the risks inherent in sea transportation made it necessary for distant operational theatres to be largely self-supporting in bulk map-printing. This applied particularly in the Middle East and East Africa after sea transit of the Mediterranean became too risky, meaning ships had to go round the Cape and up the Red Sea. For theatres closer to home such as western Europe and north-west Africa, the UK remained the principal source of bulk map-printing.

Originally the orders were for packages of assault maps to be opened and issued forty-eight hours after the ship left British territorial waters. However, if for any reason a ship had to return to port, the security risk was heightened and it was decided to issue the minimum number of maps necessary for planning at that early stage, and to issue the rest forty-eight hours before landing.

As well as flat printed maps, relief models were produced for planning purposes in theatre headquarters. Many of these were made by American planners. There were two basic types of model: those of specific enemy installations, such as the Metz forts, and area models on the scales of 1/10,000 and 1/25,000. The first were used by company commanders to identify points of attack and plan supporting fire and the use of special weapons. The second type were used to brief commanders on the nature of the terrain and the best directions for approach.

As well as strategical and tactical planning, these relief maps were used for assault landings (usually on a scale of 1/5,000), commando raids (on a scale of 1/500 or 1/1,000) and airborne landings in two scales, one covering the entire area and one of vital target areas.

The principal source of information on mapping (*Maps and Survey*, issued by the War Office in 1952) gives such enormous numbers of map production that it is difficult to believe the figures are accurate. They total some 459,000,000 over the course of the war: over 150 maps for each British soldier at the high point of June 1945. They would not all have needed maps, or not in those quantities (and it should be remembered that maps were printed on relatively heavy paper and thus bulky). Perhaps the numbers given refer to the number of passes through the printing machines when colours and overprinting were involved.

Chapter 10

Accommodation

Between the two world wars there seemed no great need for vast amounts of accommodation for troops. Even though the need to go to war was becoming obvious in 1938, with its consequent need to house a much larger army (in the event up to twenty-five times what it had been in peacetime), there was insufficient time to begin and complete major barrack-building projects. Even when these did start after Dunkirk, completion was hampered by a shortage of building materials. In February 1940 it was reported that the material available for building huts that year would only be sufficient to house 60,000 to 70,000 troops.

When the decision was made in April 1939 to start conscription, with the call-up to start in July, plans were needed for accommodation. A public assurance was given that no troops would be housed under canvas during the winter; obviously this required a big building programme. At this point there were no war emergency powers in force, and it was expected that in order to choose and survey sites, plan layouts, prepare lists of quantities of materials needed, prepare the detailed specifications and negotiate with contractors would take at least three months for each location. As many as forty different camps would be needed, and it was obvious that it would be at least November 1939 before any building could be started, and it would be fortunate if the camps were completed before spring 1940.

It was also going to be necessary to provide accommodation for the personnel of the ADGB: some 43,000 people. The peacetime situation was to provide tents on static sites, and store mobile hutting with contractors who would take it out and erect it on mobilisation. But as well as the huts, the usual basic services (water, sewerage, electric light and roads and paths) had to be provided at each searchlight and gun site.

The main quartering problem at the outbreak of war when winter was approaching, was the need to provide accommodation for twenty-six divisions after the six divisions of the BEF had gone to France. The total number of this force, when all the ancillary units such as training and administration were added, was 765,000. Existing accommodation in permanent barracks was only sufficient for 288,000. This left some 673,000 to be housed in requisitioned houses and billets until hutted camps could be built. There were numerous considerations involved in planning these camps, including the availability of materials and labour, provision of suitable training areas, mini-mum interference with agriculture and ease of dispersal in the event of air attacks.

It is impracticable to build permanent barracks for wartime troop numbers when they will be vacated when peace returns, so the quartering directorate, which had responsibility for providing the accommodation, had to make other arrangements. In order of desirability, these were hutments laid out as barracks, either built of wood, or later, the metal Nissen huts, then tented camps. The latter were only suitable throughout the year in warmer climates than in north-west Europe; otherwise they were only desirable in summer.

The next most suitable were large buildings, or blocks of them, which could be completely vacated and converted into barracks. However, hospitals had traditionally had first call on such buildings, followed by headquarters staff and then perhaps valuable or perishable supplies which had to be kept under cover. The final possibilities were blocks of small houses, but these could be problematical to administer, as could the last option of billeting troops on local households.

In July 1940 there had been a major survey of premises which might be suitable for requisitioning and billeting and accommodation that had been reserved for a War Office move out of London was put into use for troop accommodation. Much of the ancillary accommodation, such as dining rooms and recreation rooms, was reduced to allow more living accommodation, and double bunks were constructed. It was originally intended that Nissen huts would be reserved for overseas use, but the huge requirement for accom-modation at home meant that they were soon in use there too. Delivery was slow at first, but soon went up to 700 per week.

The various home commands were told that more Nissen huts were on their way and they were to concentrate on getting troops currently in tents under better accommodation for the winter. This was not fully achieved, but of the nearly 47,000 troops still under canvas at the end of summer, all but just over 9,000 had been rehoused by November 1940; 8,600 of this 9,000 were ADGB personnel. A month later there were only 4,400 left under canvas, all but forty-five of whom were ADGB personnel.

With the return of troops from Dunkirk in the summer of 1940 the immediate problem was that of accommodating and caring for an unknown number of BEF and Allied troops under disorganised conditions. Only a few Allied troops had been expected, but in the event there were over 158,000, mostly Poles but also Dutch, Belgians and Czechs. With the British troops there was a grand total of almost 523,000 evacuees. It was realised that the men arriving would probably be without their officers and NCOs, and would not know where their unit comrades were. Dunkirk evacuees, including RASC personnel, were transported to reception camps by 200 civilian motor coaches and augmented rail services. At disembarkation ports, food was provided on a buffet basis and rations were handed out on rail halts en route. These consisted of haversack rations: meat, cheese or jam sandwiches, meat pies, hard-boiled eggs, fruit (fresh or in pies) and chocolate. There were also cigarettes and matches. As the troops had no utensils for drinks, waxed paper cups were provided.

Further, in order to keep their railway journeys as short as possible, all would have to be quartered in the south of England, so no delays could be allowed at the ports. The arriving men were put into trains which pulled out as soon as they were full. Names were collected as it was realised that the public would want to know as soon as possible the names of the survivors and the missing.

It was clear that the quartering plan for evacuees would have to consist of two stages: the first being to get the men in anywhere, and to provide each one with an individual army host who would look after them and see that they were fed and clothed. The second stage would be to sort them out. Stage two took place at Aldershot and Tidworth, where tents had been erected for 20,000 and 10,000 men respectively. There were numerous French troops, and these were returned to French ports south of the Somme, after a brief period when they were hosted by the civilian inhabitants of Southampton, Bournemouth, Weymouth and Plymouth.

The threat of invasion after the return of the BEF from France meant much reorganisation was needed, and this was immediately taken into consideration in the quartering plans. Among other factors which had to be taken into account was the need for trained formations to be available in the south and south-east of England, with room to fight, so training and administration units were moved away from this part of the country. There was an increased need for aerodromes and accommodation for the RAF and other bodies, including the Ministry of Aircraft Production, and the need to house some 20,000 Australian and New Zealand troops who would otherwise have gone direct to France, plus some 25,000 troops from other Continental countries.

The priority was to get all those people under cover and more than 400,000 were accommodated in tents for the summer and autumn of 1940. Hutted camps were in process of being built, but much of the labour on these was redirected to work on defence installations. There were air attacks in late summer and early autumn which took even more labour away to make repairs.

After the Dunkirk evacuation it soon became clear that most of the British field army would have to stay in the UK for a considerable time, and that army would have to be reorganised to provide fighting units which could be stationed for defence in the most threatened areas. A much larger proportion of the RAF would be in the UK, needing accommodation, and there would also be a need to accommodate Allied troops, and then well over 1,000,000 American troops who began arriving in the UK in 1942.

There were restrictions on what types of building could be requisitioned for troop accommodation. Those used for religious purposes, municipal buildings, libraries, railway premises, schools or universities could not be used without consent of the local authority. Schools also needed the express agreement of the local education authority, and hotels, although theoretically desirable, tended to be already full of civilians whose property had been destroyed in bombing raids.

As well as existing divisions and training units, an immense number of units and formations needed accommodation: priority was given to ADGB, coast defence troops, home defence units, training units, holding camps for men who had completed their training but not yet been drafted to fighting units, AA and Royal Artillery practice camps, AFV gunnery ranges and schools, other schools of instruction, additions in new pay and records offices, internee camps, prisoner of war camps and embarkation camps.

A Central Committee was set up under Sir A. McAlpine to advise on the best division of labour and materials for the larger projects. These included an increase in road construction and water and electric light mains as well as erecting the actual buildings, which slowed construction. This allowed a tentative building programme which planned for hutting to accommodate 270,000 at an estimated cost of £60,000,000 to be drawn up; Treasury approval for this was given on 9 September 1939.

One very successful variation on wooden huts was the use of Nissen and other iron huts. These were a pre-fabricated structure made of corrugated steel as a half-cylindrical skin with a cement floor. They were tunnel-shaped with doors and windows in the end walls. Some had dormer windows. For troop accommodation they were a standard size, for ten men. There were two other metal huts, the Romney and the Marston. Rather like Nissen huts and with the same type of construction, these were larger and used mainly for storage. Originally the whole available supply was intended for France and other overseas theatres, but these were diverted to home use.

The supply of Nissen huts was used in small groups to augment the accommodation in already requisitioned buildings and billets rather than as separate camps. Typically a small village would have four or five Nissens for additional sleeping quarters with a couple as offices and storerooms. Although this did tend to split up formations, it had the advantage of being able to use existing services such as water and electricity supply instead of having to provide these from scratch.

In 1941 approval had been given for the ATS to replace men in nearly every type of unit except field force units, and they were beginning to arrive from the training centres in large numbers. Accommodating them in units was mainly a matter of readjustment: for instance they had to have separate living quarters and latrines. All this caused less difficulty than the War Office had feared, mainly because ATS officers adopted a 'don't fuss about it' attitude and everyone else adapted themselves cheerfully.

During 1942 the War Office placed orders for 105,143 16ft Nissens, which were delivered at intervals over 1942 and 1943. Some 33,680,000 square feet of 24ft Nissens, 13,203,600 square feet of 35ft Romney and 1,380,000 square feet of 45ft Marston hutting was ordered in that same year. Although some of the 24ft Nissen and 35ft Romney hutting may have been used for troop accommodation, most was for storage.

Once American troops started to arrive, the first were sent to Northern Ireland, then the southern and western commands, the British troops there being moved elsewhere. The Western Command cleared as much as it could in the Monmouth-Hereford area. This was comparatively easy, but the movements in the Southern Command were more complex. Apart from anti-aircraft and coastal defence corps and some headquarters, only training and practice corps, experimental establishments, RASC depots and a prisoner of war camp, with some ordnance units, hospitals and other miscellaneous units such as pay offices, were left. By the end of 1942, some 264,000 British troops had been relocated.

There was some irritation among British troops about the more generous proportions of accommodation for American troops, who were given minimum sleeping space of 41 square feet per man, whereas for British troops it was just 30 square feet. However, to the American troops the larger space was the norm, and they did not see why they should accept lower standards than they were accustomed to.

Billeting

A census of available billets was carried out early in 1939. It was agreed in principle that wherever possible troops should be billeted in empty houses and civilian evacuees would be billeted on other householders.

Registration of all billeting possibilities throughout the country had been carried out before September 1939 by the Ministry of Health. The specific allocation of billets in private houses was done after consultation with the local police, who would have known a little about the householders.

Billeting is expensive and the War Office stated that it should be a last resort if whole properties could not be requisitioned. The payment for a billet, which included a bed, full board, heat, light, laundry and bedding and hot water for baths was a weekly sum of 29s.2d per man. In general it was preferred to avoid hotels, licensed premises, apartments and boarding houses. If the use of these was unavoidable, a report had to be sent to the War Office. Officers were not to be billeted in expensive hotels as the proprietors complained that the rates paid were not sufficient for the services the officers required.

There was no legal ban on billeting coloured troops, whether British or Allied subjects, on the same terms as other troops, but since there was some degree of prejudice against them it was decided that they should not be placed in premises where there was joint occupation by the householder, or where the owner remained in occupation in part of the house.

Billeting was done on the basis of one person for each room in the house, so a house with seven rooms occupied by a family of five would be deemed to have two rooms which could be used for billeting. Where the household did not have sufficient beds, beds or mattresses and bedding had to be provided by the billetee's unit. Where all rooms in the house did not have blackout curtains, the unit had to provide these too.

There were some types of dwellings which could not be used as billets: those where women were living alone or with young children, those where there was somebody seriously ill, and those where the rooms were used as work rooms such as doctors' waiting or consulting rooms.

A memorandum was issued to American troops who were billeted on British householders, but the same rules applied to British troops. They were only given the right to use the room allotted to them for sleeping and should not expect to have the use of any other rooms in the house unless invited by the householder. They were not allowed to take other people into the house. They should keep their room neat and clean, with the bed made properly, and ensure that blackouts were properly used. They should not make undue noise in their room, nor in coming in or going out. Arrangements for use of the key should be made with the householder, as houses should be kept locked. Walls, furniture and floors should not be mistreated, and there would be regular inspections to check on this.

The quartering directorate spent the winter of 1941–42 working out what additional accommodation would be needed for the British army in 1942, as well as other important building works. The labour situation was still poor and the bad weather of that winter further hampered the work. An estimate of the cost of work already in progress or soon to be started was in the region of £36,000,000. The War Office listed three types of building requirements for 1942: work in progress, work approved in principle and desirable work still to be approved. The first type consisted of fifty-seven quartering projects, forty-seven projects which included quartering as part of the work, and 139 which had no relation to quartering. Of the projects approved in principle, eleven were definitely quartering projects, fourteen included quarters and eighty were for other work. Of the other desirable projects, thirty-one were definite quartering projects, fourteen included quarters and eighty were for other work.

In the War Office building programme, quartering took second place to what was seen as more important work, such as anti-aircraft defence, coastal defence and special storage depots, on the basis that troops could be accommodated in requisitioned buildings with Nissen huts erected by the service and in tented camps in summer. Meanwhile, Nissen and other larger types of metal huts were in short supply and desperately needed for storage.

They were also needed for the expected US troops and airmen. During 1942 the War Office ordered more than 105,000 16ft Nissen huts, which arrived at intervals in 1942 and 1943, but this was only a fraction of what was needed: over 33,000,000 square feet of 24ft Nissens, over 13,000,000 square feet of 35ft Romneys and 1,380,000 square feet of 45ft Marstons.

At the beginning of 1942, the quartering directorate had to deal with the arrival of more Canadian troops, the expansion and reorganisation of the ATS and the reorganisation of troops guarding aerodromes and AA commands. By 1 April 1942 all but twenty-three forestry companies of the Canadian forces were accommodated near Aldershot in the South Eastern Command. During 1942 the influx of American troops, designated Operation Bolero, led to the formalisation of a building programme to house them. This work began in August. Like all other building projects, work was hampered by the shortage of labour, which was largely caused by the increased call-up among building labour in May and June 1943. The numbers available for building work, which had been over 70,000, dropped first to 44,000 in June 1943 and then to 33,000 in December.

There was also a shortage of building materials; one of the ways this was tackled was by setting up a Works Building Priority Committee, with a Materials Priority sub-committee. The main types of building material were timber, steel, cement and tarmacadam, bricks and roofing material.

Before the war, some 90 per cent of the timber used in the UK was imported, a situation which could not be sustained. The use of timber was put under the control of the sub-committee, which promptly laid down some rules, including restrictions on its use for house-building. It was only to be released for houses which were nearing completion, or where it was essential for weatherproofing. For military purposes, especially the need for troop accommodation, it was proposed that brick construction should be used whenever possible, but this presupposed the availability of sufficient bricks. By 1940 there was a major demand by the Ministry of Home Security for air-raid shelters. Meanwhile production of bricks was falling and existing stocks were rapidly being used up.

Restrictions on private enterprise building had been considered but rejected early in 1937, but by the autumn of 1940 it became necessary to restrict this minor industry, especially in what was then regarded as a waste of materials (and labour) on 'luxury' building. Restrictions on building houses for civilians were applied, as efforts were thought to be best concentrated on military and defence building.

Hutting

Huts had to be easy to produce in large numbers, easy to erect and dismantle (to move elsewhere) with a minimum of skilled labour, easily packed for transport, able to stand rough handling, and inexpensive.

At the start of the war, the army had no stock of huts. Messrs Nissen Buildings Ltd then offered royalty-free use of their hut designs. It proved easy and quick to produce sufficient 16ft and 24ft Nissen huts to satisfy the immediate needs of the BEF. The only difficulty experienced was that of packing and transporting the curved sheets. The original huts had wooden floors and ends, but when timber became scarce this changed to brick ends and concrete floors for huts which would not have to be moved. Huts for British troop accommodation could be fitted with dormer windows.

Soon after its formation, the Ministry of Works tried to economise on steel by using concrete and plasterboard, but the concrete version was too heavy and needed skilled labour to erect, and the plasterboard version was too flimsy and tended to leak.

The 35ft Nissen hut was considered too good for ordinary storage purposes, so a cheaper version called the Iris was produced. This had tubular steel ribs, needed highly skilled labour to erect and was found not to be strong enough when many collapsed under the weight of snow in the bad winter of 1940–41.

Late in 1941, a new improved type of storage hut called the Romney was designed. At 35ft by 16ft, this had a frame of curved tubular segments of 2½in 8-gauge steel, which were bolted together to make a semi-circular arch. The tubes had flanged couplers at each end, drilled to take four bolts, and purlin supports 5½in by 3in by ⅜in. The purlins themselves were angle irons of 1¾in by 1¾in by ¼in. The huts were covered with corrugated iron and lined with plasterboard. There were also roof lights and blackout shutters. The Romney hut was a great success; although needing some skill to erect, a handbook and training courses were soon organised.

A smaller version called the semi-Romney was produced in late 1943. Using the same type of framework it was quickly covered with a fitted canvas. When time allowed, this would be replaced by corrugated iron and plasterboard. Unfortunately production of this canvas cover was slow and only fifty were made by D-Day. A further eighty-nine followed by 24 July. Their only disadvantage was that they had no windows; the door flaps could be left open to let in some light, but these were likely to be torn in high winds.

Two more similar huts were designed: the 24ft Junior Romney and the 16ft Baby Romney. These were renamed Abbey and Tufton. Although pronounced excellent on testing, neither went into production as it seemed obvious that the end of the war was imminent.

Another type of shed using what was known as 'Marston shedding' (after the main engineering store depot at Marston) was for workshops, in two types: low and high. The standard size was 200ft by 45ft. Other types included the parabolic-roofed Turran shed, or an updated version of the Armstrong hut first used in the First World War. These were invaluable for housing the BEF when it returned from France. Otherwise mainly used by the AA, this was 12ft by 6ft and portable.

France

Types of hutting sent for use abroad were Nissen 16ft, 24ft and 35ft (this last for stores), Romney 35ft and semi-Romney, Marston shedding, and large and small trench shelters. Most of the troops of the BEF were quartered in French billets and houses, but it was always intended to augment those with hutted camps. The first demand for huts was for 8,420, each to house ten men. These were to be Nissen huts and a tentage reserve was also demanded.

Middle East Command

Egypt and the Middle East (Palestine, Sudan, Iraq and the eastern Mediterranean islands) were the main overseas theatres after the middle of 1940 and were heavily reinforced by some 150,000 men, most of whom could be satisfactorily housed in tents in those warm climates. Others of these were in billets; that did not mean living with the local inhabitants in their houses, but in hired houses. By the end of 1941 the strength of the Middle East Command had risen to over 1,000,000, including 100,000 prisoners of war. There were also fifty-six hospitals with a total of over 43,000 beds and nine convalescent depots with 11,500 beds.

By September 1941 the operations of this command had resulted in a large number of prisoners of war: over 250,000 in that month alone. Some 47,000 of these were Africans, just over 2,000 Germans and the rest were Italians. In the interests of relieving the fighting troops of this command of the need to guard them, they were shipped out to camps in India, Ceylon, South Africa, Canada and Australia. They had to be housed in accommodation equivalent to that of the same ranks of their captors' armies, and the government was concerned that they would have no cause for complaint as this might lead to reprisals against British PoWs in Germany and Italy.

In peacetime, units in the Middle East organised their own laundry, using local 'dhobies', but these stalwarts were not prepared to follow their units into the Western Desert and the laundry had to be sent back to Alexandria. The laundry there had belonged to a steamship company until it was purchased by the RAOC in July 1940. It had a weekly capacity of up to 90,000 items. This was not convenient to those in the desert, as it needed transport to and fro, but the general water shortage precluded the use of mobile laundries. The solution, as far as clothing was concerned, was an ample supply of replacements, but again the shortage of transport made that difficult. Eventually a balance was achieved, with base laundries where clothing could be cleaned and repaired if necessary, and some mobile laundries operated where there was sufficient water. Otherwise, troops had to wash their own clothes as best they could and apply for replacements through the normal supply channels.

Persia/Iraq

The Persian and Iraqi garrisons increased enormously after the beginning of 1942, to a high point in March 1943 of more than 300,000 men. More than half of these were Indian troops, and there was an average of between 35,000 and 65,000 local labourers. Accommodation was almost entirely in tents, or local grass or reed huts erected by local labour.

Gibraltar

The garrison was increased from 9,152 in September 1940 to 13,629 plus 1,050 RAF personnel by December 1941. Only 250 Nissen huts had been sent out by that date and extra accommodation had been found by requisitioning some houses, but mainly in tunnels and underground shelters bored into the Rock.

Barrack services

Shortly after the war began, it became apparent that the peacetime system could not cope with the constantly increasing demands. It was therefore necessary for officers in charge of barracks to organise contracts locally. Barrack services included provision of candles, straw for paillasses and disinfectants. RAOC had responsibility for furnishings, table ware, bedding and linen.

Stores required to equip requisitioned buildings as barracks were supplied through ordnance by barrack service staff.

Each unit was responsible for the furniture and fittings in the barracks it used, and moving in and out of specific barracks involved much paperwork and inventories. Individual barracks were controlled by a barrack master and his clerks and repair and maintenance personnel. As the demand for accommodation increased, a shortage of accountants soon developed.

Barrack services were provided under the barrack department of the RASC, a situation unique to the British army. At times it was suggested that its functions should be divided between the RAOC (furnishings), and the Royal Engineers (light, heat, window cleaning, chimney sweeping and sanitary facilities), leaving the RASC with the provision of fuel. But these suggestions were rejected on the grounds that the coordinated system provided by the RASC alone was better for the welfare and, consequently, the morale of the troops, particularly those recently called up who had just left comfortable homes.

There was an inspectorate, which did not just check on minor points, but also did some good work for the benefit of the troops. One such, when inspecting a remote barracks in winter, found that the men had only two blankets each in the bitterly cold weather. On investigating the stores, he found a generous stock of good white hospital blankets being held in reserve. The expected hospital had not materialised, so there the blankets sat in the stores, neatly folded with plenty of mothballs. It took a little persuasion to get the storekeeping accountant to part with these, but he did in the end.

Chapter 11

Clothing and Personal Equipment

Until the early 1900s, with the exception of riflemen who wore green jackets, British soldiers wore scarlet jackets, often with the white straps of their equipment forming a cross on their chests. It was realised that this made them an easy target, and as a result of engagements in northern India, the colours were changed to the drab colour known as khaki (from an Urdu word for dust), the fabric being composed of a mixture of green and brown fibres.

For parades and other ceremonial occasions, especially in peacetime, elaborate regimental uniforms were worn, but in the field, the outfit worn by most soldiers in the Second World War was known as battledress* or service dress. Different regiments were identified by badges, buttons or other insignia.

Scottish regiments had kilts in the regiment's tartan, with a sporran. The front corners of the jacket were cut away. Officers might wear tartan trews, but none of this was worn in the field, where the usual service dress with trousers was more practical.

Home

The pre-war depot for army clothing was originally at Didcot, but it moved to Branston, near Burton, in 1938. In June 1939 two new sub-depots were opened at Dewsbury in the wool production area of Yorkshire and Stalybridge in the cotton production area of Lancashire. Both these depots received bulk material from manufacturers and sent it out to appointed garment-makers. Once completed, the garments were sent on to Branston, from where detailed issues were made to all UK units except those at Aldershot and Scottish commands. There, bulk supplies were received from Branston and issued in detail from the command ordnance depots. In July 1939, the inspection of army clothing was transferred from the RAOC to the Ministry of Supply, which took over the RAOC staff.

By the end of 1939 the depot at Branston was showing a huge increase of work with large quantities of items arriving from the manufacturers. New storage accommodation was constructed at Branston and four more sub-depots were opened in Cheshire, Yorkshire, Scotland and Northolt near London. Originally these sub-depots were intended to do no more than store

---

* Americans spelled this 'battle dress'.

some of the overflow from Branston, but by May 1940 they had been equipped with electric baling presses and baled and marked stocks in accordance with Branston standards and made bulk issues. A further reorganisation at Branston saw a new group formed to deal with ATS uniforms.

For many months during 1939–40 the Branston depot worked twenty-four hours a day to cope with clothing the vast numbers of new recruits and the BEF in France, sending four pack trains a week to the latter. Then they had to supply clothing to the Local Defence Volunteers (later called the Home Guard) and towards the end of 1940 began stockpiling supplies for the Middle East. Further sub-depots were opened, including one in Northern Ireland to handle stocks of garments made there.

The efficiency of the main depot at Branston can be judged from the occasion when they were ordered to issue 3,500,000 pairs of boots and almost 3,000,000 yards of greatcoat cloth to the Russian government to help them repel the German invasion of their country. These items were packed and ready for despatch by the day and time specified, despite having less than one week's notice.

When uniforms were changed in spring and autumn, the 'old' ones went back to the depots where they were cleaned and repaired for further issue. At home a few War Department mobile laundries existed before the war and others, some with trailers, were established during the war, but most of the laundry work for the troops was carried out by civilian contractors. Most units made their own arrangements with local laundries until early 1941 when local RAOC staff took over organising this. Some were dyed and issued to prisoners of war. The Women's Voluntary Service (WVS) helped to carry out clothing repairs.

Tailoring services, altering and fitting new clothing and making special size garments was normally done by contract, but the shortage of civilian tailors often made this difficult; once again the WVS were able to help.

European theatre

The version of battledress worn in the European theatre during the Second World War was introduced just before the start of the war. It consisted of a short jacket known as a blouse which was buttoned to high-waisted trousers, both items being of wool serge. Unfortunately the buttons holding the two parts together had a tendency to come off under extreme movement, so braces were issued, and sometimes a sweater was added.

The original pattern of battledress uniform (known as 1937 pattern) had a fly-fronted blouse, pleated pockets with concealed buttons and an unlined collar. The map and field dressing pockets had concealed buttons. In 1942 a further version of battledress lacked the fly front to the blouse, and had exposed buttons. Plastic buttons replaced the original brass buttons.

The sleeves were slightly curved to the front to make them more comfortable when carrying a rifle, or holding the steering wheel of a vehicle. A woollen shirt was worn under the blouse, officers leaving the top button of the blouse undone and wearing a tie. Other ranks had no tie, and buttoned the blouse right to the top, closing the collar with a hook and eye.

The trousers had a large map pocket at the left front near the knee and a special pocket for a field dressing on the hip near the right front pocket. When necessary, short puttees or gaiters covered the gap between trouser bottoms and the boots, keeping dirt and water out of the boots.

Battledress in various shades of blue were used by the RAF and RN Reserves, Civil Service Defence corps such as ARP wardens and ambulance crews. Other variations of battledress were worn by Commonwealth troops. Canadians had a flap and button instead of the hook and eye on their blouses. Their buttons were steel painted green, and the whole uniform was more green than the British version. The New Zealand version was almost identical to the British, but more brown, with the stitching in a lighter colour. The blouse had one more button than the British version. The Australian blouses were almost identical to the British version but they and the trousers were, like the Canadian version, greener. South African battledress came in either khaki wool or tan twill. They called the short jacket a 'bunny jacket'.

A version of British battle dress was made in the USA for the British army in a colour called olive drab. It had some slight variations, including plastic buttons, and was made of a finer serge than the British version, so it was often seen in the Mediterranean.

Jackets/blouses came in sizes from No. 1 to No. 19. With the exception of No. 19, which was for men 5ft 5in to 5ft 6in tall, all the others were for taller men as the number rose. Other measurements were for the waist and chest. As an example, for a man 5ft 9in to 5ft 10in tall, the No. 12 had a 35–36in waist and a 40–41in chest. Trouser sizes followed the same rules: for short men it was No. 19, and for others the heights ran from 5ft 3in to 5ft 4in, with waists from 32in to 39in and legs from 28in to 32in. If time and facilities allowed (or the man was handy with a needle), minor alterations could be made.

The standard issue blouse had fabric epaulettes, buttoned near the neck. These could be used to carry a folded Field Service cap, and were also useful to keep the shoulders of the webbing equipment set in place.

The trousers for parachutists had larger pockets, lined with chamois leather for extra strength. Fastened with a flap, a button and two press studs, these could carry more than the conventional 'map' pocket, although they were often used to carry grenades as well as maps of the drop area. These trousers also had two additional pockets on the seat, to carry extra field dressings, and a small pocket for a knife on the right.

Winter uniform included woollen gloves and a serge greatcoat. Early versions of these heavy coats were single breasted, but these were replaced after 1939 by a double-breasted version. These coats had a hip pocket on either side, and some had a belt at the back. A lighter weight rubberised coat was issued to other ranks and raincoats or mackintoshes were available for officers.

Leather jerkins provided a windproof alternative to the greatcoat. These were lined but had no sleeves, pockets or collars. Buttoning down the front, they were issued a size larger to fit over the battledress uniform.

Special overalls for tank crew men were introduced in 1942. They were made from unlined heavy cotton with a water-repellent finish. Buttoned tabs at wrist and ankle allowed for adjustments. They had a central fly-front and zipped vents on the hips to allow access to the battledress uniform underneath, and pockets at the breast and top of the legs. A later version was made of heavyweight cotton fully lined with woollen fabric. It had two long zips running from the throat down the front and on down each leg to the ankle, which made it easier to get into and out of, and if necessary to give easier access to wounds. A hood could be attached to the collar. A camouflage version was available.

Khaki denim overalls were worn for working, and being manufactured by several different firms, tended to vary a little. They were meant to be worn over the usual uniform so were issued a size larger. The Home Guard used these as their main uniform from 1940 until autumn of that year when standard battledress was issued.

Issue underwear came in two versions of 'cellular' vest and drawers: light weight with short sleeves to the vest and short legs to the drawers for spring through autumn, and a long-sleeved vest and long-legged 'long john' drawers for winter.

A camouflage suit of smock and trousers was available, initially for snipers but later used by other infantry units. It included a particoloured brown and green head net, which could also be used as a face veil.

Wounded or sick soldiers who were expected to remain in hospital for any length of time were issued with pyjamas and a dressing gown, then when they were moved to convalescent hospitals and could take exercise out of doors, they were given a suit of 'hospital blues'. This consisted of jacket, trousers and waistcoat in mid-blue serge, with a collared shirt and a red tie. Their normal uniform would have been taken for cleaning and repair and they were issued with a fresh set when they were finally discharged.

Early in the war, motorcyclists had canvas leggings to cover their trousers; these tapered at the ankle and spread out to fit over the instep of the boot. They were fastened with buttons on the outside of the ankle and had a buckled strap which went under the foot to hold them down. A rubberised version was available. An alternative was a short buckled anklet.

By 1942 the trouser legging had been replaced by breeches (often with a doe-skin inner thigh reinforcement) and a pocket. They had a standard battle-dress jacket with two breast pockets, and button-up sleeves; they also had leather gauntlets, long enough to cover the end of their sleeves and keep the wind out. Originally their 'helmet' was a close-fitting rubberised fabric affair, much like those worn by early pilots, with goggles; these were replaced by a proper safety helmet; this had no rim and was held in place by a neck and chin protector. They carried a rifle or pistol (the latter on a lanyard) and a wooden map-case to allow them to check their position.

Officers had to buy their own uniforms and equipment (known as camp kit), all as specified. The camp kit included such items as a collapsible camp bed and a bed roll. Although desirable, junior officers' camp kit was more likely to remain with the baggage train than with the officer in the field. They did receive an allowance for their purchases. Well-off officers could make their purchases from civilian outfitters and tailors; the less well-off could buy a budget version from the quartermaster. Senior officers' uniforms and equipment were more numerous and elaborate; they usually lived in billets or substantial tents and thus had room for them. There was a list of authorised outfitters and tailors.

Headgear

Hats were either peaked caps, plain caps or berets, or, in combat, steel Mk II 'Brodie' helmets, often with a cotton net cover to add twigs, grass or strips of material for camouflage. When these metal helmets were first issued in the First World War, they were found to reduce head injuries by up to 80 per cent. They had an inner lining with a rubber pad to cushion impacts, and a chin-strap of khaki cotton webbing with two metal squares to attach it to the helmet.

The berets were differentiated according to the regiment with fabric badges.

Hats for jungle or desert wear usually had wide brims to give shade or keep rain from the face, as did the standard metal helmet. The cotton 'jungle service' hat had ventilation holes and loops in a band round the brim which could be used to hold camouflage material. The cotton jungle hat (made in India) was better than the felt hat: it was rot-proofed, water-resistant and easy to fold and stow away under an epaulette. It could be soaked in water to provide cooling by evaporation. There was also a cotton General Service cap with ventilation holes and a lace at the rear to adjust size.

The Australian-style bush hat (also known as a slouch hat) had a broad brim which kept out rain and excessive sun, and was often used to scoop up water. The author George Macdonald Fraser, who had served in Burma, remarked that if you'd been able to boil water in it, you wouldn't need a hotel. A razor blade was often tucked into the band, optimistically thought to be a help if captured. These hats were mostly made in Australia by the famous Akubra Company. They were usually worn with the left brim fixed up to the crown, held in place by press studs.

Many officers bought their hats from firms in the fashionable areas of London, such as Herbert Johnson of New Bond Street or Thomas & Stones of Jermyn Street.

In most non-fighting situations, officers wore a peaked cap, or in Scottish regiments, a tartan Glengarry.

Other ranks in Iceland in 1940 and in other places with extremely cold winters were issued with woollen balaclavas and scarves. Another version was known as the Cap Comforter, which was basically a woollen tube, rolled up for a cap, or rolled down to form a scarf.

Tank crews had crash helmets with extra padding at the front to protect the forehead from bangs on the head in tanks moving over uneven ground.

Field Service caps came in basic khaki or other colours depending on the regiment, as did berets. Ski-caps had peaks and ear flaps.

Footwear

Officers wore brown ankle boots of a less heavy leather than those for other ranks. 'Mounted' officers wore either brown leather riding boots, or a buckled leather gaiter with ankle boots. Ankle boots for other ranks were known as ammunition boots because they were originally made by the Munitions Board at Woolwich. They were unlined ankle boots, usually brown for field service (and black for parades), and finished with hobnails across the sole, with toe and heel plates. These were worn by all men except storekeepers in ammunition stores for fear of sparks, or lorry drivers as the nails might damage the pedals. In 1942 this rule was extended to armoured vehicle crews and a year later to water craft RASC crews. They might have had gaiters or puttees to keep dirt and wet out of the boots. All these boots were laced.

For physical training, canvas and rubber plimsoles were worn; these were mid-brown with laces of the same colour. These shoes might be worn by infantry patrols or commando units when quiet movement was essential.

For mountain warfare, boots could be fitted with toothed cleats for grip, and for troops using skis the boots had a squared toe and a grooved heel, both designed to fit skis.

Standard issue socks were of wool and needed frequent darning. This had to be done by the wearer, who carried spare wool and needles in a 'housewife' (pronounced 'hussif') which also included thread and appropriate sized needles for sewing buttons.

Buttons

Buttons came in several sizes and materials. The largest were normally used for greatcoats, and might be domed and made in silver or what was euphemistically called 'vegetable ivory' (plastic). These had a shank on the back for attaching to the garment. Smaller metal buttons were more or less flat, with four holes in the middle to sew them to the garment.

Insignia

Soldiers and officers wore various, often coloured, insignia on their uniforms and headgear. These might indicate the regiment and/or formation to which they belonged, and were mostly placed on the shoulders. Other badges indicated rank (some of these were on the shoulders), trade, proficiency and skill at arms, and might be worn on the arms or cap. When worn on the sleeves, the actual position was designated and restricted.

The cheapest form of badge to produce was linen with silk-screen printing; the next was of worsted with the design machine-embroidered. The most expensive were badges embellished with bullion or other metallic thread, often enhanced with black or coloured silk thread. Due to the expense, and the amount of work required to produce these badges, they were restricted to full-dress or state-dress uniforms.

Most badges were sewn onto the garment, but those for wearing on khaki drill or other tropical uniforms were sewn onto a removable brassard. The commonest colours were white or cream, brown or black.

Some examples of badges are Headquarters 21st Army Group, with yellow crossed swords on a blue cross on a red shield; the Persia and Iraq Command, a red elephant's head with white tusks on a blue background; the 116 Engineer Regiment, a white bridge on a red rectangle.

Military police, when on duty, wore a red cover on their cap and a brassard with the letters 'MP' in red, below any rank markings.

Medical orderlies, who were non-combatants, being from the RAMC, wore a white brassard with a red cross and had another red cross on their field dressing packs. Although they wore the usual webbing equipment belt, the items attached to it would be extra dressings and first aid kit rather than ammunition.

Stretcher-bearers wore a brassard with 'SB' on it in red. They were not part of the RAMC, but were seconded for this duty from their battalion and thus carried their arms. They might wear a Y-shaped harness, fixed to a belt at the back, and with long straps which passed through the epaulettes and down to loops which were passed over the handles of the stretcher. This helped spread the load on their arms and provided a safeguard against dropping the stretcher.

France / BEF

The clothing and equipment provided in the early months of the war in 1939–40 was good quality, but each man had only one set of service dress uniform and thus could not change from wet to dry clothes. The leg-bottoms of the trousers could not be kept dry, puttees were useless and gaiters were needed. Gum-boots for the labour units were almost essential, but by the end of October only 700 pairs had been issued. There was no leather available for boot repairs. Demands for winter clothing began in October, less than a month after mobilisation. The supply of socks was insufficient until November. The waterproof capes only reached as far as the knees and since they had no sleeves they did not cover the trunk properly. At first only one blanket per man was issued; a second followed by the end of October but that was still not enough in that exceptionally cold winter. It was January before each man had three. Some items, such as woollen gloves, were not available until Christmas.

In midwinter the coming problems of cleaning and repairing winter clothing to be withdrawn from the BEF troops were studied. The conclusion was that there were no adequate facilities at or near either of the Base Ordnance depots, and that the answer was to contract with a large firm in Paris to do the job. Some 1,600,000 items (woollen underclothes, shirts, battledress blouses and trousers, greatcoats and blankets) would have to be dealt with. Several firms in Paris were inspected and a contract was placed with the largest, Blanchisseries et Teintureries de France, located in a western suburb of Paris. This firm had plenty of storage space, its own technical staff and civilian labour, and its own transport. It was large enough to handle two or three times the quantities from the following winter if needed. A small RAOC detachment of one officer and twenty-five other ranks was attached to the works and carried out daily checks of all the items being cleaned and repaired and baled for reissue. The firm used a trichlorethylene process. This was fast, caused hardly any shrinkage and disinfected in the process of cleaning. When the enemy occupation of Paris became too close for comfort, all stocks of army clothing still at the works were destroyed with caustic soda.

From time to time other laundering contracts were made with firms in Rouen, La Baule, Le Havre and Lille. The chief laundry requirements were for the medical base in Dieppe and hospitals at La Baule and for the returned stores depot at Doullens, which handled large quantities of summer underclothing.

Decontamination of clothing affected by gas was expected to be a major task at the beginning of the war, but the laundries of the Paris and Le Havre area refused to consider decontamination work as they feared its effects on their machinery. Space was therefore reserved in disused laundry buildings at Le Mans, Le Havre, and Isse (close to Rennes). As well as equipping the building at Le Mans for use as an ordinary laundry, large boiling tanks for decontamination work were installed.

Italy

In most of Italy, the usual serge battledress was worn, but in the mountainous areas more was needed. Windproof oversuits were made in various shades of brown or beige and were worn over the normal battledress uniform. The top part was a pullover-style smock with a hood which could be tightened round the face with draw straps. The trousers had a drawstring waist but no fly, reinforcement patches on the knees and a map pocket on the left thigh. To add a little warmth without restricting the movement of the arms, a leather jerkin was available. Woollen pullovers with drawstring necks were also issued.

For snowy conditions, white snowsuits were issued. These were just for camouflage, not to add warmth, and had to be worn over normal cold-weather uniform. They consisted of lightweight cotton trousers and a smock which had buttons to close it at the neck, and a hood which was large enough to go over a metal helmet. For the coldest conditions, a white duffel coat was available, but it was not suitable for strenuous work as it would cause the wearer to sweat. These winter garments were also worn in Norway and Iceland.

Mobile laundry and bath units were normally allocated to corps troops on the basis of one per division and one for each corps; in Italy they were used in the forward areas to provide hot baths for the troops followed by clean clothes. Sometimes, by liaising with the Army Kinematograph Services and the NAAFI, mobile canteens and cinemas were sited alongside the laundries and bathhouses; Italian women, using their own sewing machines, repaired garments, including greatcoats, battledress, khaki drill, socks and under-clothes, towels, blankets, mosquito nets and veils, and hospital bedding and clothing. They also included REME craftsmen to repair the laundry equip-ment when needed.

Equipment sets

As well uniforms, men were issued with what were known as 'accoutrements', or equipment sets. This equipment consisted of a wide belt, and braces which went over the shoulders and crossed over the back. On top of these crossed straps, a large pack, meant to carry a greatcoat and blanket, was attached. The individual items attached to the webbing were everything carried outside the clothing which was not a weapon: pouches of ammunition, pistol holsters, slings, mess tins, water bottles, an aluminium or enamel mug, entrenching tool and a haversack. This latter was to carry the greatcoat and a blanket. A waterproof cape was carried rolled up on top of the haversack. Other items were attached to or hung from the belt: loops for a bayonet and entrenching tool handle, the entrenching tool head in a canvas or web cover, a water bottle, a gas mask, and a mess tin in a cloth cover. The haversack carried a rifle-cleaning kit and personal items such as a knife and a rolled cotton pack of cutlery, shaving kit, comb and foot powder.

The belt was fastened with a simple push buckle, and the shoulder straps with a brass press stud. These studs were also used to attach various things to the belt/straps. At the beginning of the war there was concern about the use of gas, so all men carried a gas cape and a gas mask (also known as a respirator). These came in a webbing case, with spare eye shields and anti-misting cloth and tins of ointment. Another version consisted of a shaped rubber face piece with two eye-shields and a hose which went from the nose/mouth area to a filter carried on the chest.

In jungle areas the equipment consisted of a small pack containing two mess tins, an enamelled mug known as a pialla, knife, fork and spoon, needle and thread, water purification pills, mepacrin tablets, rations, and, as usual, an entrenching tool and a 5-yard length of thin rope. They also carried a broad-bladed machete or a kukri if they could get one. These were intended for clearing jungle vegetation, but also made a formidable weapon.

Made of heavy webbing, the equipment belt had to be cleaned with a product called Blanco. This came either in a cake or as loose powder in a tin, and was used with a brush and water to clean the webbing and maintain its colour. With the exception of the version for ceremonial duties of military police, or men on traffic control, it was not always white, as the name implies, but could be khaki, tan or jungle green.

An alternative to the webbing equipment belts was a large rucksack known as a Bergen (from the town in Norway where it was first encountered). This contained all the things which would otherwise be hung from the webbing equipment. Made of canvas with all edges stoutly bound, they were tear-shaped, and mounted on a metal frame to keep them from touching the wearer's back. They were waterproof lined and came in two or three variations on the khaki colour. They had a main pocket 18in high, 16in wide and 6in deep. This pocket was closed with a cinch rope. Other pockets might be zipped, but there were usually three on the outside of the main pocket: one on the back 12½ by 8 by 2in and one on each side 11 by 6 by 2½in. There were also numerous straps: two long ones to hold items under the top flap, two more to hold items such as a waterproof bedroll under the main pocket, and two 12in straps on either side.

In 1942 an alternative to the standard webbing equipment, known as a battle jerkin, was introduced. All the items needed were attached with big wooden toggles and whipcord loops. It had built-in pouches over the breast and two haversacks on the back with an additional pouch on each hip.

Produced in brown waterproof cotton duck, it was thought to look like an elaborate poacher's jacket. Lightweight in itself (weighing 3lb less than the normal webbing equipment), it could carry an enormous amount of equipment, including several grenades and mortar bombs, and 100 rounds of small arms ammunition. It was first used in the Normandy landings but very little afterwards, being unpopular with the troops, who soon went back to their webbing equipment. The remaining stocks were eventually sold off as war surplus.

Tropical theatres

In the dry parts of the hot countries where the British and Allied armies operated, the standard serge uniforms were replaced by what was known as khaki drill (drill is a strong cotton fabric with a diagonal bias in the weave). This was usually produced in a lighter shade of khaki than the serge version. It might involve long trousers or shorts, or the version known as 'Bombay Bloomers' which had a full leg that could be folded up and fastened with a button to make shorts, or tightened round the ankle with a drawstring. Purpose-made shorts came to just above the knee and had side pockets with an additional flapped pocket to hold a field dressing. They were made in numbered sizes, with measurements of height, waist and breech.

Shirts were basically a lighter-weight version of the collared jackets worn in Europe. The sleeves could be rolled up to above the elbow, or the shirts were made with short sleeves. These shirts were often made of Aertex and had a buttoned breast pocket on each side. There was also a khaki drill 'bush' shirt, with long sleeves and four pockets, two with buttoned flaps on the chest and two without buttons at waist level.

In hot weather British troops wore short sleeved Aertex shirts and drill trousers or 'Bermuda' shorts. When they moved up into Italy, denim battle-dress overalls were preferred. By 1943 the Aertex shirt was replaced by a cotton bush jacket. Khaki drill clothing was produced by numerous manufacturers, some in Great Britain and others in India.

In the Middle East, large base laundries were established using local labour; under British supervision these were used for the biannual change of seasonal clothing. However, they had to be in areas where there was electricity, and plenty of water. The first of these was in the dock area of Alexandria. Repairs were done there by some 450 local women who dealt with 30,000 garments each week. By December 1942 the number of employees had risen to 3,000 and the number of garments handled had risen to over 200,000 a week.

When the clothes arrived from the laundry at what was soon called the Clothing Repair Factory, they were first sorted into 'serviceable', 'serviceable less buttons', 'repairable' and 'unserviceable'. The latter were stripped of buttons and any serviceable sections were removed before the rest was passed to salvage. Repairable items and those needing buttons were repaired and passed on to be sized, sorted by size and type of item, folded, made up into bales and passed to a 'part-worn' department within the factory. These were always issued in preference to new garments.

Much of the laundry equipment for North Africa was lost at sea; one unit lost not only all its equipment, but also much of its personnel to enemy action at sea. Another problem was that the trailers on which the equipment was mounted were large and unwieldy and often left out of shipments.

The spring changeover from serge battledress to khaki drill shirts and shorts for men operating in the desert and long trousers for those elsewhere was made in April, but it was not easy to keep these clean in the desert. There were a number of cases of sunstroke or heatstroke in Libya and orders were issued that sun-helmets should be worn by all ranks between 0900 and 1600 hours. During the period October to March battledress was worn; although there were a few complaints of skin irritation, these stopped when the troops got used to wearing serge instead of drill.

Egypt / Western Desert / Levant

It had been decided that British and Indian troops in the Western Desert should remain in khaki drill throughout the winter, but with woollen under-clothing, which was not usually used in Egypt. But the weather in December 1940 was abnormally cold and the clothing decision was reversed; battledress was issued for winter wear, but some of the most recently arrived British troops still had their service dress, so it was mainly the Australians who had to have the woollen underwear.

Troops became deeply tanned from stripping to the waist during the heat of the day, but nights could be cold and for these they had woollen pullovers. These had a buttoned open neck, cotton epaulettes and cotton reinforced elbows; they came in several shades of beige.

East Africa and Madagascar

Clothing suited to the varying conditions was issued. The drill clothing issued was adequate, although shorts and short sleeves made the wearer vulnerable to mosquito bites. Although mosquito nets were issued for sleeping, they were not suitable for outdoor use.

Jungle conditions in the Far East

In the Far East, (mainly north-east India and Burma), khaki clothing was dyed to what was known as known as jungle green at the BODs until a stock of better jungle clothing was available. This consisted of an Aertex blouse or bush jacket with battledress trousers. In the heat of the jungles, the green items soon darkened with sweat. Full-length trousers in jungle green were issued, with canvas gaiters to close them at ankle level to keep out insects. The trousers, and shirts, were available in camouflage print.

This clothing was largely made in India, as were other items such as towels and underwear. These items, like the other clothing for troops serving in the jungles of north-east India and Burma, were dyed in various shades of dull green to make them less conspicuous in the dense vegetation. Socks were also coloured green and were oily to the touch having been treated to make them rot resistant.

A rubberised poncho was available, both gas and mosquito resistant, or a cape which buttoned down the front but had two slits for the arms. Mosquito face and hand nets were also issued, one of fine fishnet, the other of a finer mesh with bamboo hoops to keep the net from touching the face or neck, which looked rather like a modern beekeeper's hood.

Burma

For the 14th Army in Burma the uniform was all dark green, from under-clothes out; even watch straps had to be green or khaki. Puttees were used to close the bottoms of the trousers as protection against leeches, snakes and other creeping things.

Chindits wore regular tropical uniforms and army boots, but were specially equipped with Australian-type slouch hats, mosquito nets, machetes and rubber-soled hockey boots for scouting and silent marching. Their bedding was one ground sheet and one light cashmere blanket per man. Each man carried a water sterilising outfit, fifty rounds of ammunition, and six days' paratroop rations, which included salt. Salt was essential, but the men had to be constantly reminded of this.

In the Far East, the existing mobile laundry equipment was found unsuitable for use in jungles, so a new type of divisional laundry with lightweight laundry equipment and bathing equipment was provided. This was air-portable, or could be towed on a 10cwt trailer behind a jeep.

The laundry services at overseas bases were operated at first by the RAOC, but this was found to lack flexibility. In both base laundries and base hospital laundries the machinery was designed to be used in permanent locations with concrete floors, which meant that changes in locations involved long delays. The equipment was then redesigned with machinery mounted on trailers, which allowed rapid working after relocation.

ATS uniforms

Male members of the ATS wore variations of the standard battledress. Women members wore a worsted or barathea jacket with belt, skirt and/or trousers in the usual khaki. They had a pale khaki collarless shirt with a separate collar and studs to fasten it in place, with a similar coloured tie. The jacket had four pockets (two on the chest, two on the hips); the top ones were pleated with a scalloped flap and buttons. Their unit flashes were on the collar. They had a peaked cap with the unit badge centre front, and gas masks and steel helmets when working with AA units. They carried a canvas shoulder bag with a strap and a zip fastening.

Other ranks wore beige cotton lisle stockings, while officers had better quality rayon, or silk if they wanted to pay for them.

In 1945, in anticipation of the collapse of Germany and consequent reduction in necessary manpower, regulations were drawn up on the provision of civilian clothing for demobbed men. The main stocks of this clothing were held at Branston, from where they were passed on to the Civilian Clothing Depots (CCDs).

RAOC dispersal units were established at or near each military dispersal unit. Each such depot had an establishment of roughly 200, of which fifty were civilians including nine tailors, to deal with up to 1,400 men daily.

The CCDs held garments in a variety of styles and colours which were displayed for the demobbed men to choose from. If the CCD was unable to immediately meet the requirements of a man of unusual size, he was measured by an experienced tailor and his new clothes were sent to him by post. For ordinary standard-sized men, the whole process usually took no more than fifteen minutes.

Chapter 12

Food

At home

In the period between the two world wars, in the 1920s and 1930s, there was a scientific breakthrough with the discovery of vitamins and the effect which deficiency of certain of these vitamins had on human health. This discovery was followed by the commercial production of these vitamins, which were purchased for use when the food which provided them was not available. All this aided the military task of keeping the troops fit and healthy.

Improvements to ingredients

In the early campaigns of the war, the food rations received by the British empire's combat troops were little different from those the soldiers ate in the trenches during the First World War. Despite the numerous developments made in the food industry, tinned beef and biscuit remained staples, as they were easily carried by the troops. Dried ingredients took up less space (and weight) in transport and they also omitted the nonedible parts of food: bones, peels, cores and seeds. They were comparatively easy to prepare, although they did take a little care when rehydrating, but this basically meant paying attention while they were soaking. It was certainly easier to make mashed potatoes by stirring in hot water than peeling, cooking and hand mashing. Dried egg was used to make cakes and other dishes where eggs would normally be beaten first. It was also eaten, but not appreciated, as scrambled eggs, although some wily cooks disguised it by adding a little crushed egg-shell to the mixture.

'Instant tea' was useful for situations where the men made their own tea and the normal method of tea-making involved too many separate items to carry. Blocks of oatmeal, sugar and dried milk powder were used as 'instant' porridge.

Tinned bacon was available, but not popular with the troops, and was more trouble for the cooks. Tinned creamed potatoes were also tried, but were not successful; however, potato flour was found useful for thickening soups and stews.

In barracks and training camps at home, the food was generally pretty good. On a smaller scale, such as in anti-aircraft units and searchlight detachments of no more than twelve men, it was not practical to provide a cook for each unit, so after consultation with J. Lyons & Co., their food was prepared at a command headquarters and sent to them to be reheated.

Cookery manuals were produced and updated regularly. These had numerous sections, including several titled 'dietary'. The first emphasised the importance of variety, and remarked that the government ration and the daily messing allowance should serve to provide a suitable and varied diet, but added that the men could pay for extras. Whenever possible, local seasonal supplies should be used. When part of a day's meat ration was to be used for the following day's breakfast, the menus should be carefully calculated to avoid similarity of dishes (e.g. not ham for dinner and bacon for breakfast). Dinner should always include a pudding or sweet dish, and the consistency of dishes should not be the same (e.g. not a meat pie followed by an apple pie). Soup and bread could be served as a filling first course, and was also cheap to produce where a stockpot was maintained; although dried soups were available by this time, they were not much used. The final consideration in planning meals was the weather and the type of work being done; for instance oatmeal or suet puddings were appropriate in cold weather or during periods of strenuous work, but in hot weather or for light duties, fruit salad was better.

Cakes, scones, meat or fish paste, cold meat, salad or fruit should be given for the tea meal at least four times a week, also popular (and cheap) were sultanas or currants, dates, dried figs or apricots. Other popular commodities which were also cheap were sago or tapioca pudding and Indian corn cobs (sweetcorn); Cape gooseberries (physalis) were seasonally desirable. Dripping could be substituted for butter at the tea meal twice a week, but it should ideally be obtained from the meat ration rather than purchased, as the former tasted better. Frozen fish was not normally issued in peacetime, but might be in wartime if properly defrosted. Beef or mutton sandwiches were suggested as a 'haversack' ration, but of course the cooks would need notice to prepare these in time. Finally, it was suggested that pulses (beans, peas and lentils) could be sprouted and instructions on how to do this on wet cloths were given; the resulting sprouts were considered a good preventer of scurvy.

Much emphasis was placed on cleanliness, general hygiene and the handling of refuse, which should always be put in lidded bins. The ground next to the refuse bins should be regularly sprinkled with lime or creosol to prevent pollution of the ground. At temporary halting places, refuse should be buried in a pit at least 4ft deep and at least 50 yards from a well or water source. The bottom of these pits should be loose soil, and a layer of soil should be added on top of the refuse every day. When the unit moved on, these pits should be filled in and the soil rammed down. Dry refuse, including bones, could be burnt in the firebox of cookers and ovens. The simple maxim applied to all this was 'burn what you can, bury what you can't'.

Cookhouses had to have a place to wash hands with soap, a nail brush and plenty of clean towels.

Catering advisers were kept up to date by a sequence of circulars. Most of these involved administrative matters such as visitations from senior officers, reports and staffing issues, but others were more practical. For instance, one dealt with the need to use detergents in the plate-washing machines after complaints were received about dirty plates; another commented on the fact that the new Stills type of boiler, meant to supply boiling water for tea, was not being used. It transpired that this was because many units lacked teapots, and were still making tea in buckets; the teapots were being manufactured as a matter of urgency. A longer circular dealt with the care of fresh milk.

A separate section in the manuals dealt with cooking in the field. It recommended that troops should be given basic instruction in cooking in mess tins so that they could cook for themselves in an emergency, and should be shown how to build walls of mess tins round a fire to avoid waste of fuel. These tins should never be put in direct contact with hot fires without liquid in them, as otherwise the solder might melt. The outside and base of mess tins should be covered with a layer of mud or grease, which made cleaning them easier. This section also included what should have been obvious, but perhaps wasn't: that the handles should be kept out of the fire!

Rationing

The army had to comply with the overall premise of the national rationing system, but was allowed to operate it differently. Unlike civilians, who were issued with a book of coupons for specific items, each unit's catering officer was allocated a number of points relating to the number of men in the unit, that number being certified by the CO. They did not have to be 'spent' on specific items, but represented a 'value' which the catering officer then used for whatever items he thought fit and could obtain. All nationally rationed foods had to be obtained under official direction from various bodies, including the Ministry of Food. Soldiers who were billeted on civilian households were issued with ration cards, which they had to hand over to the head of the household while they remained there.

Catering reforms

As a result of a report from the Honorary Catering Adviser, the Army Catering Corps (ACC) was set up in March 1941 to take over catering for the army. Part of its work was the training of cooks; at first the candidates for courses were selected from the ranks of trained soldiers, but later recruits who had enlisted as cooks, and boy soldiers, were taken for the nine-month course. The new organisation also recruited officers and NCOs; some were men who had worked in the hotel or catering industry before being called up. Many of the student cooks were female, conscripts from the ATS, who were part of a concerted effort to recruit female cooks.

The basic course was a combination of practice and theory, covering storage, hygiene and sanitation, kitchen layout in barrack situations and the field, the use of tools and other equipment, butchery and bakery, how to cook with improvised ovens, and how to improvise cooking utensils from empty tins. A single tin cut in half lengthways could have holes punched through it from the inside, and then became a colander or a cheese grater. One with the top and bottom removed, then flattened out, became a fish slice; others could be converted into scoops or saucepans.

Much emphasis was placed on the recovery of by-products of meat preparation, and charts were issued showing what could be done with various of these, apart from the obvious sale to contractors. In February 1941 it was calculated that these sales were worth some £300,000 per year, although some of this was used to pay for by-product inspectors. There was particular concern over swine fever and foot and mouth disease, after an outbreak in 1939 had been traced to an army camp in southern Britain, as a result of which a Messing By-Products Advisory Committee was set up. Other committees included a Kitchen Waste Committee and a Fat Melters' Advisory Committee.

Heavy recruitment throughout the war meant many new barracks and training facilities had to be built, and of course these required cooking and dining facilities, which equally obviously required knowledgeable planning and design. This was specialised knowledge, so consultants and contractors were engaged to advise and assist, including the firm of Benhams. During the war Benhams provided the army with 1,060 coal-fired ranges, 600 gas ranges, 8,000 hot closets, 2,500 dishwashing machines, 860 boiling pans, 150 pastry ovens, 300 roasting ovens and 1,325 steaming ovens.

Manuals for catering advisers who would be instructing contractors were issued, giving the basics and covering all the necessary information to prepare them for the task, from the necessary administrative personnel through the fabric and layout of the working space and other facilities to storage and staff facilities. Finally came the requirements for the officers' and sergeants' messes: all of the above plus stores for table linen, glassware and the silver plate cleaning room.

Messing officers had to attend a two and a half day course at the Army School of Cookery before commencing their duties. The course included numerous practical cooking demonstrations. Attendees were given a list of 'useful don'ts', including not slamming the oven door when making cakes, not leaving taps running, not using a fork to turn joints of meat, and 'don't hide dirt'! There was also a list of sixty-three hints on what to do when taking over the duties of messing officer. These mostly dealt with paperwork, but also suggested that during the winter months messing officers ensure that dried fruit was served at least once a month, as this produced a desirable laxative effect.

NAAFI

The Expeditionary Force Canteens had done a good job during the First World War, but it was felt that something more was needed. The NAAFI came into being in January 1921. During the Second World War its numbers of personnel rose from a pre-war 4,000 operating 600 canteens to over 100,000 personnel operating 7,000 canteens. It also controlled ENSA (Entertainment National Service Association).

Officers' food

This was a time when the social division between officers and other ranks was wide and fairly rigid. Mess etiquette was prescriptive, especially on formal occasions, and although there were some things specific to each regiment, others were general. Mess dress should be worn, and transgressions such as badly tied ties were punished, usually by a fine. Lateness was seriously frowned on, as was smoking before the proper time, and improper toasting (for instance with an empty glass). Toasts always started with the 'loyal' toast ('The King'), then any foreign dignitaries present, then down in rank order of other visitors and finally 'absent friends'. If the regiment had a deed of great valour in its history, there was usually a toast to that. Finally, no dogs were allowed in the officers' mess, but one suspects that the Irish wolfhound mascot of the Irish Guards had his own place in the sergeants' mess.

Messes were run by a mess committee, consisting of a president or chairman, a vice-president who was responsible for the toasts, a treasurer, a secretary, a wines member who kept the bar stocked, a house member responsible for furniture and the infrastructure, and an entertainments member responsible for parties or other special events. His duties included organising music on special occasions, using musicians from the regiment's band.

The rooms which comprised the mess were provided by the army, and usually consisted of a dining room, an ante room, a reception room and the necessary domestic arrangements (kitchen, storage, wine cellar and so on). Most of the older regiments had a separate room where their battle honours and silver, gold, china and glassware were displayed. The army provided a certain amount of furniture, but the mess committee had to find the rest. Members of the mess paid, as in a gentleman's club, an entry fee, an annual fee and their own drinks bills.

When in the field, officers ate apart from other ranks and with as much ceremony as the situation allowed, ranging from a formal mess in permanent or semi-permanent camps or headquarters, to a little group of officers sitting together on logs in the countryside.

Senior officers had some influence on the menu; for instance Field Marshall Montgomery was fond of rice pudding with strawberry jam, but otherwise abstemious. He liked plain food, and never ate ice-cream, preferring to finish with cheese and biscuits; he drank nothing but water with a meal. However, when hosting meals for equally senior officers of other nationalities, such as two Russian marshalls in Hamburg in May 1945, he insisted that a sumptuous meal including 'caviar' should be served. This was not the real thing, but actually sago pearls cooked in mushroom juice and anchovy essence.

The bromide myth
During the Second World War, British servicemen (and also those of other countries) were convinced that they were being fed bromide in their tea to suppress sexual urges. This, although persistent, is a complete myth; apart from anything else, while it might reduce interest in sex, it would also have reduced enthusiasm for anything else, including military action.

Abroad
Planners working on providing food outside the UK had, as well as logistical constraints, to consider climate and seasons, ranging from extreme cold to extreme heat, and either drought or very wet seasons. In permanent or semi-permanent headquarters abroad, cooking arrangements were generally the same as at home.

Cooking apparatus and food storage in the field
Mobile field bakeries consisted of up to sixteen ovens and could produce 30,000lb of bread per day. They needed only thirty 3-ton lorries when moving; this impressed the US army so much that they substituted this system for their own.

Three portable cookers were produced for cooking in the field. The largest could cook for up to 125 men, but were not suitable for use in the desert.

On a large scale, 45-gallon metal oil drums made good ovens or, with a few holes banged in the sides, a topless cooker over the top of which long skewers of food could be balanced. Sawed in half lengthways, sunk into the ground far enough for stability, and with some metal mesh on top, these could be used as a barbecue, for boiling pots of water or stew, or even for making toast if someone was there to keep an eye on it. At any location, camp kettles could be massed round a central fire; this was best if the kettles were arranged in a long 'U' shape with space for the fire in the middle, and the open end facing into the wind. The food took about 90 minutes to cook, and two camp kettles would produce meals for thirty-two men: potatoes in one, stew in another, more kettles cooked meat puddings, stew with dumplings, and green vege-tables for sixteen men. If the situation and the materials allowed, a semi-permanent fireplace could be built with bricks, with the central gap narrow enough to stand the kettles on top. The manual which described this, *Cooking in the Field*, even included a method of starting a fire if no small twigs were available: take a larger piece of wood and split one end down into slivers without cutting them off the main piece, then spread these slivers out and stand the wood on them before lighting.

On a small scale, it was better to cut a biscuit or jam tin to hold a camp kettle; sand soaked with 1pt petrol when ignited gave off enough heat to boil 3 gallons of water or heat 3 gallons of food, but there were frequent accidents resulting in burns if the cooks were careless. Filtered waste oil from vehicle sumps could also be used as fuel. Cooking could also be done using a mess tin over a punctured bucket full of coke or charcoal, or by standing the tin over some stones with an open fire underneath.

Two older cooking systems were still in use: the Soyer stove and the Aldershot oven. The Soyer stove was invented by the cook Alexis Soyer for use in the Crimea; it consisted of an upright metal drum with a firebox at the bottom and a cooking pot at the top. They were often used in groups of four or more, positioned with the flue outlets together, and a central flue formed of brickwork or flattened tins.

The Aldershot oven was larger and took longer to set up, but once operational it could bake bread (its main use) pies or roast meats. It consisted of several arched metal sections which were bolted together. They had to be positioned with the door facing the prevailing wind, ideally on a site which sloped towards the back to carry off rain. A shallow ditch was dug round them to aid drainage. The oven was then covered with clay or sods of turf. They were heated by lighting a wood fire inside then raking out the embers once the oven was hot enough for use. They were usually built in banks of several ovens, each being capable of baking fifty-four 2½lb loaves. They could be moved when dismantled, but they were mainly used for more permanent situations.

One other method of producing a hot meal was the self-heating tin, usually containing meat soup or sometimes cocoa. The food was in the outer part of the tin with an inner tube containing flammable chemicals; the seal was removed and the fuel could then be lit with a match or cigarette. However, it was essential to pierce the top of the outer tin as otherwise the tin might explode.

Proper food storage in the field was essential. The main concerns relating to the storage of food were that food stores should be camouflaged (important as it was thought the enemy could calculate the size of the army by the size of its food stores), keeping out vermin and insects, keeping the food cool in hot climates and protecting it from gas. The vermin could be excluded to a certain extent by keeping food in metal containers, or in stores lined with metal, but hungry rats will even chew through metal, so constant vigilance was required. On a larger scale, an underground meat and ice store could be excavated.

A pamphlet entitled *Measures to be taken for the Preservation of Supplies* gave storage times for various items: from chilled beef to tinned sardines.

There was some early concern about gas attacks; a training pamphlet on this classified gas into two types, the most dangerous of which were the so-called 'blister' gasses: mustard and lewisite. Food should be covered with ground sheets and unprotected food should be stored away from windows and preferably not on upper floors. If necessary, a complete field service ration was available in gas-proof packs, and a reserve of these should be kept at railheads.

When the BEF went to France, each man carried two days' rations for the voyage and landing, and another four days' rations were to be carried in all personnel ships; the first RASC company that went out took 200,000 field rations with it. It was expected that much of the necessary food would be supplied by French sources, especially fresh milk, eggs, vegetables and potatoes. There was an abundant supply of green vegetables in north-west Europe, which could be purchased locally in all except the hardest frosts.

The original plan was for a much smaller force than actually went. The RASC took only two base supply depots, two field bakeries and one field butchery. This seems to have been based on the assumption that supply installations would be ready and waiting for them. In the event, the troops arrived at least two days before the supply ships. The RASC found that there were no buildings ready and such space as might be usable was fiercely contested by other services. When the supply ships did start to arrive, many were found to be only half loaded and what they did have was not properly organised.

By the middle of November things were improving. The BSDs had stock for eight days, with four more on the way. The French did what they could from their own stocks, but this was not as much as had been requested, a situation complicated by the fact that the French ration was different to the British. Many of the supply depot staff had to spend their time on sourcing local supplies.

Egypt

Port Said had the biggest cold store at 3,000 tons until August 1940, when more stores were created and forty 10-ton portable containers were acquired. By March 1943, over 17,500 tons of space was available.

Troops in this area in earlier campaigns had been obliged to subsist on the unpopular 'battle ration', which consisted almost entirely of biscuit and tinned meat. In the campaign of autumn 1942 every effort was made to provide a better diet, with fresh meat and bread being sent as far forward as possible. Daily supplies of frozen meat were sent by train to Tobruk, and two field bakeries were established there in November. Fresh fruit and vegetables were sent to Tripoli and some fresh vegetables were obtained there and at Benghazi.

When British troops arrived at Suez in 1941, mobile cookhouse vans gave each man a mugful of beef stew, a couple of biscuits and tea. About 20 miles into the country they received bully beef, sweet potatoes, rice pudding and an orange. The NAAFI supplied fried eggs, sausages, sweet potatoes and tea. Rations were issued at platoon headquarters: for each six men, there were four tins of beef, one tin of milk, one tin of cheese, six oranges and a 7lb tin of strawberry or gooseberry jam (alternated weekly with margarine). Occasionally there was a tin of treacle. Once they moved into Libya, they might also receive pilchards, baked beans, soya links, bacon or sausages, biscuits, tea, sugar, rice, porridge oats, dried fruit, dehydrated carrots and sometimes loaves from the army bakery.

Otherwise it was the staple diet of bully beef and hard biscuit, which some described as a 'cross between Cream Crackers and Dog Biscuits'. One soldier described the process of distributing desert rations in his diary. Each morning, carrying sacks, canisters and empty water cans, they accompanied their corporal to platoon HQ for rations. Basic piles of rations for each section of six men had already been assembled by the sergeants. The monotonous and unpalatable diet was made worse by the quality of the water, so heavily saline that the milk curdled. The troops in North Africa created a brew known as 'char': very strong tea drunk with condensed milk and as much sugar as possible to disguise the taste of the water. Brewing 'desert char' was a consoling ritual: thousands of little groups of men could be seen gathered round a fire tin and a brew can, their mugs arranged on the ground with tinned milk and sugar already added.

At other landings, a 48-hour mess-tin ration was available. By 21 December there were twenty-three days' of compo rations and six days' bulk rations in store, for a force of 170,000 men; this soon increased to 300,000. Philippeville and Bone had BSDs supplied by ships and trains, but the need for rapid turnaround meant unloading was hasty, commodities were mixed and there were many damaged cases and much pilfering.

These rations were only intended for short periods of time, but in Egypt the supply of fresh foods was extremely limited, and without fresh meat or vegetables the troops fell ill. There was a joke about bully beef and biscuits leading to constipation which could only be cured by a German bombing raid. More seriously, the troops began to suffer from dysentery and vitamin deficiency diseases. Huge cargoes of tinned fruit were brought up from South Africa to provide the troops with much-needed vitamins and fibre. In Egypt, Palestine, Cyprus, Syria and Iraq the British army started potato-growing schemes, provided the farmers with seed potatoes and guaranteed them a purchase price. Special vegetable farms were also set up, cultivated by African pioneer troops. These measures alleviated the health problems of men stationed behind the front line, but for those in combat a prolonged period on bully beef and biscuits affected their ability to fight. The limited transport capacity of the supply lines and the absolute priority placed on petrol to sustain the campaign meant that it was out of the question to send up bulky meat and vegetables. The men were urged to take vitamin B and C tablets along with the salt pills which were issued to counteract the effects of the heat, but the problem of ensuring that these were swallowed by small and isolated detachments was not easily solved, so lime juice and tinned fruits were issued instead. More condensed milk, margarine, bacon and oatmeal were supplied with onions and chutney to add some flavour to the food.

There was a 'vehicle' ration for use if a vehicle became stranded in the desert for several days. All carried three days' 'hard rations' and water for the crew: tins of beef, biscuits, tea, sugar and milk, frequently packed in an empty petrol tin. Their condition was not improved by bumping about the desert for several weeks.

Fresh meat and fresh bread were provided for as many men and as far forward as possible. Frozen meat was sent daily to Tobruk by rail, and a cold storage plant was built at Benghazi. Fresh fruit and potatoes were shipped from Egypt to Tripoli; it proved impossible to ship fresh vegetables satisfactorily, but supplies were available at Benghazi and Tripoli.

There was one major case of food poisoning in September 1941 when 105 men, who had all breakfasted three hours previously from the same cookhouse, were suddenly stricken with acute abdominal pains, vomiting, diarrhoea and in many cases, collapse. They were all admitted to hospital and treated within an hour of the onset of symptoms. There were no deaths and all returned to duty within three days. The source of infection was found to be the sausages issued for breakfast; the cook had taken the sausages from their tins the evening before, put them all together in one baking dish and kept them in the oven overnight. At least one tin must have been contaminated. The harm was very much aggravated by the twelve hours of incubation in the oven and consequent enormous increase in toxic output.

East Africa
Rations in East Africa were generally reckoned to be adequate and good quality. Ample fresh vegetables were available locally, but transport and distribution were difficult and fresh supplies often reached forward areas in poor condition. In addition, the army in East Africa was comprised of men from various parts of the continent and each set had its own ration scale. At one time, there two European scales, three Indian and six different African scales. This caused some supply difficulties and after a while three consolidated

scales were adopted, one for each ethnic group. Later a scale for Somalis was added. The European scale provided 4,403 calories per day (much of this from the large ration of meat and bread required by the South Africans), the Indian scale 4,258 calories and the African 3,634.

West Africa

The West Africa command was made up of what had been four separate colonies: Gambia, Sierra Leone, Gold Coast and British West Africa. Each was a separate entity and they were all widely separated geographically; there were no rail connections between them, and only a few roads which went through French territory, so sea or air was the only practical route between the colonies. The climate was problematical, with heat and damp and various pests, which all affected supplies, not to mention the unfortunate personnel. There was no supply and transport organisation except a small RAF detachment on shore.

A bacon factory was established in Gold Coast; the meat was safe if properly cured and properly handled, but other meats such as sausage meat were not and had to be consumed on the day they were issued.

Here, as well as the British troops, there were native West African troops to be fed. They were quite difficult to feed as they came from a wide area and preferred the food they were used to at home. For some the staple was rice or cassava, for others it was yam. Kola nuts were so popular that they had to be shipped to India and Burma when the 81st and 82nd (West African) regiments went there. Other items on their ration included sorghum, yam flour, cassava, plantains, palm oil, peanuts and yams.

Samples of jams from local fruits were sent to the War Office analyst. He reported that banana was not suitable, and pineapple too acid, but recommended guava as it had a high Vitamin C content, and suggested that as well as making jam with it on its own, it should be added to other types of jam.

Cattle were bought from the French at £7 per head and marched to their destination, but up to 50 per cent were lost on the march, so in 1944 new arrangements were made whereby the army paid £10–£12 per head on delivery, the contractors being responsible for the delivery. A 1,000-acre vegetable farm was set up at Media on the Gold Coast and supplied all that was needed. The Fulani tribesmen of Mauretania were reluctant to sell their beloved cattle, but finally exchanged some for cloth.

Madagascar

In May 1942 two brigades en route to the Middle East were diverted to Madagascar to keep the Japanese from spreading further west. At the close of the campaign, there were about 9,000 European troops, 400 Asians and 17,500 Africans. One of the principal industries of Madagascar was meat canning, so there was no difficulty obtaining fresh meat. However, all this beef came from the local humped cattle, and some British troops thought the hump was caused by disease, and were reluctant to eat the meat. After 9 May, when a contract for supply had been negotiated, bread was issued the day after baking, but fresh fruit and vegetables had to wait until the populace, who had hidden in the bush, were persuaded to come out. The 4- hour mess-tin ration had proved adequate, except for things like chocolate, cheese and dripping spread, which melted in the heat.

Sicily
Following the successful conquest of North Africa, Sicily was the obvious first step on the route to Italy. Operation Husky commenced on 10 July 1943. All assault troops carried the emergency ration and there were 48-hour 'compo' rations available in the beach depots from the fourth day. The initial force numbered 60,000, which grew to 172,000 by the end of the fourteenth day. There were field butcheries and field bakeries; each of the latter were set up and produced 30,000lb of bread per day.

Italy
This campaign started on 3 September 1943 and continued until November when the Italian government asked for an amnesty. The population was friendly and cooperative. The feeding strength was 450,000, a figure which included some 276,000 prisoners of war until these were sent to North Africa as a labour force.

There were ample supplies of fresh fruit, and vegetables were fairly plentiful in the country districts, but dairy produce (butter, cheese and eggs) were scarce. Other shortages included tinned bacon and other items from America. There was no supply of frozen meat until Italian ports were captured and cold storage could be arranged.

When the Allied troops advanced to Salerno, they were given a 48-hour mess-tin ration or compo rations for two weeks, then half compo and half field rations, gradually increasing to 100 per cent field rations. By the end of September, compo rations stopped, fresh bread was available and there were plenty of eggs. Meat was available on the hoof, from Sardinia; there was plenty of fish and seasonal fruit and vegetables. Potatoes were scarce but there was plenty of spaghetti.

India
Although the British army presence had been much reduced throughout the world between the wars, one place where it was still prominent was India, where many of the regiments were manned by native Indians. Given their different religious allegiances, there were some difficulties in providing food: Muslims would not eat pig meat or other meat that had not been prepared to be halal, Hindus would not eat any form of cow meat and Buddhists were

vegetarian. Added to this were various caste prohibitions, which forbade some castes from eating food that had been touched by other castes, especially the 'sweepers' and 'untouchables' who did the lowliest cleaning jobs. All this, combined with the generally poor standard of hygiene among the natives who assisted the British cooks, meant that even stricter rules pertained in this country than elsewhere.

In theory, foodstuffs produced in India should have been easily obtained, but in late 1942 food grains were in short supply and flour had to be rationed. Later that year the situation became serious, with shortages of rice, atta, ghee and tinned milk, vegetables and fruit. By the end of 1942 the supply of grain products was clearly short of the country's own needs, so it was difficult to get what was needed for British troops. Attempts to produce cheese, jam and dried vegetables were not successful, partly because of the climate and partly because the manufacturing and packing materials were not available.

When the *Manual of Army Catering* was first issued in September 1943, there were fourteen pages applicable to India, which included a detailed list of the many edible fruits and vegetables which were indigenous to the country. Salads were often forbidden by medical advice, due to the risk of tropical disease.

The section on the kitchens/cookhouses emphasised scrupulous cleanliness. Cookhouses should be well-lit and ventilated, the floors should be paved with stone, cement or tiles and the walls should be whitewashed at regular intervals. Cleanliness was the cook's responsibility, and no sweepers were to be allowed into the kitchens. Doors were to have springs so they closed automatically, and should not be propped open, the wire screens of doors and windows should be kept in good repair to keep out flies. A note adds that all personnel should be aware that flies carry disease, and so all efforts should be made to exterminate them and all food protected from them.

Fresh meat on the hoof (cattle, sheep and/or goats) was easily found. For British troops these were slaughtered at field butcheries and sent as dressed meat, but for other troops they were sent live and slaughtered under 'unit arrangements'. In warm weather the butchered meat could be sent in limited quantities in insulated lorries with ice.

By the middle of 1944, frozen meat (principally mutton) was delivered into cold store in Calcutta and flown to Benares and Assam, which enabled fresh meat to be provided three times a week.

Ceylon

In 1943 the only ACC personnel were those who had gone with the AA units or had transferred to the corps while in the command. An English lady, a graduate in domestic science, ran the School of Cookery with a capacity of six British and six East African or Ceylonese trainees. Most cooks were Indians or civilians. Although some vegetables were obtained from India, a 100-acre vegetable farm was cut out of the jungle, and a pig farm was acquired; cows, poultry and rabbits were soon added. This produced 2,500lb pork, 500 gallons of milk and 400 eggs per month, from 20 cows, 476 pigs and 90 chickens.

The vegetable farm proved popular, in more situations than had been expected: on one occasion, a rogue elephant pushed a vegetable truck on its side and proceeded to eat much of the contents.

Burma

During 1943–44 steps were taken in India to maintain a supply of fresh meat for British and Indian troops in Burma by sending train loads of cattle, sheep and goats from as far west as Benares. However, time, distance and unavoidable transhipment of animals at the changes of rail gauge, and long marches which were sometimes necessary to reach the forward areas, made it difficult to deliver sufficient quantities of meat in good condition.

Practical experience led to publication of part two of the *Manual of Army Catering Services*, which included seven pages on 'Living in Jungle Country', listing the natural foods available and the uses of bamboo to make cooking and water containers, cups, plates and spoons. The water container was a section of bamboo with a natural closure each end, one end punctured and then stopped with leaves; with a strip of the outer bark to make a carrying loop.

Details of wild food were also issued: in coastal areas these included fish and eels, shellfish and crabs. In tropical forest areas, with the exception of emergency protein substitutes such as bee and wasp grubs, ants eggs and white ant queens (scalded and fried in a little fat they were said to be quite palatable), these consisted mainly of roots (including taro and sweet potato), leaves, bamboo shoots and wild fruit such as figs, berries and nuts.

The 14th Army in Burma found that although the ration scale for troops was theoretically adequate, the rations issued were extremely poor; fresh meat was rarely available, nor were eggs. Soya 'links' (sausages with a high soya meal content) were issued as a substitute for many commodities. Fresh vegetables of the English type were available only in the four-month cold season; for fresh fruit, oranges only were issued from December to April, some pineapples in July and August, and plantains the rest of the year. However, one enterprising catering adviser initiated a scheme of air-dropping cooked rations, and for Christmas 1944 a twelve-man hamper of cooked chicken, ham, sausage rolls, mince pies, cheese biscuits and iced cakes was dropped daily. During March, April and May, a daily drop was made of 5,000 portions of sausage rolls, cakes and buns.

Orde Wingate's 'Chindit' force encountered some problems not found outside close jungle terrain; troops had to carry their own rations to sustain them for several weeks. Much of this consisted of tinned meat, tinned milk, biscuits and sugar with a little tinned fruit. Although insect-proof, gas-proof, climate-proof and bad-cook-proof, these tinned rations were heavy and un-inspiring over a long period, and delivered a mere 2,500 calories a day. Theoretically this could be made up by foraging, but in practice there was little to forage. The troops soon developed what was called 'the Chindit syndrome' of hunger and fatigue, loss of weight, vulnerability to infection, malaria and diarrhoea. They were known to other troops as 'the shitty Chindits'. Wingate himself was an advocate of raw onions, eating five or six a day, and he believed this was why he did not develop the ubiquitous jungle sores, but raw onions were not available to most of his troops.

Malaya

Until 1940 British troops were fed partly by the RASC and partly via the NAAFI. The RASC achieved their targets partly through local contracts in Australia, but also obtained preserved meat and biscuit via the War Office, shipped from Britain. Other items, including frozen meat, flour, tinned milk and butter went from the country of production through the Ministry of Food.

Field service rations

Field service rations were designed to provide food for troops on the move with no access to a fixed cookhouse or mobile kitchen. They consisted of tinned or dried items, or items such as biscuit which were naturally dry. Apart from contents, which differed according to the location, they were supplied in different sizes, from those for one man for one day, to those to feed groups of men up to fourteen or twenty strong, with a unit cook to deal with them. For these larger packs, there was some variety of contents and most were divided into three separate meals for the day.

Pacific rations

These included fruit bars, chewing gum, chocolate, lemon crystals, mepacrine (anti-malarial) tablets, salt tablets, combined vitamin tablets, cigarettes and matches, and at the end of the list, instruction leaflets and latrine paper. These rations were packed nine tins to a flat camouflaged wooden case weighing just under 40lb.

There were two versions of the Pacific ration, one for one man for twenty-four hours, the other for six men. The first was packed so that each meal used complete packages so the man did not have to carry half-consumed items.

The other was the Pacific compo ration, intended for the post-assault period and in conditions where issuing bulk rations was impractical. Each tin was packed in its own little cell, like egg boxes. There were seven versions of this ration, each containing six man-rations for one day.

Arctic or mountain ration packs were packed in a circular tin with the contents selected to provide a 5,000-calorie diet (about 1,000 more than the other packs) and to withstand extreme cold. Items included rolled oats, pemmican to replace the normal tinned meat, and Vitamin C tablets. The usual matches were replaced by special flare matches which would light and stay lit in high winds, and special fuel starters for the pressure cookers which were the standard type of heating for arctic conditions. Between September 1941 and December 1942, 2,800,000 of these packs were produced.

North-east Africa

It became necessary to reorganise the packing order of the larger ration packs, as they were otherwise opened to get at the chocolate and not closed properly, which was an invitation to pilfering.

Towards the end of the North African campaign, the quartermaster came up with a marked improvement on the endless bully beef and biscuits. This consisted of rations for fourteen men for a day, packed into one box. Inside were tinned steak and kidney puddings, steamed puddings, soup, chocolate, sweets and English brands of cigarettes and tobacco. These 'compo' rations became standard British ration issue during the campaigns in Italy and north-east Europe. Nevertheless, they were no substitute for fresh food, and once the Allies captured parts of Italy in 1943 they promptly supplemented their tins with eggs and fresh fruit and vegetables, including grapes and tomatoes from the fields.

Six-man compo ration packs weighed no more than 35lb. They were completely weatherproof and watertight, and the packaging had to be strong enough to stand heavy handling and air-dropping. They were made with rounded edges for comfort when carried on the back. Special packs included Tommy cookers, matches, water sterilising kits and insect repellent.

Later, a twelve-man pack was produced, then a one-man two-day pack, containing a tin of meat, a packet of biscuits and a portion of cheese. This was lightweight and fitted easily into a haversack, or inside a standard mess tin. There was also a small tin of mixed tea, sugar and powdered milk. This was known as the 48-hour ration pack. Later a small 'Tommy' cooker was added, then chewing gum to help saliva production, salt tablets to counter the effects of excessive sweating, and sugar tablets for those who preferred sweeter tea. Some 7,500,000 of these packs were produced.

Jungle rations

The best of all the packs were those for fourteen men, a development of the twelve-man pack. Some 10,000,000 of these were produced between 1942 and 1945. The objective was to provide three meals: breakfast, dinner and a substantial evening meal, including some items which could be used as a snack during short halts. The contents could be eaten cold, but a Tommy cooker was always included. There were seven variations of this pack, so they did not become monotonous. After a while puddings were included, the most popular being rice pudding and mixed fruit pudding as second favourite. Red salmon and tinned fruit were always popular.

There were also seven varieties of a six-man one-day pack. The actual pack was a sectionalised wooden case which protected each tin from weather and handling damage. There were three hermetically sealed containers, offering breakfast, a light midday meal and supper. There were twenty-four items altogether, including biscuits, a block of oatmeal, chocolate, a meat bar, salt tablets and sweets. Some 15,000,000 of these packs were produced from November 1944 to October 1945.

'K' rations

British troops serving alongside American troops often received 'K' rations, so-called because they were invented by Dr Ancel Keys. These were highly concentrated, but British troops found them boring.

This ration was also divided into the three daily meals, containing biscuit, sugar, meat, fruit bars, lemon powder, chewing gum, cigarettes, matches and toilet paper. When the ration was provided for Indian troops, tinned tuna or salmon was substituted for the meat and cereal for the candy. The other items were bouillon powder, chocolate bars, candy and coffee. The whole thing was self-contained, wrapped in wax paper.

Water

In India and south-east Asia, if no water was available locally, transport was needed. Each man needed 5 gallons per day, of which two were for drinking. If animals were being used, they needed 10 gallons per day each.

In Egypt, vehicle radiators in desert conditions needed 10 gallons per 2 or 3-ton lorry, and 4 gallons per 30cwt truck. Special water tank vehicles had 150-gallon water tanks, or two smaller tanks could be carried by a camel. There were also local permanent tanks called birs. None of these sufficed: the birs had no underground sources, but depended on rain. There had been many of these, some dating back to Roman times, but many had fallen into disrepair. They could be seen from long distances; spoil from the original excavation and sand from countless cleanings had produced landmarks.

For third-line bulk distribution, 350-gallon water cistern lorries were used, but these were not really suitable for second-line use because of the delay in decanting. From the second line forward, 2-gallon cans were used, specially made for this in the Nile Delta.

Water was needed for drinking, tea-making, cooking, washing up in cook-houses, plus washing of people and clothes. Eventually the Royal Engineers installed a pipeline from Alexandria to Matrah, later extending this to Mischiefa. There were a limited number of 350-gallon vehicles, so 300-gallon square tanks were bolted onto Chevrolet chassis. As a last resort, 44-gallon drums of water were carried in ordinary lorries. They also used what they called sportapools, which were like a larger version of a child's paddling pool. Despite canvas covers supposed to disguise them from the air, reduce evaporation and keep out dust, the dust got in and the end product was beverages which all looked and tasted the same.

Large stocks of new petrol cans were held at Slough until a worried movement control officer rang to say the troops on the beaches at Dunkirk were desperate for drinking water. Within a few hours, 60,000 of these new cans were on their way to Dover where they were filled with drinking water and sent on to Dunkirk.

In the Western Desert during final operations, eight Water Tank Companies were deployed. With sixty tanks per company, each of 300 gallons, this gave a total lift of 18,000 gallons per trip. Maximum tank capacity was 350 gallons, but the lower figure was used to allow for spillage during filling, or leakage en route, and there was always a little left when they were meant to be empty. Each company actually had sixty-six vehicles, to allow for 10 per cent spare.

General

The use of jerricans as water containers on mules was suggested, but Middle East Command pointed out that a mule load was 80lb each side; since a full jerrican weighed 50lb, there was 'wasted space'. A full 2-gallon can weighed 20lb, so with four of these on each side a mule could carry 160lb, and the smaller cans were also easier to handle. Other objections to jerricans were that using them for water would cause interior rusting (a major cause of can wastage), and that there was a risk of confusion, ending with water in vehicle petrol tanks. Eventually a suitable lining was found, and water containers were painted brown (petrol cans were olive drab) with 'WATER' embossed in 2in letters on each side of the can and the top painted white to aid recognition at night.

Chapter 13

Medical Matters

Rather more than had been the case in the First World War, in the Second World War both medics and military men were united in their desire to do what was necessary to maintain the army in good health. As well as ensuring that the troops were well fed, this included paying attention to basic hygiene, especially in hot countries. Dedicated units made sure that proper latrines were provided for both military personnel and local civilians, and that those civilians were inoculated against common diseases, while ensuring that local water supplies were as pure as possible.

Apart from this, the main work of the medical services fell into two basic categories: treating the wounded and treating the sick. As has been the case in most wars, including the Napoleonic Wars of 1793–1815, the number of hospital admissions from disease far exceeded those from injuries. Taken per 1,000 men on the strength, in south-east Asia in 1942 there were 702 admissions from disease, but only forty-nine from injuries, and in 1945, 418 from disease but only thirty-two from injuries. In the Middle East in 1939 it was 427 from disease and fifty from injuries, and at a similar year-on-year level to 1945 when it was 380 from disease and forty-one from injuries. In north-west Europe in 1944 it was 129 from disease and ninety-two from injuries, and in 1945, 163 from disease and sixty-four from injuries. This lower incidence in north-west Europe is almost certainly due to the climate and the lack of hot country pests such as mosquitoes and sand-flies.

Wounded

For the wounded the chain of treatment and evacuation started at the regimental aid posts. These were situated just behind the front line to receive walking wounded and those brought by stretcher from the battalion. It consisted of the battalion medical officer and some orderlies whom he had trained. Many of those who presented themselves at the aid posts needed little more than some bandaging and a few days' rest while the wound healed before they could return to duty.

For the others, the next stop was a casualty clearing station (CCS). These were the first units on the line of evacuation behind the firing line and the first at which full medical and surgical facilities were available. There was usually one casualty clearing station per division. Their staff included doctors, specialist surgeons, radiologists and anaesthetists, and also some nursing sisters. When busy, they were often reinforced by staff from general hospitals. Their main function was to sort and send on casualties as quickly as possible. Wherever possible, they were situated on main roads or railways, often relying on special ambulance trains.

Medical transport units were originally commanded by an RAMC officer. As well as their headquarters, they consisted of three sections of twenty-five motor ambulances. Their main function was to carry casualties to CCSs, which they often did in convoys of up to twenty-five vehicles. From a CCS, patients were sent on to general hospitals.

These hospitals, initially of either 600 beds or 1,200 beds, were established in large enough numbers to provide hospital beds for 6 per cent of the force. These hospitals were normally situated at the bases and on the lines of communication, but might be grouped together in a special base easily accessible to an embarkation port. They were fully equipped hospitals with facilities to diagnose and treat every kind of disease and injury, each having a medical and surgical division. Some were specialised to deal with specific types of disease or psychiatric casualties. Most casualties were treated at these hospitals, but those who required prolonged treatment were often sent back to Britain.

Men who were no longer in need of hospital treatment, but were not yet recovered enough to go back to their units, were moved to convalescent depots. These could hold up to 1,000 patients. The purpose of these depots was to prepare men to return to their units, and they received regular physiotherapy and military training under medical supervision.

Field ambulance units consisted of a headquarters and two companies, each providing stretcher squads to move casualties from the regimental aid posts. They could also establish an advanced dressing station for urgent treatment such as the treatment of shock and immobilisation of fractures. The headquarters had more advanced equipment and could establish a main dressing station a few miles behind the advanced dressing stations. Casualties were usually taken to the main dressing station by ambulance vehicles belonging to the unit, where they were inspected and their documentation was completed, and urgent attention could be given if needed. Serious medical cases and surgical cases were then sent to CCSs.

Other methods of moving casualties included ambulance trains. In France, these trains, which were made of coaches converted from LMS stock, consisted of sixteen coaches with a total length of 360 yards, pulled by a French locomotive. Each train had three medical officers, three nursing sisters and forty-five other ranks. They had two tiers of bunks on each side. They were heated by steam from the engine, but this did not always reach the rear carriages. There was a tendency for the steam to condense in the pipes when the train returned to base, and unless this was cleared by the use of compressed air from the brakes, in winter it froze and took several hours to thaw.

American jeep ambulances carried sitting patients inside and one on a stretcher secured across the top of the bonnet. Ordinary jeeps could carry three stretcher cases, on top of the bonnet or across the back seats. Three-quarter ton weapons carriers could also be used, carrying five stretcher cases: three on the top tier at right angles to the road, and two on the bottom tier parallel to the road.

For troops serving overseas, there were aeroplanes, hospital carriers and hospital ships. These were vessels specially adapted to carry casualties from overseas bases to British ports, or sometimes to large hospitals in foreign ports. The carriers operated only over short distances and had limited treatment facilities, much like an ambulance train, whereas the hospital ships were like large floating general hospitals.

These arrangements were much the same as those which had been used in the First World War, and after a couple of years it was realised that they were not right for the new type of warfare, in which troops were more mobile and needed different medical units to serve them. In October 1941, the War Office organised a special committee, chaired by Major-General W.C. Hartgill. This committee's report was issued in Decmber of that year, and stressed that surgical and other specialists should be moved closer to the fighting troops. The director-general of the army medical services, Alexander Hood, commented that:

> Modern war ... has necessitated changes in the Field Medical Units. The object has been to produce a flexible organisation of mobile and elastic units capable of treating and evacuating casualties under any conditions.

The committee had concluded that there were four main defects of the current organisation: field medical units were cumbersome, insufficiently mobile and not easily adaptable to the tactical situation; field ambulances lacked adequate means of communication internally or with their parent formations; casualties were not sent straight to appropriate units but passed through a chain of evacuation which caused congestion in the forward areas while insufficient transportation led to delay in the distribution of casualties to selected centres; and finally surgeons with their assistants and equipment were located too far to the rear.

The committee revised the evacuation system to reduce the number of stages through which casualties should pass. The main feature of the new system was to classify the casualty as far forward as possible, and evacuate him straight to the most appropriate medical unit in the rear. For this purpose, casualties were divided into groups:

- Group one was those exhibiting severe shock and urgently needing resuscitation. They were sent immediately to a field dressing station which had facilities for resuscitation, usually based on a field transfusion unit. They were manned by one medical officer and three other ranks.
- Group two cases were those needing immediate surgical attention, including wounds to the chest or abdomen or severe or complicated fractures. They went straight to the advanced surgical centre.
- Group three, which constituted the majority of cases, were sent to a CCS.

The field dressing stations might have different functions depending on whether they were located in a corps or divisional area. They were provided at a rate of one for each armoured division and two for infantry divisions; their primary function was the treatment of severe shock. In corps areas they were allocated at a rate of one per corps, but were employed mainly in surgical centres.

Casualty clearing stations were given some mobility by adding a platoon of RASC men and more large lorries, which allowed these stations to be moved in no more than three days. With this mobility, the CCSs added a second surgical team. As they were intended to function closer to the fighting than before, the nursing sisters were withdrawn. These new CCSs were allocated at the rate of two per corps with one extra for each army.

Motor ambulance units were reorganised as a unit of the RASC, since they were primarily transport units and it was thought it would be better for them to be commanded by an officer with experience of the technicalities of transport and vehicle maintenance. They still included a platoon of RAMC other ranks to attend casualties.

The role of the general hospitals was revised. Those of 600 or 1,200 beds were felt to be too cumbersome for mechanised warfare, and new 200-bed hospitals were created at a rate of one per corps. They were situated at railheads or airheads.

In the Western Desert of North Africa, there was a strong feeling that casualties from the forward CCSs should be evacuated by air, but until late in 1942 little provision had been made for this. There were no forward aerodromes, and even the few casualties who could be taken by air had to go on returning transport aircraft, and often had to be driven long distances to them.

In Italy, most casualties were evacuated by air to Naples: some 4,670 in eleven days at the end of May and beginning of June 1944. As before, this was dependant on convenient airfields and many patients had to begin their journey by road.

As the Allies moved north through Italy, pushing the enemy before them, air evacuation continued, but care had to be taken over the routes used by the pilots. The routes up the eastern coast and across the central plain were good; as long as the weather was kind they were able to fly below 2,000 feet without changes in atmospheric pressure, ensuring a smooth passage. The route across the Apennines was a different matter, as they had to fly above 7,000 feet, and the journey was so turbulent that it had to be restricted to limb and flesh wounds only, as patients with head, chest and abdominal injuries suffered too much from the turbulence.

By the middle of 1940, the medical services were seeing numerous burn cases from igniting fuel and flash burns, especially in tank crews. This was not a surprise and the first aid kits issued to tank crews included tannic jelly. When applied quickly this improved the patient's outcome. However, Vaseline was better for facial burns as the tannic solutions tended to leave deep stains. Later, in North Africa, it became standard practice to use penicillin, often in the form of a powder which could be dusted on and helped prevent infection in burns and other wounds. Plastic surgery was often needed for severe burn cases, which were common among tank crews. They rarely wore anti-flash clothing because the interiors of tanks were especially hot. But most burns were the result of accidents from using petrol as a cooking fuel.

During the period between the two world wars, medicine, and in particular wound care, had been developing steadily. One 'new' method which showed particularly good results was that of treating compound fractures (i.e. those where there was an open wound as well as the broken bones), by what was called 'the closed method' of treatment. Instead of frequently examining and redressing the wound, the damaged limbs were completely covered in plaster and left to heal without frequent applications of antiseptics. With this method, not only did the limbs heal more quickly, but there was also a very low incidence of sepsis and gangrene.

Another major event which improved treatment of the severely wounded was the setting up of the Army Blood Transfusion Service. Collection of blood donated by civilians began in Bristol in the summer of 1939, but later supplies had to be obtained from soldiers in the field. It had been discovered at the beginning of the war that it was best to transfuse blood as soon as possible after the wound was received, as this helped minimise shock. After some field trials it was found that plasma had the same effect of reducing shock, but this required supplies of plasma which had to be provided from Bristol, while whole blood could be obtained more or less on the spot from willing troops. A number of Field Transfusion Units equipped with refrigerators for storing blood were established in 1942. These consisted of one medical officer and three other ranks, all specially trained in blood transfusion. They were allocated to other units as required, normally to field surgical units to form an advanced surgical centre.

Work at the end of the First World War and between the wars had shown that shock was not just caused by loss of blood through wounds, but also by concentration of blood in the capillaries, thus removing it from circulation. Transfusion of whole blood, plasma and saline solution helped maintain good blood pressure and relieved the consequent shortage of oxygen.

In the mountainous terrain of Greece and Crete, evacuated wounded could take up to twenty-four hours to reach the ports or railways, so they were taken in stages, stopping to rest at CCSs along the way, often being transported by mule. But the hospitals in Athens were full of wounded men from the fighting in Macedonia, a situation which not only created medical difficulties, but also made the hospitals vulnerable to bombardment. Many patients were evacuated from Greece to Crete, but then had to be moved again when Crete itself had to be evacuated, with many men going to Egypt.

Evacuation of casualties from the interior of the Western Desert over the long lines of communication was difficult, and it was equally difficult to site hospitals as it was rarely possible in the desert to find places with adequate water supplies and electric light. Most of the main hospitals were in the Canal Zone, the Nile delta or Cairo. Where the lines of communication were very long (up to 500 miles in Libya) it became necessary to provide more forward treatment centres. There were ambulance trains on the railways and these were given priority, but the railways were a prime target for attack. There were also hospital ships at Mersa Matruh and Tobruk, but at Tobruk the patients had to be transferred by lighter as the harbour was not big enough for the large hospital ships. Evacuation by train was slow, despite daily trains, but the average journey was six days. A few patients were moved by air.

In a few cases, looted Italian lorries were converted into mobile surgical units. Mobile operating theatres could be improvised by putting two motor ambulances back to back, with a canvas awning closing off the gap. These, and the other casualty clearing stations, were known as Field Surgical Units (FSU), and made it possible to give surgical attention in no more than twelve hours. These units were gradually modified to improve their mobility until by the end of the desert campaign the main dressing stations were reorganised with additional vehicles to provide one medical unit at brigade headquarters. However, the only vehicles allocated to regimental medical units were more 15cwt lorries with no protection from hostile fire of bullets or artillery shells. At the insistence of medical officers, medical units were finally issued with armoured scout cars to enable them to keep up with the rapid movement of troops. Until Montgomery was appointed these medical officers were rarely informed in advance of movements, but Montgomery insisted that they should be properly briefed.

By 1941 it had become standard practice to conduct preliminary operations on patients with facial and jaw injuries. These were then evacuated to specialised maxillofacial units. It was said by the army's standing committee on maxillofacial surgery that it was 'only by the earliest treatment that severe deformity and loss of function could be obviated or mitigated'. The War Office had decided in 1935 that a special unit maxillofacial hospital should be located in every theatre of war.

In major cases, the first event on a patient's arrival at these units was dental treatment, followed if necessary by skin or bone grafting. The most difficult skin-grafting cases were evacuated to the UK, where there were more facilities and speedier recovery than in the Middle East. There was also less scarring in cases treated at home, although Vitamin C was found to help. Wags renamed the maxillofacial units 'Max Factor Units'.

In north-west Africa the British army landed its medical units at the same time as the troops and they were able to handle battle casualties straight away. The Americans did not take sufficient hospital accommodation with them and so had to rely on the British. The British had 9,300 beds in general hospitals in or close to the coastal bases at Algiers, Bougie, Philippeville and Bone. There were also smaller units such as casualty clearing stations, field surgical teams, neurosurgery and maxillofacial surgery units. They met with some resistance from the French medical teams, many of whom were Vichy sympathisers, and ended up staffing the hospitals with their own people.

The first task was dealing with casualties from the Tunisian plain. The troops were fairly static and this enabled the casualty clearing stations to group together and pass wounded between them. Low priority casualties went straight to the general hospitals, while others received immediate surgical attention. In one week in early May 1943, over 5,600 casualties were seen at the hospital group at Thibar and over 1,040 surgical operations were performed. Evacuating casualties was easier there than in the Western Desert; there were ambulance cars and hospital trains, and American aircraft evacuated over 16,000 British and American troops during the battle for Tunisia. The field surgical units were also better than those in the Western desert, having good electric lighting and twenty beds apiece.

First aid was carried out close to the battlefield, with broken limbs immobilised by the 'Tobruk splint'. This was a variation on the Thomas splint, which had two side bars with a padded ring at one end and a cross bar at the other, allowing traction to be applied. It was modified by an unknown medical officer, who having applied the Thomas splint, covered the whole thing in plaster of Paris. This allowed the patient to be moved in comfort.

This was particularly valuable as many of the wounds were the result of shrapnel, with complex lacerations.

In Italy in 1944, the hospital at Anzio filled with patients suffering from multiple shrapnel and bullet wounds and surgeons had the ongoing and unenviable task of triage. By early June the Germans had retreated beyond Rome and the field surgical units had moved forward with the Allied troops; during this time the field surgical units had little to do, as the ambulances often found themselves stuck in traffic jams. The roads were narrow, with mines on the sides, and many bridges had been destroyed. None of this was helped by the result of several weeks of heavy rain, making minor routes unusable with embankments washed away. Once the roads were usable again, most cases were brought to field surgical units within sixteen hours.

There was a marked difference in the casualties from the two main types of tank: the Cromwell and the Sherman. In tanks hit by artillery fire, an average of 55 per cent of the crews in Cromwells escaped unhurt, as opposed to 35 per cent in Shermans, and a greater number of casualties died from their injuries (46 per cent) as opposed to 33 per cent in Cromwells. However, the Cromwells were more vulnerable to mines as their floor plates were only half as thick as those of the Shermans.

For the Army Radiological Service in 1939–40 in France, unreliable electricity supplies in hospitals meant the old X-ray sets could not be used until the Royal Engineers reorganised the supply. However, it was found that experienced surgeons did not need X-rays before operating unless it was necessary to locate foreign objects in the abdomen.

One other change, which took place in June 1940, was the removal of doctors from the list of reserved occupations, so they could be conscripted if necessary. The British Medical Association's Central Medical War Committee chose the doctors they considered most suitable to fill the quotas.

France and Belgium
Medical stores in France were initially located along the lines of communication, but it was not long before the threat posed by enemy aircraft meant that the medical services also had to be spread out because troops were no longer concentrated in large numbers.

At the end of April 1940 the fighting force numbered some 400,000. At this point the medical services consisted of thirty-four field ambulances, eighteen hygiene sections and seven motor ambulance convoys. The advanced air striking force had twelve CCSs, twenty-three field transfusion units and five mobile bacteriological laboratories. There were twenty general hospitals, some of which were in tents, four convalescent depots, two base medical stores (at Dieppe and Boulogne), four advanced medical store depots and nine ambulance trains.

Complicated cases, in which it was expected that the treatment would require more than twenty-eight days, were given preliminary treatment in specialised hospitals in France before being sent home. On 10 May 1940 Germany invaded the Low Countries; the British, after a brief forward movement, had to retreat through Arras to Dunkirk. Despite efforts to save their equipment and stores, the medical services had to abandon much of it.

The medical services did take some valuable lessons with them from the retreat from France, not least the limited usefulness of the old type of CCSs, which were too heavy to be moved frequently, as was needed in the new style of fully mechanised warfare.

Sick

Another worrying medical problem at this time was the incidence of venereal disease. There were several forms of this, and the term 'full house' was used to refer to patients who had syphilis, gonorrhoea, lymphogranuloma and soft chancre simultaneously. Venereal disease had always been common among British troops in India, despite a well-established system of medically regulated prostitution. General Slim applied the same rule as he did for malaria: forward treatment units to prevent cases escaping to the comforts of India. In Burma many men arrived already infected with at least one type of venereal disease picked up in India.

Sulphanilamide drugs came into use for treating a range of bacterial infections, including gonorrhoea. Penicillin worked well on syphilis and gonorrhoea and also sulpanomide for gonorrhoea.

In France, punishment for contracting venereal disease was counterproductive, as men tried to hide it and treat it themselves. Post-sex cleansing was complicated and difficult without adequate clean water and few bothered. Regiments that made condoms available had the lowest rates of venereal disease.

One viewpoint at home was that morality and chastity should be encouraged; the Archbishop of Canterbury William Temple spoke out against the issue of condoms to troops on the grounds that it would be 'an inducement to fornication'. Of course, this made no difference to fit young men with nothing better to do than frequent bars and pick up women.

There was an initial shortage of paratyphoid vaccine and tetanus toxoid and it took until January before all the units were vaccinated. The Assistant Director of Medical Services suggested that some additional items should be added to the standard equipment of field ambulances, including a range of suture needles and sizes of catgut and silk, and the means of sterilising swabs, dressings and towels.

The winter of 1939–40 was exceptionally severe. Rain and storms gave way to heavy frosts, but despite an influenza epidemic, admissions to medical units stayed below 3 per cent of the total strength. The principal causes of these admissions were, in this order: gastric disorders, scabies, venereal disease, respiratory disorders, tonsillitis, pediculosis and impetigo. There was constant demand from France for aspirin and cough mixture. During this period, just over 11,000 patients were evacuated to the UK.

Field ambulances had to treat lobar pneumonia and broncho-pneumonia, as well as acute abdominal conditions, which were outside their usual remit.

Far East

The situation here, where the medical services were already stretched, degenerated rapidly once the Japanese began their offensives. Hospitals and medical stores saw staff butchered and female nurses raped, and those patients who were transferred to prisoner-of-war camps suffered, as did the other prisoners, from dietary deficiencies such as beri beri. The prisoner-of-war camps in Germany were nowhere near as bad. Although the Allied prisoners were treated fairly well, those from Eastern Europe and Russia were not. Many of the latter were viewed as racially inferior; of the 5,700,000 Red Army captives during the course of the war, over 3,300,000 died, some executed and some from disease and starvation.

Egypt and Libya

In the Western Desert, the wide expanse of the theatre and the constant movement of the fighting force created some logistical problems. As always in desert conditions, sanitation and insect control were major issues for the medical services.

There had been much inter-war research into the prevention and treatment of heatstroke. The obvious prevention was to avoid exposure to the sun; hats were to be worn and working without shirts was forbidden. Adequate drinking water and salt were to be taken, and salt tablets were issued. Later on it was found that hats were not necessary if the salt and water were taken regularly. At first sunbathing was forbidden, but then encouraged as it was found to help prevent prickly heat. Light clothing was issued, including uniform shorts. However, fly-bites and minor injuries often turned septic, and in areas where this was prevalent, long trousers were worn, with short puttees to close off the bottoms.

In Libya medical stores were sometimes difficult to obtain until the depots moved closer to the troops and units were able to collect what they needed direct from the depot. They were lucky in being able to capture large amounts of medical stores, including quantities of bandages and dressings. The salvaging of captured enemy medical stores and equipment was conducted systematically, by field ambulance detachments at Benghazi. The salvaged stores were collected in Tobruk.

The only item which was lacking for a while was stretchers. A large number of these 'disappeared'. The Red Cross supplied medical comforts, including Dunlopillo mattresses, for patients being transported by ambulance cars. These could be fitted into a stretcher frame with a webbing attachment.

The health of the troops was mainly good; this was fortunate, as climatic conditions were not conducive to aerial evacuation. In the autumn months of October to December heavy rains in the coastal region flooded the landing grounds, so aircraft could not take off. Exceptionally cold and wet weather in Cyrenaica during the last week of the year caused considerable hardship to the troops, but did not appear to affect the incidence of disease.

An alarming increase in the incidence of dysentery in November 1941 was thought to be caused by hot weather continuing and producing a third fly season when troops were moving into the forward areas and had few facilities for protecting food and constructing fly-proof latrines. Many units new to desert conditions arrived and had a lower standard of hygiene discipline than was desirable. Such few cases of malaria as presented were contracted outside the region. Diphtheria continued to appear sporadically.

The principal diseases affecting the troops during July to September 1941 included desert sores, sandfly fever and influenza, ear, nose and throat conditions, accidental injuries, dysentery and enteritis, malaria, chest conditions and several others. Desert sores were treated by immediate covering with Elastoplast, but winter clothing which protected the skin solved the problem, with the number of cases of infective hepatitis falling off rapidly with the onset of winter. Many cases of pediculosis were wrongly diagnosed as scabies and many medical officers were ignorant of the habits of the louse *Pediculus corporis* and failed to examine clothes for eggs.

In the civil population dysentery was common, and typhoid was endemic as the public aqueducts were polluted. Relapsing fever was endemic in some regions, as was undulant fever. Typhus was endemic everywhere. Malaria was very prevalent and there was a high incidence of venereal disease among the population.

Burma and north-east India

The superiority of British medical arrangements, especially those which kept malaria at bay, as opposed to the inadequate way in which the Japanese dealt with it, was one of the most important reasons why the 14th Army was able to defeat the Japanese. Admissions to hospitals from malaria dropped from 1,850 per 1,000* men per year to only 500 in 1945. This was partly due to preventive measures, and partly to the rapid recovery of those who did contract malaria and other diseases, thanks to the development of facilities for forward

---

*This figure is correct as many men were admitted more than once.

treatment, including the formation of several cooperative medical centres made up of units from many Commonwealth countries. As well as enabling rapid treatment and return of casualties to active service, this discouraged men who thought sickness would be a ticket back to the relative comfort of India.

The British army found itself forced into retreat by a series of moves from the Japanese. On 14 December 1941 the airfield at Victoria Point, on the southernmost tip of Burma, was captured; five days later the Japanese crossed the border from Thailand and by 8 March Rangoon had fallen. The British soon realised that sick and wounded men and medical staff could not be left behind as they would be killed. Good evacuation facilities were scarce; there were few compartments on the trains and many wrecked vehicles were left on the lines, which had to be cleared. Infectious cases had to go up the Irrawaddy on barges and hospital ships.

The original plan was to take the sick and wounded by air from Schwebo (just north of Mandalay) to Calcutta, but the rapid Japanese advance prevented this and they had to be flown from Myitkina (just north of the border) to Dinjan in Assam. There were few medical facilities there and little transport to take patients to other hospitals in India. Measures were immediately put in place to reinforce the medical units at Dinjan and send a hospital to Tijpur on the Brahmaputra. This was soon to be linked by a metre-gauge railway, which would enable all serious cases to be sent to larger hospitals in Bengal. At Dinjan medical and surgical cases were treated in a small military hospital and in the planters' hospital a few miles from the airfield. Facilities were poor and eventually several trainloads of sick and wounded were forced to rely on local civilians for food. This was deeply embarrassing to the British authorities, as most of these patients were Indian and there was a risk that there would be accusations of lack of concern for the lives of Imperial subjects. As soon as news of this situation reached Eastern Command, steps were taken to effect improvements: more money was spent to improve way-stations, and additional medical facilities were situated along the lines of evacuation. Despite this, medical provision in north-east India remained inadequate. A nurse at the hospital at Ranchi wrote to her sister-in-law in June 1942, telling her that despite the hospital being intended for 250 patients, there were at that time 788 and as many as eighty were arriving each day. This was largely due to the monsoon, which fed breeding sites for mosquitoes and caused rainwater carrying infection to flow into the drinking water.

This hospital had no modern lavatories, only one water tap and virtually no drugs, including aspirin. This nurse's sister-in-law was the wife of R.A. Butler, then the Minister of Education. Mrs Butler passed the letter to the Secretary of State for India L.S. Amery, who promptly wrote to the viceroy demanding that the situation be dealt with. The viceroy replied that he was well aware of the situation, but that it was the same throughout India. He said he would soon have to request further medical staff and supplies from Britain. None were sent.

The War Office was also aware of the situation in India. The adjutant general had made a tour in 1942 and was horrified at what he saw there, worrying that there would be a complete breakdown of the medical services. There was a shortage of nearly 800 medical officers, but none could be sent from Britain without undermining civilian medical arrangements at home. He suggested that India should be pressed into introducing conscription for doctors. This proved impossible, and the salaries were inadequate compared with the earnings available in civilian practice. The medical supply situation did improve, but had civilians such as planters not worked voluntarily in the hospitals, and taken convalescents into their homes, the whole thing would have collapsed. As well as caring for sick and wounded troops, the British and Indian medical staff assisted in the care of the numerous refugees who fled from the advancing Japanese. Many of these refugees were suffering from malaria, typhoid, dysentery and cholera, and as well as their humanitarian concern, the military medical services were anxious to prevent these diseases spreading to troops.

As many as 80 per cent of the troops evacuated from Burma in 1942 had some form of disease. The 14th Army was fortunately able to take advantage of research conducted by the Australian army into malaria prophylaxis. The most useful of the findings at that time was the effectiveness of daily small doses of mepacrine. General Slim had a simple way of ensuring that these doses were taken. He was convinced that it was the responsibility of regimental commanders to see that the dose was taken. If they did not, he sacked them. Despite all this, it was not always easy in the heat of battle or on long patrols to ensure that the drugs were taken, and malaria continued to affect large numbers of the troops, often more than three times those wounded by the Japanese.

In 1943 Brigadier Orde Wingate's 'chindit' force operated behind the Japanese lines in Burma. Although comparatively successful, about a third of his force was lost, mostly to disease. A second operation in 1944 was more successful, but also ended with much of the force incapacitated by disease. Although Wingate's public reputation survived the war, many doubted the wisdom of his operations, calling him fanatical and unstable. But some of Wingate's junior commanders did pay attention to the health of their men, especially when it came to drinking water.

Wingate's thinking on disease was fatalistic; he believed that his soldiers should put up with the inevitable diseases of warfare in the tropics. This, and his contempt for hygiene and sanitation, meant that his troops suffered a higher than normal incidence of disease, and there was some controversy about his fitness to command. He had written a training pamphlet in which he stated that it was a waste of labour to dig latrines unless the force expected to be in place for more than seven days. In the interim, soldiers should relieve themselves in the surrounding countryside at least 100 yards from the camp. It caused some amusement when he almost died from typhoid contracted after drinking water from a flower vase.

North Africa

In hot countries the common diseases were malaria and typhoid, where there was standing water in which mosquitoes breed; in sandy desert conditions sand-flies and the fever they carried were also prevalent. Another epidemic disease in the North Africa theatre was the louse-borne typhus, which was often fatal. Most effort to combat typhus was directed at the civilian population; as one medical officer remarked, 'It had long been appreciated that a close connection exists between the health of an army overseas and the presence of civilian communicable diseases'. For this reason the French authorities were urged to disinfect all the villages and nomads they could reach, and Allied soldiers were not allowed to travel on public transport, attend cinemas or other public places or fraternise with civilians. Despite this, there was a high incidence of scabies and lice among the troops. Mobile bath houses helped with the latter.

One infectious complaint which reached epidemic proportions in this theatre was ear infection, or *Otitis media*. The specific cause was not known, but dirt, sand and sweat running into the ear, dirty towels, sea water and infected swimming pools were suspected. There was also a problem with infective hepatitis (also called infectious jaundice) in all the armies in North Africa; Rommel himself suffered from hepatitis and had to be evacuated home twice for treatment. The disease showed with anorexia, general weakness, fatigue, aches and nausea. Sometimes it only lasted a few days, but could take up to three months. Sufferers could be hospitalised for up to six weeks. It was not until 1944 that research showed there were actually two forms of jaundice: Type A which is a virus found in faeces, and Hepatitis B, which is a virus spread by dirty injection needles. The wholesale vaccination against yellow fever may have been a contributory factor. Inoculation against typhoid was available after 1940. All American troops were inoculated on arrival, and British troops as soon as possible. This treatment was 90 per cent effective. By the time the Allies moved into Italy, DDT had been introduced and found to be effective against lice and flies. It was also effective against malaria-carrying mosquitoes when applied to their breeding grounds in wet areas such as the canals round Salerno and Naples.

Quinine and mepacrine (also known as atabrin) were effective as a prophylactic as well as treatment, but a rumour spread that quinine caused sexual impotence and many who took atabrin suffered from vomiting, so neither were taken as they should have been. Malaria was also a problem in north Italy in the delta of the Po river until DDT was sprayed aerially.

Sickness among the Allied troops accounted for twenty times more patients than did combat wounds, with sickness amounting to 585 per 1,000 men, and wounds less than 50. The main causes of sickness were skin problems, digestive problems, malaria, sand-fly fever, inflamed tonsils and venereal disease.

Hygiene

In November, mobile bath units began to arrive and by January six units, attached to field hygiene sections, were available for use, doing much to control the incidence of pediculosis. The hygiene sections soon found themselves very busy. Troops were billeted in all sorts of buildings, from convents to barns, and the construction of latrines, disposal of rubbish and selection of water points had high priority. The standard of hygiene among the poorer groups of town dwellers was low and the use of human dung for agriculture did not help in the country. All drinking water had to be continually tested and treated. Over-crowding in the billets was common, especially where troops were billeted in small villages, but by January hutted camps were being built.

'Bucket' latrines were constructed from the wooden containers of the 4-gallon petrol tins, the tins themselves sometimes taking the place of the regulation buckets. Bucket latrines were found preferable to deep trench latrines, especially in rural areas, as the heavy rains and high water levels of the sub-soil made them unusable, and also because the troops preferred the bucket type which could be put indoors.

Specialised hygiene units made latrines and cleared rubbish, and with military police they attempted to educate the civilian population. This helped prevent typhoid, dysentery and diarrhoea, and the troops were given instruction on the importance of good practice. 'Don't murder your mates' was one of the slogans coined and used in radio broadcasts. Inoculation was used to fight typhoid and tetanus and the anti-malarial drugs quinine and mepacrine were issued. Water filtration and purification plants were used, and men were urged to wash their hands after using the latrines, and to ensure that food was properly covered so that flies could not get at it. One medical officer wrote that they killed flies by the ten thousands, but as they lacked effective sprays they could not do the job properly. Another reported that the Bedouin were major carriers of infection (not to mention theft) and whenever possible they were to be kept away from the camps and replaced by British personnel in the kitchens. There were very few cases in this Western Desert theatre of the louse-borne typhus, due to regular issues of louse-powder and anti-louse belts of pleated cotton impregnated with chemicals. All prisoners of war and native labourers were also routinely disinfected.

East Africa

In Sudan, transport for evacuation of the sick and wounded was almost entirely confined to the railways and the river. It was generally possible to drive anywhere in dry weather, but the tracks were unsuitable for ambulance cars. A second ambulance train was needed and soon provided.

The enemy here was Italian; their healthcare authorities were not active in Abyssinia except in the control of epidemic diseases. They had hospitals, laboratories and quarantine stations, but had done little to improve the health of the native population. The diseases of most importance to the military were malaria, typhus, venereal disease and the enteric group. Less common were epidemic meningitis, relapsing fever, dengue, leishmaniosis, tuberculosis, brucellosis, leprosy, myiasis, tropical ulcers, smallpox, trachoma, diphtheria, worm infections and rabies. Insect vectors for these were mosquitoes, lice, fleas, ticks and the common housefly. It was reported that some 80 per cent of the native population had either syphilis, gonorrhoea or soft chancre, syphilis being the most common.

Ambulance trains were limited at the beginning of this campaign; sleeping accommodation had to be provided for all patients as the distances between the forward areas and base hospitals were great. Eventually there were four ambulance trains designed to take seventy-six stretcher cases each, and by adding extra coaches, as many sitting or lying cases as needed. The maximum capacity for any one train was reached when fourteen extra coaches were added, allowing the train to carry more than 350 patients.

Dental service

It was found that mobile dental units were more useful than the older system of dental officers attached to field ambulance units. Many dentists attended a special maxillofacial course and another on anaesthetics. The war establishment was one dental officer per 3,700 men. The daily dental sick parade averaged eleven cases per day. During and immediately after the Normandy landings the dental officers of the mobile dental units worked 2 to 3 miles behind the line. Before these mobile units arrived, dental work at general hospitals and casualty clearing stations was heavy, mainly to repair dentures. Dental officers with field ambulances provided maxillofacial first aid. The movement in Belgium in August and September saw 19,172 attendances for dental treatment; all the dental officers of the 2nd Army were instructed to maintain one month's supply of stores to make them independent; maintain close contact with their parent units in the absence of movement orders and arrange for liberal signposts to the unit. The incidence of maxillofacial casualties rose during the assault crossings of the Rhine, Weser and Aller, mostly caused by small-arms missiles. In the ten months from June 1944 to March

1945 there were 57,660 attendances at dental clinics, 25,167 new dentures supplied and 26,354 dentures repaired.

In the Army Directorate of Psychiatry there was a widespread belief that most 'nervous' cases were malingerers or cowards often referred to as having 'LMF' (Lack of Moral Fibre). Now these men would be diagnosed as suffering from Post-Traumatic Stress Disorder.

Medical stores

As well as the drugs and unguents used to treat patients, medical posts needed a wide range of items. As well as the larger material such as tents and operating tables, these included signalling flags for directing incoming ambulances, stretchers, blankets and groundsheets and pyjamas. Equipment carried by ambulance trains included bedding, mugs, plates and cutlery, hurricane lamps, water bottles, sets of splints and surgical haversacks.

Rations for the sick

For emergency situations in hospitals in the field, a special pack of supplies for 200 men was designed to be packed into a bomb-like casing and dropped by parachute. It contained meat extract, arrowroot, condensed milk, sugar, cocoa, tea, boiled sweets, chocolate bars, cigarettes and matches, all packed into two kegs, plus a tin of biscuits and chocolate bars and a box containing two bottles of brandy. The total weight of these packs was 200lb.

Until the end of the war, diets were described by their main ingredient content: chicken, fish, beef tea and milk diets. This was replaced by the 'light diet (solid)' and the 'light diet (fluid)'. The solid version was designed for three situations: convalescent patients not yet ready for ordinary diet, for instance post-operative cases in the later stages, a bland low-residue diet for gastric and dysentery cases after the acute stages, and for TB cases, which had small additions of the ordinary diet. The fluid version was designed for four situations: patients too ill to eat solid foods (such as those with acute fevers), early-stage post-operative cases, first-stage gastric cases, and acute stage dysentery cases.

The fluid diet consisted of milk, cereals, oatmeal, arrowroot (made into a thin sauce-like consistency, and flavoured with brandy, wine, or citrus peel and sugar), oatmeal gruel (with a little brandy, rum, or wine and sugar), sago or tapioca, calves' foot jelly, mutton or chicken broth, beef tea, cocoa, Bengers, Horlicks and Ovaltine (mixed with milk), barley water, sugar water or toast water (steep a well-browned slice of toast in two pints of boiling water for half an hour and strain), fruit juice and meat extract.

The solid diet consisted of the above, with the addition of bread, sweet biscuits, jam or syrup, eggs (scrambled or as an omelette), egg blancmange, onion porridge (just a Spanish onion boiled until soft, mashed and thickened with flour, sago or cornmeal), baked egg custard, junket and egg flip cheese or fish and potato pie, fish soufflé, macaroni and cheese, milk soup with strained vegetables, stewed fruit and custard, milk or sponge puddings.

Hospital cooks could indent for 'kitchen sundries' if needed: 12oz curry powder, 2oz essences, 1oz gelatine, 1oz dried herbs, 2oz pepper, ½pt salad oil, ½oz spices, ¼pt vinegar per 100 diets, and 1oz mustard for 20 diets which included beef, ½oz salt per diet, and ½oz flour for sauce per diet.

Chapter 14

Invasion of North-West Europe – Operation Overlord

In June 1944, an enormous military force of over 3,000,000 men moved from Britain into north-west France, then eastwards through Belgium and Holland and into Germany. This force involved the armies, air forces and navies of several Allied countries; the largest numbers of men were from Great Britain and America. Such an endeavour required vast amounts of stores and equipment, from food and weaponry to medical equipment: the classic 'beans, bullets and bandages', and in order to have all this in place at the beginning, the planning and provision of support personnel had to commence over eighteen months in advance. Given the size and complexity of this task, it is impressive that, with a few minor hiccups, it all worked extremely well.

One of the hiccups with providing supplies related to miscalculations on the speed of advance after the landings. This expected the force to reach the Seine in ninety days; they did so in seventy-nine days, and continued their progress so fast that the line of communication had difficulty keeping up, leading to some shortages at the front. Some of this was due to the damage inflicted on the large Channel ports by the retreating enemy; given that the weather would deteriorate rapidly through autumn, opening those ports took on greater importance. Boulogne was reopened on 10 October, Antwerp on 28 November; the delay being due to the large number of mines which had been laid on the approaches to the ports. Until these ports were opened, most supplies continued to be landed in Normandy.

It was not until the end of 1941 that America entered the war, although before that it had been aiding Britain with various types of supplies and equipment. But with the Japanese attacks on Pearl Harbour and invasion of the Philippine islands, America realised that it could do little to eject them at that time, and decided instead to take a more active part in the conflict against Germany. Almost immediately meetings took place between Roosevelt and Churchill to discuss a mutual attack on the Germans, first in North Africa and then in north-west Europe. Although the desirability of the latter was agreed, it was not until a year later that serious planning began. During that process, a series of high-level conferences took place, with other meetings of various Allied planning committees.

By April 1943 a meeting in Washington put a proposed date of May 1944 on the assault and the serious planning began. An organisation called Chiefs of Staff to the Supreme Allied Commander (COSSAC) was formed. This consisted of the joint chiefs of staff of each of the two main Allies, which functioned through a staff secretariat and seven committees and boards, one each for Staff Planners, Military Transport, Intelligence, Munitions Assignment, Communications, Meteorology and Civil Affairs.

One of the first decisions was to damage the production capacity and morale of Germany by a major bombing offensive, to damage or destroy German installations, equipment and peace of mind. In April 1943 COSSAC stated their objective as being 'to defeat the German fighting forces in North West Europe' and asked for a full-scale plan of assault for early 1944, and an elaborate camouflage and deception scheme for that summer to encourage the Germans to expect a large cross-Channel operation focussing on the east Kent–Pas de Calais route. This plan led to the production of inflatable ships to lie in the harbours of Kent and Essex and wooden and inflatable tanks and aircraft to sit in the fields of Kent and southern East Anglia.

A further meeting in Washington in May 1943 began to define the assault, the aim being to gain a foothold on the Continent from which further operations could be launched. A target date of May 1944 was fixed, and it was agreed that forces and equipment should be established in Great Britain as quickly as possible. Lieutenant General F.E. Morgan was appointed chief of staff to the Supreme Allied Commander (designate) and tasked with submitting an outline plan for the invasion, now named Operation Overlord.

This operation is often referred to as 'D-Day', which implies that it was a unique title; this is not quite right. The day on which the assault commenced was indeed D-Day, and the days before referred to as 'D-Day – (number) and those after as 'D-Day + (number)', but the designation of D-Day was given to the commencement of all operations, not just this one.

Most historians describe the campaign as being in four phases:

1. Preparation, including planning and mounting arrangements.
2. The assembly of Operation Overlord including landings and operations in the bridgehead.
3. The breakout, covering the move first to Antwerp and Brussels (25 July to 26 September 1944).
4. The 'last round' including the winter campaign, crossing the Rhine on 23 March 1945 and the final sweep into Germany, culminating in victory.

However, the first two phases were far more complicated than these simple statements suggest. These processes took more than eighteen months, and the very first part, invading the Continent by a joint force, meant that as well as British troops, some 1,500,000 American soldiers and airmen were expected to move into Britain, and it took some time to organise the logistics of this; these plans were approved in May 1942.

General planning for the operation began in June 1942. The detailed planning began even before the plan of the invasion was defined, with preparations based on the total possible capacity of the English coast ports from the Thames to the Bristol Channel. This meant that the essential part of planning, i.e. the number of troops involved, was not available. Upon that number usually devolved the provision of rations and other essential supplies, and the method of movement of the troops and their equipment. The two main aspects of the operation were defined as 'planning' and 'mounting', the first being the provisioning and maintaining of the force, and the second being the actual movement of the troops and their equipment.

During 1943 General Morgan set up COSSAC headquarters in St James's Square in central London. An outline of the invasion force and first order of battle was finalised and had been agreed in December 1943, but General Montgomery and his 8th Army returned to the UK in January 1944, which immediately increased the size of the available force by 50 per cent. Accommodating them meant that ports on the Humber and Mersey had to be added to the plan. This, and the previous coastal preparations, defined the operation as amphibious, and it was obvious that the enemy would be expecting this. There was no definite information on their likely reaction, but the use of gas was anticipated, so gas masks had to be supplied.

During 1943, preparation of intelligence for planning, and engineering advice on planning, was done by the staff of the engineer-in-chief at the War Office. Some exercises to assist in this work were carried out; part of the result of these was the realisation of the need for special units and equipment. These were rapidly organised and plans were produced with estimates of engineering stores and equipment needed, including those for bridging.

The reasons for the dates selected for the assault were two-fold. There had to be a good moon to allow sufficient visibility for the airborne troops to land at night, and at the same time, the tide had to be low to expose as much as possible of the beaches for the land assault troops. The chosen beaches on the Normandy coast were shallow and went out a long way. The Germans had blocked the beaches with steel structures rather like giant caltrops, and any unsuspecting craft which encountered these under the water would have their bottoms ripped out. The British mathematician A.T. Doodson had invented a prediction machine which could identify and combine all these factors, and this came up with an exact time (known as H-hour) between 5 and 6 June for the landings. If they had to be postponed there would be a two-week delay.

This covered preliminary deployment of troops as well as the divisional engineers. Much of this could only be decided after the full list of tasks had been decided: tasks for engineers placed with the assault troops and arrangements for rallying; bridging policy including considerations of the levels of destruction by the enemy; allocation of heavy equipment and arrangements for material dumps; road maintenance and repair with material dumps for this, and the construction of pontoon causeways.

Once the main plan for the invasion had been decided and issued, detailed plans could be prepared at all levels. The main points to be considered included producing a list of engineering tasks and their priorities, including deployment of engineering troops. The final details of this would include the chain of command in each case, and the time when central command would be resumed, allocation of mechanical equipment and of responsibility for each section of road and railway, including those needed for beach maintenance. Finally the amounts of water which would be needed, both for drinking and for engineering work. Drinking water had to be purified; for other purposes such as cement mixing, filtration and an adequate flow were important.

Expecting that some men would inevitably fall into the sea on the assault, kitbags were made up at Branston ordnance depot with clothing, arms, ammunition and food. These were to be issued to individuals as they were rescued. They included two 24-hour rations, a tin of self-heating soup, a water sterilising outfit and an emergency ration. Other provisions had to be gas-proof, and also had to be waterproof as it was realised that the landing would inevitably involve scrambling out of the landing craft through shallow water. It was intended that the rations would be issued to each soldier to carry in his pack, so they also had to be compact and lightweight. For this reason dehydrated foods were included in this pack; this reduced bulk, but rations had to be easily cooked and included cigarettes, matches and toilet paper. (At the beginning of the invasion, toilet paper was provided on the basis of six sheets per man, but this was later reduced to five sheets per man.) Some 7,500,000 of these packs were produced and just over 5,000,000 were used; the rest were sent to hospitals in London after the war for use in casualty wards.

For a big operation like Overlord, orders had to be placed with manufacturers nearly twelve months before D-Day.

The RASC received approval for six headquarters supply units and twenty-five base supply units; most of these were formed and trained six months before D-Day. They included eighty detailed issue depots and eighteen port detachments, with twenty-five bakeries, producing over 55,000lb of bread a day, and fourteen field butcheries and cold storage depots.

As well as 24-hour rations, 1,000,000 Tommy cookers and 21,000,000 refill tablets were ordered, and more than 1,000,000 water sterilising outfits. Next the fourteen-man compo pack was considered; it was assumed that half of the force would need these for six weeks, and so a month's reserve should be held. The RASC added fourteen days' ration for French patriots, then the navy demanded 1,250,000. The final estimate for compo rations was 58,000,000. AFV packs for armoured crews had to be organised, of a special size and design to fit into the receptacles inside tanks. The RAC (Royal Armoured Corps) thought it might have 85,000 men in actual operations, so a total of thirty days per man were ordered, varying between two, three, and five-man packs: a total of 2,500,000 rations.

All this involved not just the food itself, but also tinplate, lacquer and case-boarding, all going to packing factories on a fixed schedule. RASC officers were situated at all the most important factories to make regular checks. Every case of food had to be marked 'RASC Supplies'. Once packed, these had to be moved out of the factories quickly to make room, but the V-rocket threat meant storage had to be outside London. The Ministry of Food helped find places for 60,000 tons, much of this eventually in 400 separate small civil depots.

Cold storage might have been a problem: on the premise that the Germans would destroy all existing storage on the Continent, four 500-ton cold storage plants were ordered and five 200-ton and thirty portable 10-ton plants for use on the Continent. In the event, only a few of the 10-ton plants were needed as the cold storage plants at Antwerp and Hamburg were captured intact; the latter with a bonus of 8,000 tons of meat, and German technicians who were willing to cooperate.

Anxious to keep tinned food for the Continent, the RASC arranged special trains full of potatoes and other vegetables to go from East Anglia to Aldershot. By the middle of August, a trial of sending carrots and turnips (200 tons of each) and 600 tons of potatoes was started. By 12 September fresh supplies sent from the UK totalled 4,000 tons of fresh supplies, 3,000 tons of potatoes, 1,999 tons of root vegetables and 400 tons of mild cured bacon.

The RASC also supplied sacramental wafers for chaplains of various denominations. They even worked out ration scales for war dogs and carrier pigeons, and ordered stocks of these.

After the decision had been made to have everything ready for the invasion of the Continent by May 1944, the planning included collecting the invasion units of the two forces into concentrated areas for final training and then to prepare for embarkation. The final count of American troops was set at 1,446,000, plus 45,300 operational replacements. In May 1943 the first tranche of about 672,000 arrived in England, and the British army arranged to house more than 531,000 of them. By the end of 1943, the War Office had to cater for more than 2,500,000.

One major planning factor was that it was expected the Germans would extensively destroy ports. This would not be too bad at the beginning, as the beaches were able to handle men, vehicles and stores (weather allowing), but priority was to be given to port clearance for maintenance, replacement and further build-up.

It had been decided that the whole of the force would be gathered in the UK, so the first task was arranging accommodation. Altogether, accommodation had to be provided for 1,350,000 Americans, together with about 70,000 hospital beds. The first wave of American troops was housed in Northern Ireland and the rest in various places throughout England. Hutting was needed for 200,000 men and 1,500,000 square feet of covered accommodation for other purposes. Some 60 per cent of this accommodation was transferred to the Americans by requisition, the rest was purpose-built. Equally, the American Air Force had to be provided with airfields, and again over half of these were transferred from the RAF and the rest purpose-built.

The Americans supplied most of their own vehicles and mechanical equipment, but the additional numbers of these items needed for the British and Canadian armies had to be calculated well in advance.

Camps for 100,000 refugees and prisoners were prepared, later this grew to 200,000.

For a while it was thought that it might be necessary to transfer the entire population of Caen to a refugee camp at Shoreham where they would stay for forty-eight hours before being billeted on English homes. Around 30,000 men and women were expected, but in the event, only seven arrived, including one elderly lady with her goat.

The original number of British army troops expected to leave from the UK was about 900,000, plus another 250,000 Canadian, French and other non-American Allies. To this must be added over 500,000 Air Force personnel who had to be housed and fed in the UK and on the Continent. Food also had to be provided for some 23,000 naval personnel.

A depot at Marchwood, near Southampton, was set up in February 1944 to hold the stores being collected for Operation Overlord. These included 10,000 tons of special equipment for the Mulberry harbours and large quantities of material for repairing damaged quays, lockgates and so on. It consisted of 18 acres of open and 1 acre of covered storage with nearly 8 miles of railway sidings and forty-three roads. It also had a deep-water jetty capable of berthing steamers of up to 17ft draught and was equipped with four 6-ton diesel-electric portal cranes. There were railway sidings and storage areas, and a concrete slipway for constructing and launching concrete pontoons.

Maps were needed for the post-assault period and the priorities were set as:

- Normandy coastal area and inland as far south as the River Loire (inclusive).
- Pas de Calais coastal area, from 1941–42 air photographs, and again later when better photographs were available.

- Brittany, to show position of enemy guns.
- North-eastern France and Belgium on a central axis running approximately from Paris towards Brussels and Antwerp.
- Holland.
- The Atlantic seaboard of western France.
- Germany, as far east as approximately Berlin, where it was anticipated that the Western Allies and Russia would make contact.
- Denmark and parts of Norway.
- Numerous town plans, some full, others showing 'through ways'.

Some 3,200 reconnaissance missions were flown before D-Day to take photographs to aid the mapping project.

As sufficient inflatable lifebelts had not been made to provide one per man, a system had to be organised on how these should be returned after use, serviced and re-issued.

All vehicles landed up to D+42 were to be waterproofed. For some, this required tall metal plates to be attached to the sides, front and rear of the vehicles so water could not slop in, while for others, waterproofing compounds were applied to vulnerable parts of the engines. Rubber air intakes and exhaust hoses were fitted to form snorkels.

In December 1943, General Eisenhower was appointed Supreme Commander Allied Expeditionary Force, and his headquarters was designated Supreme Headquarters Allied Expeditionary Force (SHAEF); General Montgomery was Commander 21st Army Group, and was to command all land forces (British and American) in the assault and immediately after; for this period it was recognised that the tactical situation would necessitate a single battle commander. From August British and American ground forces would each have their own separate commander, each reporting to the Supreme Commander. When that happened, General Bradley took over command of all American ground forces and Montgomery retained the British 21st Army Group.

21st Army Group's function was to be the control of the British advanced base on the Continent, notification to the War Office of bulk maintenance requirements for the period during which 21st Army Group were in administrative control of Allied land forces, initiating return movements of troops, casualties, prisoners and refugees, and demanding reinforcements up to authorised establishments.

The directive to the Supreme Commander on logistics stated:

In the United Kingdom the responsibility for logistics, organisation, concentration, movement and supply of forces to meet the requirements of your plan will rest with the British Service ministries so far as British forces are concerned. So far as the United States Forces are concerned, this responsibility will rest with the United States War and Navy Departments. You will be responsible for the co-ordination of logistical arrangements on the Continent. You will also be responsible for co-ordinating the requirements of British and United States forces under your Command.

By the time the Supreme Commander was appointed, much of the detailed planning for Overlord had already been done by COSSAC and the general plan was substantially approved and adopted by Eisenhower. The original date chosen for the assault was 1 May, but gliders carrying jeeps and other items too large to drop were needed. Known as Horsa gliders, these were built entirely of wood, with a hinged nose and detachable tail for easy loading; they could carry troops or goods/stores and could be modified to carry bombs. They were made by Aircraft of Christchurch Hants and sub-contractors. Some 5,000 were made; they could be towed by various aircraft, and were used in other campaigns besides Normandy, including Arnhem.

The cargoes were strapped down and secured to plywood floors. Pilots and glider troops had only canvas and light wood to protect them from attack. Supplies were also dropped from powered aeroplanes. The RASC had to do its own packing for aerial drops, using special packs with points to attach inside planes for balance and trim. If they had no specific orders, they took standard loads.

It was pointed out that another month's production of assault craft would make up the perceived deficiencies of what was needed for seven divisions. Eisenhower was convinced that the success of the whole operation was dependent on a sufficiently strong invasion force, and he agreed to postpone the target date by a month.

The first task for the movements branch of the quartermaster general's staff was to work out, with the navy and Ministry of War Transport, a system for the vast numbers of men and vehicles to be transported, with their stores and equipment, in the exact order required by their commander. Even the way each individual craft was loaded had to be worked out so that items came to hand as needed.

There were some difficulties over finding adequate shipping for stores. The tonnages could not be stated with accuracy until items were packed, so bids for shipping had to be made on a 'best guess' basis, and were inevitably over stated on a 'better safe than sorry' basis, but all went well in the event. There was some concern about how to deal with emergency requirements, but these were sent air freight or by express coaster.

While this was in progress, the 'V' rocket attacks were about to start, according to intelligence, and it was thought that this might mean a semi-paralysed London, so the RASC arranged for America to hold a bulk reserve of 15,000,000 rations in New York. When the attacks did come, they were not as bad as feared, thanks to the RAF and Bomber Command.

Replacement vehicles were to be shipped unaccompanied, their drivers meeting them on the beaches. It was assumed that normal reinforcement demands could be expected before D+18. Some other potential problems included the need for drivers to clear reserve vehicles from ships to vehicle parks, and the need to control shipment of unaccompanied equipment and its reception on the beach head.

There was a shortage of tank transporters, so all tanks 'walked' to embarkation ports on their own tracks. Other vehicles had been 'stored' on the sides of roads well away from the embarkation ports to await their call for departure.*

The detailed plan required that the whole of the coastal fleet allocated to the operation should be pre-loaded for stores needed up to D+7. Some 82,000 tons were loaded in 136 coasters; this was completed by D-11. Fast turnaround was important, but it was not always possible to know the location of empty ships, so fast launches went into the Solent to see what was anchored there. By D-7 supplies had been loaded at Glasgow, Lancaster and York, and from D+8 to D+30 supplies had been loaded at Ascot, Reigate, Hereford, Bedford, Tilbury, Victoria Dock, Southampton, and Barby (Northants).

The advent of Landing Ships and Landing Craft made the vehicle shipping techniques needed for combined operations very much easier and the use of ordinary cargo ships carrying vehicles was only used in Normandy for increasing the rate of build-up of vehicles in later phases. But military materiel was different as there were no ports available. The assault was expected to lead to immediate fighting so it was necessary to use whatever size of ships were available, often small ones; if 150-ton capacity it took one day to discharge via DUKWs; if 2,000 tons, it took four or five days so the order of loading (and thus unloading) was important. Some shuffling was involved with 'one' day or 'two' day ships being slotted in between bigger ones.

Troops were moved in batches from their regimental 'homes' towards the coast, first into what were known as marshalling areas, where they were split into battle groups and then moved to the embarkation ports. In the latter areas, where troops had been briefed on the invasion, they were completely enclosed in barbed wire fences to prevent any contact with outsiders. In some marshalling areas accommodation had to be built for the purpose, all roads had to be surveyed and some repaired or improved.

While troops were waiting to be moved to the embarkation areas, they were kept entertained by ENSA performances, concert parties, cinemas and games, and canteens with supplies of beer were provided whenever possible.

---

*The author's husband recalls seeing miles of these on roads in South Wales.

The main movement control difficulty was allocating accommodation available in shipping and craft to the units travelling, concentrating the units behind the ports and hards, marshalling them into ship loads and moving them out in time for embarkation.

The movement of troops through marshalling areas towards embarkation was done by splitting them into numbered 'parties', one per vessel load. This meant they lost the ability to draw and cook their rations, so each camp had a staff which provided what was called 'hotel service'. Men arrived at all hours of the night and day and had to be fed; this was done by a 'buffet line'. The hotel service was provided by twelve officers and 400 other ranks including sixty cooks.

By the end of May, all the supply requirements up to D+7 had been loaded into sixty vessels.

There were some sixty-four units dealing with ammunition, several of which handled repairs. An effective system for supplying ammunition was operated throughout the campaign; this handled the receipt of over 1,000,000 tons; 700,000 tons of which was actually used. The BADs sent daily statements of issues and returns to Ordnance headquarters, as did all ports clearing ammunition. One minor problem was that improved types of ammunition left the depots with stocks of 'dead' ammunition of the older types. Other returns after battles often consisted of opened boxes, which had to be examined and possibly passed to the repair units. Very little ammunition was lost by enemy action, but 400 tons were hit by shell fire during June. Extensive use of pioneer companies was made in handling the large tonnage of ammunition.

British forces were to be maintained over the beaches until sufficient ports were captured, two road heads were to be formed and a Rear Maintenance Area (RMA) to be established as soon as possible.

Although none of the large Channel ports were available for the assault, there were several smaller ones: an example was the fishing port at Coursevalles, which was not suitable for shipping, but was used for the barges which unloaded ships in the anchorages. Port-en-Bessin was used as a bulk petrol port, and shallow-draft small coasters. Cherbourg was reopened by US forces on 16 July and a rail connection was made on 21 July. British forces were allocated 500 tons per day through this port. Ouistreham was captured on D-Day, but was initially too close to the front to use as a port, but work was started on building quayside berths and hards, and from 21 August minesweeping began and it was opened fully on 3 September.

It was expected the Germans would extensively destroy ports. This was not considered to be too bad at the beginning, as the beaches would be able to handle men, vehicles and stores (weather allowing) but priority was to be given to port clearance for maintenance, replacement and further build-up.

DUKWs were particularly useful when conveying cargo from ships to beaches. Stores were carried in two cargo nets, which were lifted by crane, put on pallets and empty nets returned to the DUKW. This had its hazards. Some beaches on the north-facing Channel coast were mined, but it turned out that personnel actually in DUKWs were not injured when they hit a mine, but those outside and standing close were injured. The water close to the beaches and the beaches themselves were littered with debris and the landing sites had to be moved frequently. The DUKWs took casualties with them when they returned to the ships. Once the landing was complete, the DUKWs continued to work on land as general transport.

It was estimated that after D+60, for each fighting division ashore (about 16,000 men) another 24,000 would be needed in the field for support duties. They also needed some 8,000 vehicles, consisting of prime movers, tanks, guns and trailers and motorcycles. Five motorcycles were deemed to be equivalent to one other vehicle, and one vehicle to hold five men.

According to certain broad assumptions (e.g. 50 miles per vehicle per day, 6lb supplies per head per day), an average daily maintenance requirement per 'gross' division would be 700 tons per day. By August this figure was modified to 675 tons.

The assault

After a 24-hour delay to wait for bad weather to subside, the assault started on 6 June. It took forty-eight hours to land 150,000 troops on the beaches. In the first thirty days, 1,100,000 men, 200,000 vessels and 750,000 tons of stores were landed.

The first REME elements ashore cleared beaches and recovered what vehicles they could (sometimes under fire and attack from enemy aircraft). They established parks for 'drowned' tanks, guns and other vehicles. There were eleven second and four third-line workshops. Armoured brigade workshops had first priority, followed by gun repair.

Beaches and ports were not the best for combined operations from the point of view of the slope; the gradient varied from 1/100 to 1/250, a rise/fall of tide of 20ft. The surface was good except for some patches of blue clay exposed at low water and the soft sand above the high-water mark, which needed a lateral beach roadway of Sommerfeld track. It was impossible to discharge motor transport from craft for two hours either side of low water, and on a falling tide it was rare for craft to be able to beach and retract due to the speed of the ebbing tide, so causeways were created using US navy pontoons sunk to make piers for discharging. Due to the gentle slope of the beaches, the closest anchorages were well offshore. This could be up to 1 mile for coasters, 2 miles for motor transport ships and 5 miles for fully laden store ships. This all caused delays, especially on turnaround time.

To provide sheltered water for the numerous small craft, thirty blockships in groups of five called 'Gooseberries' were sunk off the beaches to make breakwaters. This was done from D+2 to D+4.

It was known there would be no major port facilities available for Allied use until Cherbourg was captured and reopened. This would make the supply of vehicles and large quantities of stores difficult, if not impossible, as while the gently sloping beaches of Normandy were good for putting assault troops ashore, the shallow water beyond them went out a long way and it was almost impossible to deliver stores or vehicles from ships moored there. The solution was to create two massive artificial harbours, one each for the British and American beaches; these were known as 'Mulberrys'.

The Transportation Directorate designed and supervised the construction of the whole Mulberry project, dividing the design work between branches handling the breakwater units for the floating piers, linkable spud units for pierheads and other steelworks. They worked with the National Physical Laboratory at Twickenham on research into the behaviour of various items in rough water, with an experimental station at Cairnhead for tests, and trained two floating equipment companies to assemble the equipment during experimental stages and finally at Normandy.

When the Mulberry project was agreed in the autumn of 1943, more facilities were provided for the assembly of floating bridge spans and the construction of 'Whale' links. These sectional pier units for the submersible concrete breakwaters known as 'Phoenix' formed a part of the Mulberry harbours. Camps to house 1,500 men were also built at this time, and the Marchwood depot assembled Mulberry equipment in the first half of 1944.

The two harbours were designated 'A' and 'B'; A was to be located at St Laurent for the US sections, while B was for the British sections, at Arromanches. Knowing it would take up to forty-two days to complete the building, outer breakwaters were constructed first to provide some shelter until the rest was finished, which was why the Mulberries were so valuable. The original intention was for the Mulberries to be used for only 100 days, or until a deep-water port was captured, but this did not happen until Antwerp was captured several months later at the end of November.

When Mulberry harbours are mentioned, they are often described as having been towed into place and they are often referred to as floating, which is not quite right. The impression gained is that of two giant structures, whereas in fact each of them consisted of several separate sections of breakwaters, cement caissons, piers constructed on pontoons and floating roadways, all spread along a wide area just offshore. It was these component parts which were towed across, as were floating cranes and dredging plant.

The breakwaters were made of enormous concrete caissons known as Phoenix; these were equipped with light AA protection. The size of the caissons ranged from 2,000 to 6,000 tons, and they were 'planted' so the tops of all were level. Used to make a broken line of piers, some of these were connected to shore with floating roadways. There were three types of piers: barge pier, LST piers with one floating roadway, and stores piers, with two floating roadways.

An advanced party arrived at Arromanches on 8 June and construction work began the next day. Discharges on artificial breakwaters began on 11 June and the stores pier on 18 June. However, a massive storm began on 16 June and blew for three days and nights, totally wrecking Mulberry A and badly damaging Mulberry B. The remains of the US Mulberry left after the storm was diverted to the British one.

One seldom mentioned advantage of Mulberries was that they allowed some 100,000 vehicles to be unloaded dry from ships so they did not need to be waterproofed, thus saving countless man-hours. During the period 6 June to 31 July, Mulberries handled 56,000 personnel, 4,200 vehicles and 274,000 tons of stores.

Hospital ships were brought alongside the LST pier so they could be loaded direct from ambulances; this was quicker, more comfortable for the wounded and thus helped morale.

Once a bridgehead been established, the force settled down for the long slog to Germany, assisted by the usual stores and support services. Although the general principle of these was the same as elsewhere during the war, there were some aspects which were specific to the invasion.

Fire protection and defence
On the land assault on D+2, there were six firefighting companies: headquarters had two first-class fire brigades, each with four standard fire tender lorries. They started with Leyland fire engines laid up before the war, then used four-wheel drive Bedfords on 3-ton chassis, which could tow a medium trailer fire pump. They carried a smaller pump, portable dams, ladders, foam-making equipment, hoses, ropes, axes and breathing apparatus and a 300-gallon water tank with hose reel and a small capacity pump driven by the vehicle's engine.

These units were used to protect beach sub-areas, Mulberries, rear maintenance areas and local petrol installations. Water supply was often in static tanks delivered through pipelines, shell-holes lined with tarpaulin and filled with water, and fire tenders. One major cause of fires inland, apart from bombing in towns, was French civilians tapping into bulk petrol lines.

Between 27 September 1944 and 14 January 1945, they were called to 1,191 fires, 188 of these due to enemy action. The most serious was from a V2 rocket at Hoboken, which set fire to two petrol can-filling sheds, two trains of full cases of petrol and three bulk storage tanks. The whole installation lost

102,618 tons of fuel. It took fifty hours to extinguish with eighteen pumps, three fire boats with Army Fire Service personnel, five pumps from the US army and six from the Belgian civil fire service.

Railways

The first railway line to be captured was from Bayeux to Caen; it was in good repair and included some usable rolling stock, but there were not sufficient locomotives. Some additional diesel locomotives were landed on the beaches in early July and the line was gradually restored. A slight problem occurred when the US wanted to use right-hand running; the British, and the rest of Europe, used left-hand running. There was prolonged argument over this until it was pointed out that the lines were designed and built for left-hand running.

Railway workshops were needed for clearance and repairs of machinery. An advance party of a railway workshop company arrived in Caen on 23 July, with the rest of the company arriving four days later.

The train ferry at Dieppe was made operative in September by two railway workshop companies. An ambulance train maintenance company arrived at Bayeux on 1 September and as well as other work refurbished some of the British wagons left behind in 1940.

There were also some large general goods wagons, mainly operated by the Canadians, using parts imported from the US. The initial target was 1,000 per month; this was later doubled.

The Belgian railways were in better condition than those in France. By the end of October, most lines on the line of communication had been repaired and despite an ongoing shortage of locomotives, it was possible to send stores all the way from Le Havre to Brussels and then Antwerp. This had required a great deal of bridge repair and replacement.

Between D-Day (6 June 1944) and VE Day (8 May 1945), railway repairs had been carried out successfully throughout northern France, Belgium, Holland and northern Germany. Not counting work done by civilian rail workers, the Transportation Corps had constructed or repaired 122 railway bridges, repaired 1,030 route miles of damaged main line, laid 24 miles of new track in depots and 29 miles of new track on main lines, and carried out over 500,000 cubic yards of earthwork.

Medical

It had been decided that the services of all the participating nations should be integrated and before the landings British and American medical officers exchanged places to learn each other's procedures.

On the first day of the invasion, nine medical units were landed on each beach. These comprised two field dressing stations, two field surgical units, one field hygiene section, two field transfusion units, a small corps field dressing section and one company of pioneers for stretcher-bearing. It had been intended that a CCS should be landed on each beach, but they did not arrive until the second day due to bad weather. There were four field ambulances across the Channel; three along the south coast and one on the Isle of Wight. Hospitals at the British Channel ports provided surgical centres for urgent operations.

The Normandy assault produced a great number of casualties, but this had been anticipated and the medical services had their full complement of medical staff and plenty of medical and surgical stores. Over 100,000 wounded men were evacuated by air to base hospitals within a few hours of being wounded and there was also a well-organised sea-evacuation process in place. Staff of LSTs (Landing Ship Tanks) were trained in handling casualties from amphibious craft and seventy of these craft were adapted for medical work.

All but the slightest casualties were evacuated to the UK. The policy on this was that all but those whom it would be dangerous to move would be evacuated to the UK immediately. Others were to receive such life-saving surgery as could be provided by the medicinal units in the beach organisation. Once the force had advanced as far as Brussels, many casualties went from the airport there, where a steady stream of Dakotas came, loaded, and went. As soon as hospital accommodation ashore was adequate, all cases requiring not less than seven days' treatment were to be retained on the Continent, then as more hospitals became available, fifteen days, thirty days and perhaps longer. Casualties arriving at British ports were sent on by ambulance trains or ambulance coaches or ordinary civilian ambulances.

LSTs and other designated casualty-carrying craft were, as soon as they had discharged their cargoes of stores, to be used for evacuation over the beaches and the Mulberry harbours, and hospital ships were later used for evacuation from major ports. Fifteen hospital ships were provided for the first phase, with 600,000 pints of plasma, 600,000 doses of penicillin, 100,000lb of sulphur and 8,000 doctors.

Almost all the hospitals for the US forces in Britain were built by contractors. Although hutted, the construction was of a semi-permanent type and of a high standard. Covered paths went from the surgical wards to the operating theatres, and these paths were smooth and without steps. The original programme was for 94,000 beds, but it was recognised that these would not all be needed immediately, most not until the invasion had begun, so they were built in two types of camp: all-purpose or convertible, the latter arranged to be easily converted to hospitals as needed. The hospitals were for either 834 or 1,084 beds, these costing £187,000 or £250,000 respectively.

The medical organisation of the British airborne forces at Arnhem consisted of two field ambulances and an air-landing ambulance. Each had two surgical teams, with forty-seven medical officers and 545 other ranks. These were soon working flat out, tending German as well as Allied casualties. By the end of September there were so many casualties that some had to be passed to the Germans, who put them in the care of captured medical officers. In general they were well looked after.

PLUTO

The Pipelines Under The Ocean (PLUTO) delivered 15,000 tons of petrol per day. Planning for the Pluto cross-Channel high-pressure pipelines started in November 1939. There were two routes: one via Sandown on the Isle of Wight to Cherbourg, where the UK terminal was known as Bambi and the French terminal Bambi-far. The other was Dungeness to Boulogne, with the terminals known as Dumbo and Dumbo-far. Dumbo supplies originated from Walton on Thames and there was a storage facility on the Isle of Grain.

The total amount of petrol and oil for 21st Army Group during the campaign in bulk shipments alone was nearly 1,200,000,000 gallons and RASC was operating 300,000 tons of bulk storage. Also 2,500,000 jerricans and more than 4,500,000 4-gallon tins were sent over for filling.

Pumping started from Dumbo on 27 October 1944 with a total of 111,000,000 gallons received in France to 22 May 1945. Pumping started from Bambi on 18 September 1944, which sent nearly 1,000,000 gallons to Cherbourg by 10 October 1944. The system eventually consisted of sixteen lines delivering an average of 3,500 gallons per day.

As the armies advanced, the pipelines were extended at a rate of about 3¼ miles per day.

Other bulk petrol for the invasion was sent by sea. On 30 June, in spite of bad weather and high seas, the first load was pumped from ship to shore at a rate of 80 tons per hour, when the first Mobile Filling Centres were established. Before D-Day, 200,000 tons (60,000,000 gallons) of petrol were filled into 4-gallon containers.

Coal/solid fuel

In north-west Europe, much locomotive coal went through Cherbourg, but was in desperately short supply in Europe in the winter of 1944–45. In the first four months of 1945, 140,000 tons of pitch were shipped to north-west Europe for the manufacture of briquettes (with coal dust) for use on the railways.

It was feared that the Germans would destroy coalmine shafts, as they had done in the First World War, and plans were made before the landings to take enough emergency mining equipment to produce 3,000,000 tons of coal. Fortunately the coal mines had been left intact by the retreating Germans, and British mining engineers took over. The emergency equipment included portable winding engines, wire ropes, pit props, electric pumps and so on; the list of what was needed had been produced with the assistance of a mining engineer who had experience of the Nord and Pas de Calais coalfields. Some 250,000 rot-proof 80lb sacks were also provided, by which supply would be maintained by man-carrying the coal over the beaches, this size being selected as a one-man load. A buffer stock of 5,000 tons of coal in bulk was laid down at Swansea.

The War Office was responsible from D-Day to May 1945 for the supply of all solid fuel to both the British and American forces taking part in Operation Overlord. Requirements were planned up to D+270, about the end of February 1945. It was clear that the Normandy landings would take place a long way from any coalfields and the general plan did not expect it to be possible to draw from the northern French coalfields for over six months.

Printing and stationery supplies

With 21st Army Group there were two Advanced Storage Depots, one stationery depot, one publications depot, two mobile duplicating sections and a printing press at GHQ. The Canadian army had one mobile printing section and one advanced stationery depot. Demands for P&SS stores received from the theatre were met by express coaster consignments and then the advanced stationery depot for 2nd Army began to function on 7 July.

By 14 July the main depot was functioning to capacity, but the unprecedented rate of consumption of some forms (especially those used in the production of fire plans) meant considerable shipments of stores had to be brought in by express coaster.

Considering the size and nature of the operations, surprisingly few typewriters were lost or destroyed. The only printing unit in the theatre at first was the mobile duplicating section attached to headquarters 2nd Army. This arrived 2 July and started functioning at Vaux-sur-Selles on 6 July when it produced the first issue of 'Second Army Troops News', which was then published daily. All other printing was done in the UK, including weekly 21st Army Group general routine orders, and messages.

The Directorate took over responsibility for providing all printing and publishing for 21st Army Group headquarters. P&SS units were landed in July and August (none in June, but by the end of June many of the express coaster consignments were P&SS loads). On 18 August a printing press was found in Caen and taken over, but there was no power so generators had to be installed. The first section to arrive was operated in tents near Bordeaux, but in winter the site degenerated into a quagmire and a section of pioneers was assigned permanently for maintenance. At Dunkirk a stock of paper had been left behind at Arras, much of which was still usable.

A three-week supply of green envelopes for uncensored letters per unit was kept.

Ordnance build-up and maintenance
The first ordnance units to land on D-Day were six OBDs with some expert units. Reconnaissance was rapidly carried out to locate suitable depot sites. The first mobile laundry and bath units landed on D+12. They concentrated on providing clean clothes and linen for hospitals until relieved by hospital laundries. Ammunition was stored in dumps divided into areas, each capable of holding up to 20,000 tons, these subdivided into six groups, containing AA ammunition, forward artillery ammunition, tank and anti-tank ammunition, medium and heavy artillery ammunition, infantry ammunition, demolitions and associated RE stores.

For the first four weeks the force was maintained from special packs of stores, known as Beach Landing Reserves (BLR), each comprising about 8,000 cases calculated to maintain a brigade group or equivalent formation in ordnance stores for thirty days. For planning purposes, and to allow for losses, delays in off-loading and heavy demand, it was assumed that each pack would maintain a brigade for fifteen days only. The quality and nature of these stores was based on experience gained in previous operations.

From D+26 the force was maintained from Beach Maintenance Packs (BMPs), similar to BLRs but containing a more comprehensive range of stores sufficient to maintain a division or equivalent formation for thirty days. One BMP weighed approximately 500 tons and contained about 12,000 cases.

From about D+100 on, maintenance was to be carried out in the form of Standard Maintenance Packs (SMP), which included spare parts for heavy artillery, signal wireless stores, clothing and general stores. The residue of stores from one period was carried over to the next.

In addition, all formations ashore were supported by Ordnance Field Parks (OFP), which landed complete with spare parts and complete equipment such as spare guns, small arms, wireless sets and so on. These OFPs were mobile and sited well forward so that their stocks would be readily available.

Maintenance of the force in ordnance stores was based on the UK being the main base and only advanced ordnance depots holding a limited range of stores being located in the theatre of operations. Other stores were sent by fast boat or air from transit depots.

The first tranch of reserve stocks was to be landed by midnight of D+3. This consisted of four days' ammunition, 50 miles of POL per vehicle ashore on D+3 and two days of supplies for forces ashore on D+5. Ordnance stores at maintenance level were to be landed from D+1 to D+9, dependent on landing reserves. From D+10 maintenance was to be by BMPs.

For planning purposes before D-Day, reserves to be immediately available were taken as being:

- By D+3: two days' reserves for forces ashore.
- By D+41: fourteen days' reserves for forces ashore, these to be held in Rear Maintenance Area (RMA) temporary depots.
- D+42 to D+90: one half day's reserves to be landed each day for forces ashore making reserves up to D+90 of twenty-one days and a seven-day working margin.
- After D+90: twenty-one days' maintenance entered with each divisional slice.

Engineering work

At planning meetings before the assault, the chief engineer was surprised to find that the planners had received his comments on the necessity of bulldozers with which to work on the beaches with astonishment. On one of the Normandy beaches, ten bulldozers landed with the first assualt team, followed within a few hours by several more. This points up the necessity for intelligence on aspects of any campaign which involves civil infrastructure, for instance the width of roads or the strength of bridges.

The Allied armies had plenty of heavy machines, many of which (armoured or unarmoured) were landed early in the assault when they were used to clear obstacles from the beaches, cutting exits through the sand-dunes and clearing rubbish from the roads. However, 'clearing rubbish' included burying numerous dead cows (and sometimes men), which left the machine smelling of dead cows for many days, despite much washing down with diesel oil. One machine was sent forward at night to bury some cows on the defence line, but encountered a German fighting patrol; burying cows had to be postponed while the German patrol was buried. Before the bulldozers arrived on station, some airborne engineers were using explosives to make craters and pushing the cows in before covering them by hand, but one group made the mistake of setting the explosives on the bodies of the cows.

It was decided soon after the bridgehead was established that they should maintain only two forward routes: Bayeaux to Mantes with branches to Les Andelys and Vernon; and Bayeaux to Rouen.

Engineer planning for Operation Overlord was dealt with by the engineer-in-chief at the War Office. One of the major technical aspects was rapid building or repair of airstrips. During this campaign:

- 125 airfields were constructed or repaired, equivalent to 2,020 miles of 20ft roadway.
- 1,445 bailey bridges were erected.
- More than 2,000,000 tons of stone was quarried.

- 750,000 tons of engineering stores and 25,000 items of plant and machinery were imported.
- More than 180 miles of 20ft span hutting equivalent were erected, of which some 30 miles was locally made.
- 420 electricity generators producing 10,000 hp were installed with 280 miles of overhead cable and 3,000 miles of insulated cable.

Tunnelled accommodation was constructed for staff at Portsmouth and other embarkation ports vulnerable to bombing. 'Hards' were built at embarkation points for LCTs and other vehicles, and road connecting and solid turning points at sharp bends and junctions, with turning circles on some other roads.

Some 20,000,000 square feet of covered and 33,000,000 square feet of open depot storage and workshop accommodation were prepared. Some British depots were handed over for US stores and several new ones were built, including one near Cheltenham in 1942. It had more than 1,000,000 square feet of covered storage and 9,500,000 square feet of open storage. The whole cost £1,650,000. In all there were ninety-four US depots.

Forestry/timber

Provision of 12,000 tons of timber was included in the planning for Phase 1, but once the Allied engineers arrived in France, they found plenty still standing and in sawmills and dumps. But timber suitable for pilings was needed and four months before D-Day rafts of timber were stored at Southampton and Barry. At 120ft by 60ft, these rafts were towed across the Channel by tugs. In France, 250,000 tons of timber, 50,000 of which were pit props, was felled by forestry companies.

Bridging

Bridges across the Seine were built and maintained: one each at Rouen, Pont de l'Arche and Les Andelys, and two each at Elbeuf and Vernon. All these were Bailey bridges on pontoons except the one at Rouen, which used the piers of a demolished bridge.

Between 15 January and 8 May 1945, the main task for engineers was bridging the Rhine. This also required much sorting out of approach roads: 50 miles new, 400 miles repaired. Roads had been badly damaged by heavy frost and thawing and the abnormally heavy use by operations traffic. Intensive efforts by Belgian repair teams, contractors, national road authorities and some British army troops managed to keep the main advance route open.

For the Rhine crossing, engineers used:

- 22,000 tons of assault bridging equipment, which included 2,500 pontoons.
- 650 storm boats.
- 2,000 assault boats.

- 60 river tugs and 70 small tugs.
- 650 outboard motors, 600 other propulsion units.
- 260 miles of wire ropes.
- Numerous blocks and tackles for semi-permanent bridges.
- 15,000 tons of material.
- 250,000 items of spare parts.

During the campaign, 1,445 Bailey bridges and eighty other bridges were installed, as was 19,000,000 square feet of hutting. Some 250,000 tons of timber was used, 2,000,000 tons of stone was quarried, and 750,000 tons of engineers' stores were used.

Electricity
The high-tension line from Caen to Bayeaux was repaired during October 1944 and hospitals could then be provided with electricity. As Bourg-Leopold became more important, 10 miles of low-tension mains were laid for the town supply. Temporary lighting was supplied to all quays in Antwerp dock in December 1944 and it was decided to provide night lighting for store dumps. Twenty-one lighting sets, consisting of a 3 KVA three-phase generator were made up and mounted on a small bogie with a 10ft high platform with floor-lights with blue glass. Some cranes were also fitted with boom lights.

Salvage
Much abandoned and damaged material was left on the beaches and imme-diate assault areas. Salvage dumps were rapidly established, but there was much pilferage for souvenirs.

In 1944 the assault operation offered tremendous opportunities for salvage, starting with immense quantities of abandoned and partly damaged material on the beaches. Salvage dumps were quickly established and a very acceptable amount of material was collected. By the end of July the base salvage depot alone had collected over 7,000 tons of serviceable stores. One problem that arose was the lack of an efficient plan for the storage of the rescued equipment. Later, at Arnhem, there was no plan for salvaging the valuable equipment used by the airborne forces. Some of this was recovered and returned to the UK, but one item which was rarely found was parachutes. Made of silk, it was pointless to expect the average soldier to return such a prize, which was guaranteed to make him popular with the female members of his family.

There was a general lack of spares, so it was necessary to cannibalise from what started out as a scrap section. This soon became known as a 'help your-self' park; some 20 per cent of spares were obtained from this source.

Provisioning
At Arnhem, one catering officer recorded that by 22 September their rations were exhausted and water was in short supply. They found some tinned food

in a cellar and a tin bath full of water. They also found some tame rabbits, and one small goat which was reckless enough to run across the lawn of one of the houses and was promptly brought down. Elsewhere in northern France, one unit found a pork factory stocked with sides of dressed pork and other pork meats. Looking further afield, they found abandoned trains with some trucks full of food for the French army, and some supply dumps. Where these had guards they were taken along. One potential problem was a shortage of bread, but this was alleviated when an empty bakery and nearby stocks of flour were found. A quick screening of the troops found over twenty bakers who quickly set to work and were able to provide bread for the whole division.

Germany

After the Allies moved into Germany, the medical services had to deal with the inmates of concentration and prisoner-of-war camps. The sheer number of sick and dying men and women was such that at first the medical services could do little but distribute food and water. After a while it was possible to conduct triage and begin the treatment of these cases. At Belsen, the medical staff took over a large German military hospital and the buildings of a Panzer school. These provided accommodation for about 10,000 patients. There was also a smaller hospital called the Glynn Hughes Hospital, after the RAMC officer in charge of medical relief for the camps. The hospitals were run by the RAMC and the Red Cross, with nurses from the Irish army and a team of British Quakers. Many patients did not survive the first few weeks, but the death rate dropped rapidly in May, from 600 to sixty per day.

As well as basic starvation in these camps, typhus was rampant, as were diarrhoea, skin diseases and pulmonary tuberculosis. The typhus was tackled by mass delousing. As well as louse-borne typhus, common diseases were tuberculosis, influenza and hepatitis.

This put a bit of a damper on the jubilation of the success of the mission, but by the middle of May the Germans had surrendered and it was all over.

Weights and Measures

As I find it cumbersome, I have not included conversions from imperial to metric in the text. For those younger readers who are not familiar with the imperial system:

1 acre	= approximately 0.4 hectares, or 4,840 square yards
1 mile	= 1.609 kilometres
1 yard	= 0.9144 metres
1 foot	= 0.305 metres
1 inch	= 25.4 millimetres
1 ton	= 2,240 pounds or 1,016 kilograms (not to be confused with the metric measure of 1 tonne, which is 1,000 kilograms)
1lb (avoirdupois)	= 16 ounces (oz) and 454 grams
1 ounce	= 28.34 grams
1 knot	= 6082.66 feet (used as a measurement of speed over distance, or as maritime people like to say, 'a little longer and a lot wetter than a land mile')
1 gallon	= 4.546 litres
1 pint	= 0.5682 litres

Medical Terms and Diseases

Dengue – like yellow fever, this is caused by a virus carried by *Aedes* mosquitoes. Shows as severe fever, skin rashes, nausea, headaches and joint pains. Symptoms subside after a few days but may recur in a milder attack.

Leishmaniasis – transmitted by sand-flies, causing a dangerous fever or localised infection such as severe boils.

Lymphogranuloma venereum – a long-term chronic infection of the lymphatic system, a form of chlamydia, rarely seen in heterosexuals. Often located in the groin, or around the anus, it shows with buboes or abcesses.

Otitis media – a group of inflammatory diseases of the middle ear which cause redness and swelling and a build-up of fluid behind the ear-drum.

Relapsing fever – carried by ticks or lice, shows first as a severe fever which lasts for several days, then fades only to recur a week or so later.

Sand-fly fever (or Phlebotomus fever) – is carried by the fly *Phlebotomus paptasi*. It shows with lassitude, headaches, joint and muscle pains and a fast heart-rate. This lasts for a couple of days, and may be followed by low blood pressure and a slow heart rate with fatigue which can last several weeks. There is usually a complete recovery.

Trachoma – severe and prolonged inflammation of the membrane lining the eyelids, often known as conjunctivitis. A disease of hot dry climates, and can lead to blindness.

Tropical ulcers – chronic open sores, usually on the lower leg and often following a minor injury. Large sores may need skin grafts.

Undulant fever – now known as brucellosis. Usually mild, but the fever can recur.

Yellow fever – a virus carried by Aedes mosquitoes, showing with fever, chills, loss of appetite, nausea, headaches and muscle pains. In 15 per cent of patients it can cause liver damage.

Appendix 3

Vitamin Deficiencies

The commonest of these deficiencies were as follows:

Vitamin A. A deficiency of Vitamin A, although not as debilitating as the other deficiencies, affects the sight, often leading to night-blindness. This last discovery was used to mislead the enemy by hiding the development of radar and explaining the 'good night vision' of the British as a side-effect of carrots in the diet. Vitamin A is present in liver (including fish liver), carrots, butter, some types of cheese, kidneys, suet and watercress, and yellow fruits including apricots and mangoes.

Vitamin B. There are several important B vitamins, including B1 (thiamin), B2 (riboflavin) and B12 (niacin). Deficiencies of these vitamins can lead to beriberi, pellagra and nervous complaints.

Vitamin C. Prolonged deficiency of Vitamin C leads to scurvy, the results of which show as teeth falling out, old wounds opening up again, and general debility. It was common in sailors, especially those who were at sea for a long time, until the British navy added citrus juice to the diet. This problem was not truly solved until fresh fruit and vegetables, or citrus juice, became a part of the regular diet of military personnel. As well as citrus fruit, Vitamin C is found in blackcurrants, raw cabbage, sauerkraut, rose hip syrup, watercress and scurvy grass (*Cochlearia*). In some places, 'acid' (actually lemon) drops were issued instead of Vitamin C tablets.

Vitamin D. Deficiency of Vitamin D, which regulates calcium and phosphate production in the body, in children leads to rickets, often because the child is rarely exposed to sunlight. In adults, deficiency of Vitamin D impairs muscle function. If not possible to expose the body to sunlight regularly, cod liver oil supplements are advisable. It can also be found in oily fish and egg yolks.

Abbreviations, Acronyms and Operation Codewords

Bodyguard – Cover and deception plan for Allied strategy in Europe.
Bolero – Build-up of US forces and supplies in UK for cross-Channel operations.
Market Garden – Operation to seize bridges at Nijmegen and Arnhem, 1945.
Overlord – Allied campaign in north-west Europe 1944–45.
Torch – Allied invasion of north-west Africa.

AA – Anti-Aircraft
ACC – Army Catering Corps
ADGB – Air Defence of Great Britain
AFHQ – Allied Forces Headquarters
AFV – Armoured Fighting Vehicle
ALFSEA – Allied Forces South East Asia
AOD – Advanced Ordnance Depot
AOW – Advanced Ordnance Workshop
AP&SS – Army Printing and Stationery Services
ARH – Advanced Rail Head
ARV – Armoured Recovery Vehicle
AT – Anti-tank
ATS – Auxiliary Territorial Service
AVRE – Assault Vehicle Royal Engineers
BAD – Base Ammunition Depot
BAS – British Army Staff in Washington
BEF – British Expeditionary Force
BLR – Beach Landing Reserves
BMP – Beach Maintenance Packs
BOD – Base Ordnance Depot
BOW – Base Ordnance Workshop
BSD – Base Supply Depot
BTI – British Troops in Iraq
CAD – Central Ammunition Depot

CCS – Casualty Clearing Station
CIGS – Chief of the Imperial General Staff
COD – Central Ordnance Depot
COSSAC – Chiefs of Staff to the Supreme Allied Commander
DFW – Director of Fortifications and Works
DOS – Director of Ordnance Services
DST – Directorate of Supplies and Transport
ESBD – Engineering Stores Base Depot
ESO – Embarkation Staff Officer
ETOUSA – European Theatre of Operations, US Army
FSU – Field Surgical Units
GHQ – General Headquarters
GSGS – General Staff Geographical Section
LVT – Landing Vehicle Tracked
MGO – Master General of the Ordnance
OBD – Ordnance Beach Detachments
OFP – Ordnance Field Park
PIAT – Projector Infantry Anti-tank
PLUTO – Pipelines under the ocean (across the English Channel)
POL – Petrol, Oil and Lubricants
RAMC – Royal Army Medical Corps
RAOC – Royal Army Ordnance Corps
RAPC – Royal Army Pay Corps
RASC – Royal Army Service Corps
REME – Royal Electrical and Mechanical Engineers
RMA – Rear Maintenance Area
ROF – Royal Ordnance Factories
RT – Radio Telephone
SEAC – South East Asia Command
SHAEF – Supreme Headquarters Allied Expeditionary Force
SMG – Sub Machine Gun
SMP – Standard Maintenance Packs
WVS – Women's Voluntary Service

Bibliography

Books

Allen, J., *Burma, The longest war 1941–1945* (London, 1958).

Ambrose, Stephen E., *The Supreme Commander* (New York, 1970).

Brayley, M. & Ingram, R., *The British Tommy in WWII* (Marlborough, 1998).

Brayley, M. & Ingram, R., *Khaki Drill and Jungle Green* (Marlborough, 2000).

Boileau, D.W. (compiler), *Supplies and Transport*, 2 vols (War Office, 1954).

Buchannan, A.G.B., *Works service and Engineer Stores* (1953).

Campagnac, R. & Hayman, P.E.G., *Fighting, Support and transport vehicles and the War Office provision for their provision, Pt 1 Common problems* (1951).

Carter, J.A.H. *Maintenance in the Field*, 2 vols (1951 & 1952).

Chamberlain, P. and Ellis, C., *British and American Tanks of the Second World War* (1969).

Chappell, M., *British Infantry Equipments 1908–80* (London, 1980).

Clough, A.B., *Maps and Survey* (1952).

Cole, Howard N., *The Story of the Army Catering Corps and its Predecessors* (Army Catering Corps Association, 1984).

Davis, Brian, *Uniforms and Insignia of the British Army* (1983).

Davis, Brian, *British Army Cloth Insignia: 1940 to the present* (London, 1985).

Dorish, Michael, *Dressed to Kill* (2001).

Dunn, C., *The Emergency Medical Service*, 2 vols (1952).

Ehrman, et al, *Grand Strategy*, vols I–VI.

Ellis, L. *Victory in the West* (1962).

Ferneyhough, A.H., *History of the Royal Army Ordnance Corps 1920–1945*.

Fraser, George Macdonald, *Quartered Safe Out Here* (London, 1993).

Gander, T., *Allied Infantry Weapons of World War Two* (Marlborough, 2000).

Gordon, David, *Uniforms of the World War Two Tommy* (2005).

Gordon, David, *Equipment of the World War Two Tommy* (2014).

Granby, B., *Signal Communications* (London 1950).

Harrison, Mark, *Medicine and Victory* (Oxford, 2004).

Hastings, M., *Overlord: D-Day and the Battle for Normandy 1944* (London, 1984).

Hay, Ian, *The Story of the Royal Ordnance Factories 1939–1948* (London, 1949).

Hornby, William, *Factories and Plant* (1958).

Howlett, O., *Fighting with Figures: Statistical Digest of the War* (London, 1951).

Higham and Knighton, *Movements*, 1939-45.

Hurstfield, Joel, *The Control of Raw Materials* (1953).

Jewell, B., *British battledress 1937–1961*.

Kohan, C.M. *Works and Buildings* (1952).

Macdonald, Janet, *From Boiled Beef to Chicken Tikka: [etc]* (Barnsley, 2014).

Macdonald, Janet, *Project Management* (Kingston-upon-Thames, 1999).

Magnay, A.D., *Quartering* (1949).

Magnay, A.D., *Miscellaneous Q Services* (1954).

Micklem, R., *Transportation* (1950).
Napier, Gerald, *Follow the Sapper*.
Nicholls, T.B., *Organisation, strategy and tactics of the Army Medical Service in War* (London, 1937).
Norris, John, *Infantry mortars of the Second World War* (2002).
Norris, John, *The Second World War tanks & trucks*.
North, John, *NW Europe 1944–45*.
Pakenham-Walsh, R.P. *Military Engineering (field)* (1952).
Postan, M.M., *British War Production* (London, 1952).
Savage, Christopher I., *Inland Transport* (London, 1957).
Scott, J.D. & Hughes, R. *The Administration of War Production* (1955).
Sutton, J. (ed), *Wait for the Waggon: The story of the Royal Corps of Transport and its Predecessors, 1794–1993*.
Thompson, J., *Lifeblood of War: Logistics in armed conflict* (London, 1991).
Wells, Edward, *Mailshot: A History of the Forces Postal Service* (London, 1987).
Various authors, *Grand Strategy*, 6 vols.
Williams, G.W., *Citizen Soldiers of the [RE] Transportation and Movements and the Royal Army Service Corps, 1859–1965* (Camelot Press, 1966).
Wolmar, Christian, *Engines of War* (London, 2010).
Wilson, H.W. (compiler), *Administrative Planning 1939–1945* (WO, 1952).

Periodicals and War Office pamphlets

RASC Quarterly, *Supply planning for Operation Overlord*.
The administrative history of the operations of 21 army group on the continent of Europe 6/6/44–8/5/45
Notes on the handling and storage of packed petroleum products (War Office, 1942).
Ammunition Pt I, movement and distribution by road (War Office 1942).
The Jerrican, notes on its care and use (War Office, 1947).
RASC orders for drivers (Egypt) (BPTC, 1942).
Middle East Training Pamphlet No. 0, Part VII, Cross country driving (War Office, 1942).
Alexander, Field-Marshall Viscount, 'The Conquest of Sicily from 10th July to 17th August, 1943', published in *London Gazette*, 10 February 1948.
Ince, C.E.R, 'Supply Planning for "Overlord"' in *Royal Army Service Corps Review*.

PhD thesis

Johnstone, Rachel S. (Oxford, 2006), *Operational Rations and Anglo-American Long-range Infantry in Burma, 1940–1944: A subcultural study of combat feeding*.

The National Archives (London)

War diaries of the Second World War – all War Office (WO) section:

- 165 War office directorates
- 166 Home forces
- 167 BEF
- 168 N W Ex force
- 169 Middle East
- 170 Central Mediterranean
- 171 N W Europe
- 172 SE Asia command
- 173 W Africa forces
- 174 Madagascar
- 175 N Africa
- 176 Various small theatres
- 177 Medical services
- 178 Military missions
- 218 Special services

Index